AF539475

Practising the Symbolic

Pierre Bourdieu's Contribution

Practising the Symbolic

Pierre Bourdieu's Contribution

Sheena Jain

Practising the Symbolic: Pierre Bourdieu's Contribution
Sheena Jain

First Published, 2013

ISBN : 978-93-5002-231-3

Published by
AAKAR BOOKS
28 E Pocket IV, Mayur Vihar Phase I, Delhi 110 091
Phone : 011 2279 5505 Telefax : 011 2279 5641
info@aakarbooks.com; www.aakarbooks.com

Printed at
Mudrak, 30 A, Patparganj, Delhi 110 091

To the memory of my parents
and sister Indu

Contents

Preface and Acknowledgements

This study is the outcome of a process set in motion by a reading of Pierre Bourdieu's *Outline of A Theory of Practice*. The book was an introduction to a veritable revolution in sociological thought and practice that led to a profoundly original and thought-provoking corpus of work challenging many conceptions about the discipline that one had learnt to accept over the years. It was soon evident that to engage with Pierre Bourdieu's thought was a project that would involve considerable time and effort, but which would be richly rewarding.

The research work on which this study is based commenced with the attempt to grasp the basic contours of Bourdieu's thought by traversing through writings which are ethnographic, theoretical and methodological. From this initial exploration, the theme of symbolism emerged as a nodal concern of the author, exemplifying what makes his sociology so richly innovative. The absence of a study examining Pierre Bourdieu's theory of the symbolic in a sustained and systematic manner offered a challenge which this work seeks to meet. Additionally, a review and appraisal of this theory seemed to have the potential to bring to bear a powerful conceptual framework on hitherto unexplored social realities. This study, therefore, examines the intellectual warp and woof that makes the theory and also, though in a small way, tries to see how far it works in a context other than the one in which it was conceived.

The articulation of Bourdieu's theoretical contribution with his role as a public intellectual forms part of this study as well, and has inspired the phrase 'practising the symbolic' in the title of this book. It condenses and brings together two distinct but related aspects of Bourdieu's engagement with the symbolic: the 'theoretical', as in making it part of his theory of practice, and the 'practical' as in his activism in the fields of symbolic production and in his resistance to neoliberalism It therefore signifies, symptomatically, the ideal of a unity of theory and practice.

This book crystallised and was written over several years, nurtured by many persons and institutions.

My parents, Shrimati Kuntha Jain and Shri Lakshmi Chandra Jain, provided the nourishing environment in which it was conceived and initiated, and pampered me with their affection and care when the going was rough, as it sometimes was.

To my brother and teacher, Professor Ravindra K. Jain, many thanks for inspiration, guidance, and intellectual stimulation, throughout, and especially at all critical moments.

A scholarship awarded by the Commonwealth Trust for research on Pierre Bourdieu's social theory took me to the University of Cambridge, UK, where Professor John Thompson guided me towards a close analysis of Bourdieu's work, was tireless in providing suggestions and criticisms, and readily made available translations of Bourdieu's writings from French into English as they were being published by Polity Press. Many thanks to him.

I am grateful to Darwin College for providing ideal facilities for work and residence during my stay in Cambridge.

Professor Mohini Anjum at the Jamia Millia Islamia, New Delhi, inspired me, with characteristic care and concern, to complete my PhD thesis on Bourdieu's theory of the symbolic, which forms the initial rubric for this study. I am deeply grateful to her.

Thanks to my sister Indu Jain and brother-in-law Madan Mohan Jain for providing the heady brew of regular evening walks, lively discussions, and constant moral support while I was writing.

My sister Champak Bagla and brother Ashok Jain averted a lapse into solipsism by generously providing many occasions for sociality and helped order emerge out of chaos. My heartfelt thanks to them.

For friendly and scholarly inputs at different stages, thanks to Arvinder Ansari, Saugato Bhaduri, the late Teresa Brennan, Biswajit Das, Jayati Ghosh, Sameera Jain, Shuka Jain, Jennifer Jarman, Bruno Moncorge, Madawi Al-Rasheed, Isabelle Vallin, and Punam Zutshi.

Thanks to my sister Runjhun Gaggar for bringing her inimitable typing skills to bear on a disorderly manuscript.

Thank you, Mridula Sharma, for providing the welcome distraction of hot and nourishing meals when work was arduous.

A version of the chapter 'Bourdieu's Theory of the Symbolic: Traditions and Innovations' was published in the book *Reading Bourdieu in a Dual Context: Essays from India and France* (Routledge, New Delhi, 2006), edited by Roland Lardinois and Meenakshi Thapan. I thank the editors for permission to include it in this book.

I would also like to acknowledge the permission given for republishing, in a slightly modified form, the article entitled 'Bourdieu's Theory of the Symbolic and the Shah Bano Case', published in the *Sociological Bulletin* (Vol. 56 No. 1 Jan-April 2007).

I am grateful to the K.K. Hebbar Art Foundation for permission to reproduce the drawing on the cover of this book by the artist K.K. Hebbar. It portrays the multifaceted genius of the Kannada author Shivaram Karanth, instantiating 'practising the symbolic' in a context nearer home, and invoking Bourdieu's figure of a 'métier militant' striving for genuine universalism.

1

Introduction

The term 'symbolic' refers, broadly speaking, to that which relates to mental processes that represent some feature of external reality. Symbolism therefore forms part of all human practice, from the most mundane to the most esoteric. Since social life is constituted by human practice, it is inconceivable without symbolic practice. Thus, most sociological theories contain, in implicit or explicit form, at least the rudiments of, if not a full-fledged theory of the symbolic.

Generally, symbolic practices have been conceptualized under the rubric of cultural practices, as part of culture. Though, for some time, the concept of culture was posed in alterity to that of social structure, contemporary sociology is marked by a resolution of this debate in favour of a dialectical complementarity between the two. Thus, the realm of symbolic figures as a constituent element in most theories of society.

In recent years, the concept of discourse has replaced the concept of culture in the work of some scholars. Thus, for instance, with reference to anthropology in particular, Oivind Fuglerud writes ...

> I see discourses as linguistically mediated configurations of meaning, systematically constructing and reconstructing the objects which they speak of. Seen against our traditional understanding of 'culture', the concept of 'discourse' has two characteristics, which should be emphasized. The first is that it helps overcome the timelessness, which has been part and parcel of our anthropological concept of culture. Discourse is something,

> which by nature is always changing and any outline given should openly admit only to be a freezing of history at a particular moment in time. The second is that it questions the distinction, built into the culture concept, between a realm of ideas and material realities. Discourses are never totally coherent, they are not closed universes of meaning, but always strive toward tantalization by aligning themselves with aspects of reality — demarcations, regulations, institutions, practices, which also legitimate non-linguistic means of control. They are in other words intrinsically linked with the exercise of power. [1]

While the dimension of power has undoubtedly been brought sharply into focus in discourse analysis, the link between the material and the symbolic is less clearly conceptualized. The work of Pierre Bourdieu, it may be argued, marks the transition to a theory of the symbolic, which fills this lacuna by unraveling the complex relations between symbolism and the economy.

Indeed, while the initial significance of symbolism in social life lies in its universality, it interweaves with social institutions in diverse ways in different times and places, mediating processes of reproduction and transformation, consensus and conflict. Thus, it becomes essential to move beyond generalities to historically and empirically specific contexts to appreciate the social significance of symbolism.

If we pause to consider the current conjuncture of human history, for instance, we witness, among other things, the continuing hegemony of the United States of America on the one hand and an emerging world order characterized by plurality, where there is no linear development from multiple traditions to singular modernity on the other; and together with these, diverse movements of resistance to imperialism and neoliberalism are evidenced. These phenomena urge an inquiry into the symbolic systems and processes that sustain and subvert relations of power and constitute culture, including the continuous invention of traditions. They also point to the complex linkages between material and symbolic realities, that belie equally attempts at economic reductionism and culturalism, or conceptual idealism.

Yet another general feature seen as characterizing the new social order is a constant process of internalization and externalization of groups or individuals[2]. While the processes of the construction of 'others' is acknowledged to be universal, its development in a more systematic way is identified with the emergence of social science in the nineteenth century and particularly with the invention of 'primitive society'. Manifest in class relations, gender relations, race relations, and ethnic relations of other kinds, as well as in relations between nations, and between groups within nations, at the core of this process are systems of belief, which point to the significance of symbolism in social life, and to a compelling area of study with important implications for the human condition.

Also, in the realm of belief, and as an institution too, religion has similarly seen a resurgence and transformation over the years. Among other aspects of the phenomena, analyses have looked at the gender dimension of religious beliefs and practices, and at the effects of electronic media on new forms of spirituality, highlighting yet another dimension of symbolism in social life. Thus, for example, a recent study argues that the diversities inherent in earlier religious traditions were overwhelmed by the ascent of an archetypal male heroic consciousness, which saw conquest and subjugation, not persuasion and accommodation, as the only meritorious goal.

> What was symbolic, polytheistic and emotional was transformed into literal, monotheistic and hyper rational understandings of spirituality and by extension, religion. It is with the rise of the latter consciousness that charges of heresy proliferated and women's spirituality was repressed and marginalized.[3]

Another study looks at the techno-spiritual world of the Internet, video and the charisma of the Indian god-man, Satya Sai Baba, and its implications for the traditional Hindu notions of *darshan* and *bhakti*.[4]

Still nearer home, in the Indian context, the electronic media throws up conundrums arising from the widening access to the media on the one hand, and the politics of representation that features only a selected segment of reality on the other. Thus, as Uma Chakravarti writes,

> Rural India has virtually disappeared from the media, except to

> figure as disaster arena in the news. On an everyday representational basis rural India, where the majority of our population still lives, has been reduced to a trope figuring in a new ethinicized glossy or comic depiction depending on the product being advertised.[5]

The link between power relations and symbolic systems that the above examples suggest, have indeed been a major concern of post-structuralist sociological theory. This has yielded enormous insights into processes structuring societies today, ranging from the role of international agencies and the state in creating systems of classification and identities to the micro-processes of power in the context of local cultures, and also the links between them. A recent collection of essays on the politics of cultural mobilization in India, for instance, validates the observation that the issues of politics (defined in its broad sense in terms of power relations, and not confined to the activities related to the running of the institutions of government) and culture have come to dominate actual politics as well as theoretical debates. A major argument put forward is that 'national politics is increasingly being shaped by local politics, and is often described by its protagonists as lying in the sphere of culture'.[6] The top-down approach to political analysis focused on formal processes, is giving way to studies that look at discursive structures and symbolic systems, just as these structures and systems are assuming a greater significance in the political arena, and more generally in social life.

A recognition of the phenomena of multiple identities in processes of identity formation also throws into relief the salience of symbolism in social life, as well as the need for sophisticated theories of the symbolic to comprehend it. It puts forward the challenge of offering correctives to the orthodox Marxist insistence on subsuming all complexities within class. In the context of the Indian working class, for instance, we have analyses such as those of workers in the Kolar Gold Mines, about whom it is observed that their memories of indignities as low caste workers in the countryside served to exaggerate the relative freedoms of the capitalist workplace. The continuance of caste identities despite this, cannot, according to the author, be adequately understood by a 'mere recognition of intermittent or intertwining identities', but by taking account of the actual conditions from which the workers came, and by analysing how caste was reconstructed in the process of migration, the labour processes in mines, and in the social and political movements of workers.[7] The complex links between symbolic structures that go into the construction of identities and the material and social conditions of existence, are sharply highlighted by such analyses. Conceptually, they draw attention to how a focus on the symbolic blurs the sharp lines usually drawn between the mental and the material, body and mind, cognition and emotion, and the conscious and the unconscious.

As these random examples of the social significance of symbolism suggest, the search for an adequate and powerful theory of the symbolic is a meaningful task, as much for Indian sociologists as for sociologists anywhere. One prominent trail in the search leads to the work of Pierre Bourdieu whose contributions have made him a major intellectual of our times. That symbolism was for him a central concern, is clear from his statement that

> the object of social science is a reality that encompasses all the individual and collective struggles aimed at conserving or transforming reality, in particular, those that seek to impose the legitimate definition of reality, whose specific symbolic efficacy can help to conserve or subvert the established order, that is to say, reality.[8]

What it also clarifies is that the symbolic figures in his work as part of the larger and more general project of understanding society.

The significance of what he achieved in pursuing this project can be gleaned from the fact that his wide-ranging work has been described as 'one of the most imaginative and fertile bodies of social theory and research of the post war era'.[9] In particular, it is distinguished by the way in which theory, epistemological reflection, and empirical research are integrated in it, to address an astonishing array of subjects across conventional disciplinary boundaries. Substantively, its central and unifying concern is social class and the reproduction over time of class-based power and privilege, with which it engages in a profoundly innovative way, developed in dialogue with classical and contemporary intellectual traditions, some of which are critiqued and surpassed. In the process, several dualisms characterizing social science, such as those of objectivism versus subjectivism, the material versus the symbolic, theory versus research, structure versus agency, rationalism versus historicism, and micro versus macro analysis, have been transcended.

The duality of subjectivism and objectivism engaged Bourdieu initially through his immediate intellectual milieu, dominated as it was by existentialism when he was a student of philosophy, on the one hand, and subsequently, as a social science researcher, by Levi-Strauss's structuralism, on the other. In fact, as Rogers Brubaker points out, the 'exemplary confrontation' between Sartre and Levi-Strauss, was doubly significant for Bourdieu.[10] To begin with, it furnished divergent models of intellectual vocation. It opposed what Bourdieu calls a kind of 'metascientific enthusiasm for science' that characterized Levi-Strauss's approach, to the figure of the politically committed 'total' intellectual represented by Sartre.[11] It led Bourdieu, with his training, social personality, and the peculiar circumstances of the Algerian War in which he found himself in the 1950s, to conceptualize for himself the role of a *métier militant*, or the practitioner

> of a kind of militant craftsmanship, signifying the ambition to bring together the scientific and the ethical or political vocation in a humbler and possibly more effective way. Unifying theoretical and practical aims, beginning with his analysis of Algeria, Bourdieu regarded his sociological work as one of demystification and de-consecration, committed to revealing the hidden basis of domination and thus to undermining the misrecognition of the mechanisms on which it is founded.

A combination of scientific autonomy and civic engagement that characterized Bourdieu's intellectual project throughout, thus had its roots in his particular response to these early influences.

The confrontation was significant in a second way in that it set two radically different approaches to the study of social life against one another. On the one hand was Sartre's voluntarism with its emphasis on creativity, freedom and undetermined power of choice of the individual subject, and on the other, Levi-Strauss's emphasis on the causal power of structures operating independently of the consciousness of agents. The opposition between the two, which Bourdieu terms that of subjectivism versus objectivism, was understood as characterizing the entire history of social thought, and as posing a major obstacle to the construction of an adequate science of society. Bourdieu, in his work, attempts to transcend the antagonism, which sets these two modes of knowledge against each other, and at the same time, to preserve the insights gained by each position. He does this by maintaining that to understand social life, one must do justice both to objective, material, social and cultural structures, as well as to the constituting practices and experiences of individual and groups. Thus, for example, both structuralism and phenomenology are critiqued as well as appropriated by Bourdieu to construct his theory of practice, constituted by the interrelated concepts of habitus, capital, and field — a seminal contribution to sociology.

As a corollary of overcoming the opposition between objectivism and subjectivism, Bourdieu also offers a critique of the dualism of the material and the symbolic. And once more, he shows a way out of a conceptual impasse found in social theory, with objectivist variants of Marxism, including crudely reductionist interpretations of historical materialism, on the one hand, and semiologism and other forms of idealism on the other. Thus Bourdieu insists that social science has to take account of two kinds of properties that are attached to individuals

> on the one hand, material properties, starting with the body, that can be counted and measured like any other thing of the social world; and on the other hand, symbolic properties , which are nothing other than material properties when perceived and appreciated in their mutual relationships that is, as distinctive properties.[12]

Furthermore, he argues that

> The spurious alternatives of social physics and social

> phenomenology can only be superceded by grasping the principle of the dialectical relationship established between the regularities of the material universe of properties and the classificatory schemes of the habitus, that product of the social world for which and through which there is a social world.[13]

While we will discuss Bourdieu's concept of habitus in some detail in Chapter 3, what is notable here is the emphasis on the material and the symbolic and their interrelationship. At this point, we must also clarify that while Bourdieu is a materialist who views the ultimate conditioning factors of all practices as being material, the 'generalized' or 'radical' materialism that he advances refers more precisely to what Brubaker suggests might better be called 'the sociology of interest' whereby even the most ostensibly disinterested practices are conceived of as 'economic' (that is interested) practices, directed (though often unconsciously) toward the maximizing of material and symbolic profit.[14] In this regard, Bourdieu marries Marx with Weber in a distinctive way, developing a non-economistic theory of the economy of practice.

Indeed, a significant feature of Bourdieu's contribution to sociology is the way he adapts the theoretical legacy of classical social theory to the empirical study of contemporary society. Strongly critical of the tendency to treat Marx, Weber and Durkheim as denominationally discrete intellectual totems, he identifies, to begin with, the commonalities between them as regards a theory of sociological knowledge. These are, firstly, the principle of non-consciousness, which is apparent in Durkheim and Marx, but is also expressed in Weber by his refusal to reduce the cultural meaning of actions to the subjective intentions of the actors; secondly, the rejection of attempts to define the truth of a cultural phenomenon independently of the system of historical and social relations in which it is located; and thirdly, the conviction that social facts are constructed rather than given 'out there' as naive realism would have it.[15] However, Bourdieu engages with these thinkers beyond the acceptance of these features, modifying, linking, and extending their contributions in a novel way.

Thus from Weber, as Brubaker suggests, Bourdieu

appropriates

> the conceptual resources for a theory of the social functions of symbolic goods and symbolic practices. From Weber's conception of the particular styles of life and attributions of honour or dishonour that define status groups, he develops (most fully in *Distinction*) a systematic theory of the relation of life styles and their attendant marks of distinction to material conditions of existence—a theory, in Weberian terms, of the relation of stratification by status to stratification by class. From the Weberian notions of charisma and legitimacy he develops a systematic theory of symbolic power and its relations to economic and political power. And from Weber's notions of ideal goods and ideal interests (as well as other themes and concepts developed by Weber in his sociology of religion) he constructs a general theory of the economy of symbolic goods; and its relation to the material economy—a theory of the production and consumption of symbolic goods, the pursuit of symbolic profit, the accumulation of symbolic capital, and the modes of conversion of symbolic capital or power into other forms of power.[16]

As for Durkheim, while Bourdieu critiques his objectivist and apolitical epistemology, he nevertheless finds in his work the starting point for a sociology of symbolic forms. While we will discuss this link in some detail in Chapter 2, we may note here with Wacquant that what Bourdieu does is to supplement the Durkheimian structural analysis with a genetic and political sociology of the formation, selection, and imposition of systems of classification.[17]

Regarding Marx, it may not be incongruous to suggest that Bourdieu's oeuvre represents a serious attempt to solve some of the aporia of Marxist materialism in relation to the analysis of superstructures. This Bourdieu does while extending Marx's own insight into the need to focus on practice to overcome the shortcomings of both idealism and a reductive materialism. Thus Bourdieu quotes Marx's first thesis on Feuerbach before he begins his seminal work, *Outline of A Theory of Practice*. As noted earlier, Bourdieu relates the material and symbolic realms in his analysis, and he does so in a way such that the theoretical understanding of symbolic production and consumption does not require a radically different mode of reasoning from that required for a theoretical understanding of the economy. To do so, he brings together Weber and Marx, and introduces new concepts, such as those of symbolic power, and cultural and symbolic capital, which partly bridge the gulf between the two traditions, even as they go to constitute part of a new theoretical framework. Indeed, the 'vexing yet obdurate relationship of collision and collusion, autonomy and complicity, distance and dependence, between material and symbolic power' has been described as a universal principle that has been explored by Bourdieu in more than one work.[18]

More generally, Bourdieu inherited from Marx an alignment with the project of human emancipation through freedom from domination. However, the identification of the proletariat as the agent of this liberation was initially clearly articulated only in his work on Algeria, after which the focus was on how sociology can potentially contribute to the process of the demystification of power relations, not least, relations of symbolic power. Subsequently, in his engagement with the movements opposing neoliberalism, he was once again, this time in a very active way, and not just conceptually, concerned with 'the reconstruction of a viable progressive agenda true to the historic ideals of the left betrayed by the neoliberal turn of socialist and labour parties everywhere'.[19]

Bourdieu's activism was a coming together of theory and practice via a reflexivity which simultaneously linked theoretical practice with reflections on the practice of theory, and the practice of theory with social practice in general, whereby he extended the influence of sociology in the public sphere 'like no one before him'.[20] Crucial to his project of a reflexive sociology was the attempt to break with what he termed the scholastic fallacy that inheres in the intellectual who mistakes the things of logic for the logic of things, and tends to treat the social world as a spectacle. This involved using the method of participant objectivation, as he termed it, by which the attempt is to achieve a full sociological objectivation of the object *and* of the subject's relation to the object. Thus, Bourdieu believed that the sociology of sociology is a fundamental dimension of sociological epistemology. His work, exemplifying this particular form of reflexivity, is a trailblazer for future generations of sociologists.

Bourdieu's contribution to sociology also lies in his role 'as a sort of intellectual entrepreneur', as Roland Lardinois puts it.[21] As Director of Studies at the Ecole des Hautes Etudes en Sciences Sociales and founder of the Centre for European Sociology, he trained and assembled a team of prolific scholars who investigated varied questions with a focus on the relations between culture, power and social inequality. Their work was a blend of rigorous theory with systematic observation, against both the empiricist tendencies of US sociology and the theoreticist bent of the French intellectual milieu. In fact, he may be said to have founded a sociological school in the Durkheimian sense,

> which since 1975 has had its own journal *Actes de la recherche en sciences sociales*, where one finds the affirmation of alternative forms of intellectual communication that militate against the arid academism of the usual journals. He was series editor for a number of presses, and it is in this avatar that he intervened to publish translations of a number of major authors in philosophy and the social sciences (notably Ernst Cassirer, Erwin Panofsky, Edward Sapir, Erving Goffman and Quentin Skinner).[22]

Furthermore, in the closing decades of the century Bourdieu guided numerous groups of activist intellectuals who could be termed as 'so many small scale incarnations of the "collective intellectual" that he dreamed of building across disciplinary boundaries and national borders'.[23] Indeed, he believed not only in social science as a knowledge enterprise, 'but also in sociology's capacity to inform a "rational utopianism" needed to salvage institutions of social justice from the new barbarism of the unfettered market and withdrawing state'.[24]

The quality and scope of Bourdieu's intellectual project and his contribution to sociology in particular encourage the attempt to identify the salient features of his theory of the symbolic, as a potentially rich repository of methods, concepts, and analytical insights for studying symbolism in society. This aspect of his work derives its significance not only from the outstanding nature of the intellectual project in which it is embedded but also from the fact that it represents an area marked by considerable intellectual ferment in the social sciences in recent years. In France itself, the post structuralist generation to which Bourdieu belongs, also includes Foucault and Derrida, whose work represents a major engagement with the symbolic. The work of Clifford Geertz has also been extremely influential in the same terrain and at about the same time. A brief look at what distinguishes Bourdieu's work from that of these scholars may thus be meaningful.

Insofar as the scholars belong to the tradition of postmodernism, it should be clarified that Bourdieu does not identify with the anti-Enlightenment, anti-modernist project of post-modernism, but also that he does nevertheless share certain elements of the post-modernist critique of earlier thought such as the critique of positivism, of representation and of structuralism's binary oppositions. However, each of these criticisms has a particular place in Bourdieu's own work, sometimes taking the form of a creative reinterpretation which does not necessarily converge with the postmodern critique. Thus, for example, binary oppositions are seen by Bourdieu to be a particular form of the workings of practical logic (rather than unconscious structures of the mind with a universal reality as in structuralism). So also, the critique of positivism does not lead him to anti-scientism, but to an appreciation of what modern science in the post-positivist sense is all about. The critique of representation, in the sense of political representation, is rooted in a social analysis of forms of political mobilization, and the critique of representation in theory (given what he calls the many sidedness of social reality) is tempered by a call for giving rationality its full force and power through disseminating ways of overcoming dominance and misrecognition.[25]

As regards Derrida and Foucault, according to Loic J Wacquant, Bourdieu agrees with them that knowledge must be deconstructed, that categories are contingent social derivations and instruments of (symbolic) power possessing a constitutive efficacy – and that the structures of discourse on the social world are often politically charged social preconstructions.[26] But there are important differences as well.

Derrida, of course, works in the domain of philosophy which is a subject of Bourdieu's criticism as a field given over to the illusions of a scholastic discourse claiming to talk about reality but actually and constitutionally unable to do so. Yet, insofar as the symbolic, more specifically in the sense of signification, is a central concern of Derrida, and insofar as his deconstruction claims to move forward from the material ontology of the production of signs and meanings to the analysis of texts of all kinds, his theory of the symbolic has to be taken seriously when considering any conceptualization of the realm of the symbolic in contemporary social theory. It has been pointed out, for example, that although from different perspectives and with considerable differences, Derrida's and Bourdieu's texts both deal with the problem of symbolic-social inequality in a critical way.

The differences, however, become apparent when we look closely at Derrida's deconstruction. Peter Dews in his *Logics of Disintegration* notes the fact that Derrida's deconstruction rests on a philosophical strategy akin to that of Schelling in the history of German idealism.[27] Offering a philosophy of *differance* as absolute, Derrida posits a transcendental structure more fundamental than that of consciousness. Through the use of the term *'differance'*, Derrida suggests the impossibility of closing of the differing and deferral of meaning in language, a suggestion in which the potential endlessness of the Husserlian *Ruckfrage* the striving to recover an original sense, combines with Saussure's insight into the different structure of language, according to which the meaning of each terms depends on its contrast with all others. For Derrida the movement of *differance*, language as writing, undermines the interpretive aim of grasping the coherent and unitary meaning of a text, of revealing its definitive truth.

Discerning idealism in Derrida's deconstruction, Dews notes that Derrida in his evocations of 'differance', 'arche-writing', the 'trace', has not escaped the 'idea of the first', even though this first cannot take the form of 'presence'.[28] Adorno's characterization of the vapidity of a philosophy of origins well captures the weakness of the thought of 'differance', for:

> The first of the philosophy of origins must become more and more abstract: the abstracter it becomes, the less it explains, the less it is able to do its job of grounding.[29]

For Adorno, any reduction of opposition to a *single* principle must have this idealist consequence. Thus, while both Adorno and Derrida are concerned with demonstrating how apparent philosophical contraries surreptitiously depend on each other, and both are concerned with reversing the traditional hierarchical relations in which these contraries have been placed, in Adorno, the need for this reversal results from the genuine primacy of one of the terms, a primacy which is specified by the materialist critique of metaphysics which begins with Marx, and which places thought within the overall development of social-historical life. In contrast, in Derrida, the reversal of emphasis *within* the hierarchy is portrayed as being merely a stage on the way to its overcoming.

While Bourdieu does not share with Adorno his forays into philosophical speculation, his approach to the symbolic does also exemplify a materialist concern with placing thought within the overall development of social-historical life, and converges with his in regarding the fundamental illusion of philosophy as being the illusion of the autonomy and primacy of the concept, an illusion to which Derrida's work succumbs.

As regards Foucault, the realm of the symbolic as representations of features of external reality is what his oeuvre is centrally concerned with. It has been pointed out that on the question of historical discontinuity and the temporal rootedness of historical categories or *epistemes*, there are many parallels between Bourdieu and Foucault, some of which can be traced directly back to their common training in the history of science and medicine under Canguilhem. But Bourdieu does not conflate the politics of science (knowledge) with that of society (power) and argues instead for taking into account the historically instituted autonomy of the scientific field. To quote:

> While Bourdieu shares with Foucault a Caesuralist and constructivist conception of rationality and a historicist understanding of knowledge, he rejects his *epoche* of the question of scientificity. Where Foucault, embracing a form of

> epistemological agnosticism, is content to suspend the question of meaning and truth by means of an 'orthogonal double bracketing' of the questions of causality and totality, Bourdieu recasts them by reference to the functioning of the scientific field.[30]

Moreover, in his analysis of the articulation between practices, representations, and the social world, Bourdieu's conception of 'strategy without a strategist' is not unlike Foucault's 'except that the latter lacks the dispositional concept of habitus to link the objective structures bequeathed by history to the historical practices of agents and therefore a mechanism to account for the social patterning and objective meaning of strategies.'[31] It can be argued that while both Bourdieu and Foucault share a non-idealist theory of the symbolic with reference to a transcendental idealism, with his concept of habitus, Bourdieu foregrounds the links between the material and the symbolic, whereas in Foucault's Nietschean framework, ideas are foregrounded in a manner that makes him a crypto-idealist.

Bourdieu's theory of the symbolic can also be seen fruitfully against the backdrop of problems in another major tradition in the analysis of symbolic forms—that of Clifford Geertz. The symbolic is central to Geertz's concept of culture which, it can be inferred, he defines as 'the pattern of meanings embodied in symbolic forms, including actions, utterances and meaningful objects of various kinds, by virtue of which individuals communicate with one another and share their experiences, conceptions and beliefs.'[32] Geertz's interpretive anthropology is a significant departure from structuralism and brings centre stage the importance of actors' meanings which are conspicuously neglected by the former. However, it has been pointed out that Geertz does not consider the relationship between symbolic systems and the life that they talk about or to the material conditions and activities for maintaining (or changing) life. Thus, for instance, in the way he defines religion, it is isolated from social practices and discourses and regarded primarily in terms of consciousness. Moreover, symbols are regarded as 'sui generis' rather than as a condition of social life, and there is a hiatus between 'cultural system' and 'social system'.[33] The attempt to work with a universal definition of religion, seeking its essence, is symptomatic of the a-historical, idealist conception underlying Geertz's theory of the symbolic, to which Bourdieu's theory provides a striking counterpoint. Grounded in a theory of practice, Bourdieu's theory transcends the dichotomy between society and culture, and offers a critique of the intellectualocentricism that conceives of social reality as a text.

Given the social significance of symbolism and the indisputable importance and distinctiveness of Bourdieu's work in sociology, his theory of the symbolic calls for systematic understanding and appraisal. Such an attempt must be made bearing in mind that his theory is an open-ended construct, providing a set of heuristic conceptual tools which may be modified by application in new contexts. It must also take cognizance of Bourdieu's immersion in the vital and urgent issues facing the world today, since sociology for him had an important role to play in politics and society. In fact, his work represents an endeavour to redefine the boundaries of the sociological field, relating intellectual activity to the human condition through an energetic blend of scientific rigour and inventiveness, and humility and compassion.

In this study, I will first delineate, in Chapter 2, the nature of the links between Bourdieu's theory of the symbolic and earlier traditions of analysis. In particular, I will examine how he critiques them, and innovates with them, to create a new theory. The major reference points for this are the traditions of neo-Kantianism, of structuralism, of phenomenology, and the Marxist and Weberian traditions. A significant feature of the relationship of his theory to these traditions is that critique simultaneously leads to a synthesis of aspects of these divergent perspectives into theoretical theses about symbolic systems in general. Thus, Bourdieu arrives at the formulation that symbolic systems exert a structuring power insofar as they are structured; and that it is as structured and structuring instruments that they fulfill their political function as instruments of domination. Furthermore, the fact that structuralism, including what Bourdieu calls relational structuralism, and phenomenology, are incorporated in the theory, exemplifies how Bourdieu transcends the opposition between objectivism and subjectivism in his work. One is led to conclude that Bourdieu's theory is much more than a mere eclectic putting together of diverse perspectives, whose originality seems to stem from the novel theory of practice in which it is embedded.

It is precisely how Bourdieu's theory of the symbolic forms part of his theory of practice that further constitutes the theme of the next two chapters.

In Chapter 3, I begin with a discussion of the concept of practice itself, identifying the importance of Bourdieu's reflections on the practice of theory for his theory of practice. The formula {(habitus)(capital)}+field=practice} is noted as being a useful starting point for viewing the conceptual framework of his theory. The concept of habitus is analysed next, beginning with an understanding of what Bourdieu means by describing the habitus as structured structures predisposed to function as structuring structures. The relation between social structures and the habitus, the implications of the fact that they are embodied structures and their dialectic with the context in which practice takes place, are examined. The significance of practical logic as part of the workings of the habitus is explained, in which context, the relevance of Bourdieu's method of participant objectivation is highlighted.

Moving next to the concept of capital, I attempt to clarify its precise meaning in Bourdieu's oeuvre. His conceptualization of various forms of capital and the interrelationships between them is examined. The salience of cultural and symbolic capital for his theory of the symbolic is explicated.

In Chapter 4, the specific attributes of Bourdieu's concept of fields are first identified, and the importance of the invariant features of fields, as well as of their variation along the axis of their degree of autonomy, is explained. How the relationship between habitus and field leads to a rejection of the duality of action and structure, and exemplifies Bourdieu's relational mode of thought, is also clarified. Finally, in the context of Bourdieu's overall argument for the possibility of a unified political economy of practice, his notion of an economy of practice is examined by contextualizing his articulation of this proposal in the trajectory of his work.

Since Bourdieu's theoretical framework 'was constructed through and for the production of new research objects aimed at unraveling the multisided dialectic of social and mental structures in the operation of domination', in Chapter 5, I attempt to put to work Bourdieu's theory of the symbolic in relation to a new empirical context.[34] In particular, the concepts of misrecognition, of doxa, orthodoxy and heterodoxy, and of the state as an institution with a monopoly over legitimate symbolic violence, are used to analyse the Shah Bano case in India. In the process, the strengths of Bourdieu's theory become apparent, as well as some aspects that require further work, given the transposition of a theory originating in work in Algeria and France to a new context.

In Chapter 6, I turn to Bourdieu's critique of contemporary society, as clearly exemplifying his role of a métier militant. As a prolegomenon to this, I sketch his trajectory as a critic of society and note how his is a theory with a critical intent. In particular, I discuss his identification of the links between intellectual pursuits and activism, noting certain problems in his conceptualization of the same. I move on to an exposition of his critique of neoliberalism, highlighting how symbolism is an important dimension of this global phenomenon. I conclude with a few critical observations regarding how Bourdieu's critique and his theory of the symbolic do not cohere entirely.

In Chapter 7, I first discuss the impact of Bourdieu's social theory on sociological theory in general and in the context of French social theory in particular. I then identify the main features of his theory of the symbolic and consider certain assessments of it. Finally, I discuss my own encounter with Bourdieu's work and consider its relevance for further research in the Indian context.

ENDNOTES

1. Fuglerud, Oivind, *Life on the Outside: The Tamil Diaspora and Long Distance Nationalism*, London, Stirling, Virginia, Pluto Press, 1999, pp. 15–16, quoted in Ravindra K Jain, 'The Dynamics of Indian

Diaspora and Vision for a Museum, Unpublished Paper, 2004, p. 7.

2. See T.K. Oommen, *Pluralism, Equality and Identity: Comparative Studies,* New Delhi, Oxford University Press, 2002.
3. Ayesha Jalal, 'Women and Religion', review of *Gendering the Spirit: Women, Religion and the Post-Colonial Response,* (ed) Durre S. Ahmed, New York, Zed Press, 2002, in *Economic & Political Weekly,* 8 February 2003, p. 529.
4. See Rahul Srivastava, 'Power of the Image', review of Christiane Brosius and Melissa Butcher (ed) *Image Journeys: Audio-Visual Media and Cultural Change in India,* New Delhi, Sage Publications, 1999, in *Economic & Political Weekly,* 24 July 1999, p. 2069.
5. Uma Chakravarti, 'State, Market, and Freedom of Expression: Women and Electronic Media', *Economic & Political Weekly,* 29 April 2000, p. WS–17.
6. Usha Thakkar, 'Culture & Politics' review of *The Politics of Cultural Mobilisation in India,* (ed) John Zavos, Andrew Wyatt and Veron Hewitt, New Delhi, Oxford University Press, 2004, in *Economic & Political Weekly,* 25 September 2004.
7. Samita Sen, 'Recast(e)ing Class' review of Janaki Nair, *Miners and Millhands: Work, Culture and Politics in Princely Mysore,* New Delhi, Sage Publications, 1998, in *Economic & Political Weekly,* 1 May 1999, p. 1027.
8. Pierre Bourdieu, *The Logic of Practice,* Cambridge, Polity Press, 1990, p. 141.
9. Pierre Bourdieu and Loic J. Wacquant, *An Invitation to Reflexive Sociology,* Cambridge, Polity Press, 1992, p. 2.
10. Rogers Brubaker, 'Rethinking Classical Theory: The Sociological Vision of Pierre Bourdieu', in *Theory and Society,* Vol. 14, No. 6, November 1985, p. 746.
11. Pierre Bourdieu, *The Logic of Practice,* Cambridge, Polity Press, 1990, p. 102.
12. Ibid., p. 135.
13. Ibid., p. 140.
14. Pierre Bourdieu, *Outline of a Theory of Practice,* Cambridge University Press, 1977 p. 183.
15. Pierre Bourdieu, et al. *The Craft of Sociology,* Berlin, New York, Walter de Gruyter, 1991, pp. 15, 19–20, 32.
16. Rogers Brubaker, 'Rethinking Classical Theory: The Sociological Vision of Pierre Bourdieu', in *Theory and Society,* Vol. 14, No. 6, November 1985, p. 747.
17. Pierre Bourdieu and Loic J. Wacquant, *An Invitation to Reflexive*

Sociology, Cambridge, Polity Press, 1992, p. 14.

18. Pierre Bourdieu, *The State Nobility*, Cambridge, Polity Press, 1996, p. ix.
19. Loic J. Wacquant, 'The Sociological Life of Pierre Bourdieu', in *International Sociology*, vol. 17(4), December 2002, p. 556.
20. Ibid., p. 549.
21. Roland Lardinois, 'Pierre Bourdieu (1930-2002), A Sociologist in Action', in *Economic & Political Weekly*, 16 March 2002, p. 121.
22. Ibid.
23. Loic J. Wacquant, 'The Sociological Life of Pierre Bourdieu' in *International Sociology*, Vol. 17(4), December 2002, p. 556.
24. Ibid.
25. Pierre Bourdieu, *In Other words*, Cambridge, Polity Press, 1990, p. 21.
26. Pierre Bourdieu and Loic J. Wacquant, *An Invitation to Reflexive Sociology*, Cambridge, Polity Press, 1992, p. 47.
27. Peter Dews, *Logics of Disintegration*, London, New York, Verso, 1987, p. 24.
28. Ibid., p. 40.
29. Ibid., pp. 40–41
30. Pierre Bourdieu and Loic J. Wacquant, *An Invitation to Reflexive Sociology*, Cambridge, Polity Press 1992, p. 48 note 86.
31. Ibid., p. 25 note 46.
32. John Thompson, *Ideology and Modern Culture*, Cambridge, Polity Press, 1990, p. 132.
33. Talal Asad, 'Anthropological Conceptions of Religion: Reflections on Geertz' in *Man*, 18 March 1983, pp. 237–59.
34. Loic J. Wacquant, 'The Sociological Life of Pierre Bourdieu' in *International Sociology*, Vol. 17 (4), December 2002, p. 552.

2

Bourdieu's Theory of the Symbolic: Traditions and Innovations

Introduction

The practice of symbolization is as old as human history, and permeates all human activity. A part of the history of reflections on symbolization is the emergence of theories of the symbolic, first in the domain of philosophy, and subsequently in the fields of art history and art criticism, literary criticism, linguistics, psychology, sociology and anthropology. More recently, certain symbolic phenomena have become important objects of analysis in the field of cultural studies, which includes studies of the media. Not surprisingly, Bourdieu's theory of the symbolic taps some of the rich resources of existing traditions. Yet, as we shall see, it is a singularly original contribution. In fact, it reflects a general feature of Bourdieu's sociological craftsmanship which he describes as the attempt to adopt a fair attitude toward theoretical tradition, affirming as inseparable both continuity and rupture as a precondition for truly productive thought.[1]

The range of symbolic phenomena that Bourdieu's various sociological analyses encompass is very wide, including myth, language, arts and science, as well as revolutionary and magical forms of consciousness (in the context of the Algerian subproletariat), and also what he terms practical logic, practical sense, and common sense. It also includes the symbolic aspects of religion, of ritual, of kinship systems, education, law, philosophy, gender, politics, literature, the media, the state, systems of tastes in lifestyles, political preferences and aesthetics. It is therefore helpful to note, that at a general level, the realm of the symbolic in Bourdieu's work refers to mental structures, including schemes and categories of perception, thought, evaluation, and action, both conscious and unconscious, as well as to activities, institutions, and objects pertaining to the same.[2]

Underlying Bourdieu's various analyses is a theory of the symbolic, whose originality stems from the original theory of practice in which it is embedded. The theory draws attention to the fact that symbolism is intrinsic to human practice, and that symbolic phenomena are both products of the material and social environment in which human practice takes place, as well as contribute to the creation of this environment. The basic conceptual framework of Bourdieu's theory of practice, consisting of the interrelated concepts of habitus, fields and capital, is informed by this understanding of the symbolic.

This chapter attempts to identify the various traditions of analysis that have gone into the making of Pierre Bourdieu's theory of the symbolic, and to specify the way in which he innovates with them, to surpass them in power and scope. His article entitled 'Symbolic Power' provides a particularly clear framework for viewing the relationship between previous approaches and his theory of the symbolic.[3] It discusses explicitly (albeit schematically), the neo-Kantian tradition and its sociological version in the writings of Durkheim and Mauss, the structuralist tradition, the contribution of Marx and the work of Weber. It also implicitly but clearly indicates how relational structuralism and phenomenology are relevant for a full appreciation of how he reconstructs tradition in his theory. Its argument, in summary form, is as follows:

Bourdieu identifies three types of symbolic instruments each of which has been the focus of a distinct mode of analysis. Thus, we can distinguish between symbolic systems: (1) as instruments of knowledge and construction of the objective world, being thereby **structuring structures** usually apprehended as various symbolic forms; (2) as means of communication, perceived as symbolic objects, and described as **structured structures;** (3) as instruments of power in so far as they contribute to the formation of a dominant culture which functions to integrate dominant classes while creating the false consciousness of the dominated classes: in other words, legitimating the established order by establishing distinctions or hierarchies and in turn legitimating these distinctions. From this perspective, symbolic systems are **instruments of domination**, phenomena usually designated by the term, ideology, or qualified as being ideological.

In Bourdieu's conception, all symbolic systems share the three qualities noted above. They are symbolic forms capable of structuring structures, they themselves constitute structured structures, and they serve the ideological function of maintaining the dominance of the dominant and the domination of the dominated. The coming together of these aspects in Bourdieu's theory is not, however, a simple additive process. It is an alternative proposal based on a critical rethinking of the implicit assumptions and methodological features of existing traditions; a rethinking we will discuss now.

Relationship with Preexisting Traditions

Symbolic systems as symbolic forms or structuring structures

While recognizing the cognitive function of symbolic systems, Bourdieu's theory differs from the tradition which views them as structuring structures alone. This is the approach of what he terms the idealist Kant–Humboldt–Cassirer tradition and its American Sapir–Whorf version which treats the different symbolic universes (myth, language, art and science) as instruments for knowing and constructing the world of objects.[4] While granting that this tradition has moved beyond Kant in giving the mind a greater role in constructing its own reality, thereby recognizing, as Marx notes in his *Theses on Feuerbach*, the 'active aspect' of cognition, Bourdieu chooses to go further along with Marx.[5] He argues that this tradition is a form of idealist intellectualism that fails to recognize that the principle of the construction of objects of knowledge is real concrete activity – that is practical activity oriented towards practical functions. This links Bourdieu's theory of the symbolic clearly to his theory of practice, a link we will discuss in detail in

Chapters 3 and 4, after completing our exploration of its relationship with earlier traditions in this chapter.

Though also within the neo-Kantian tradition, the work of Panofsky is seen by Bourdieu as being more cognizant of history, and therefore an exemplary contribution to a social history of conventional modes of cognition and expression.[6] However, while breaking with the notion of transcendental forms, it does not make a radical break with the idealist tradition, by relating historical forms of perception and representation systematically to the social conditions in which they are produced and reproduced.[7] From this point of view, though still within the Kantian tradition, the work of Durkheim and Mauss is the proper starting point for a sociology of symbolic forms.[8] For with Durkheim's *The Elementary Forms of The Religious Life* and Durkheim and Mauss's *Primitive Classification*, symbolic forms or forms of classification cease to be universal transcendental forms, and become social forms that are arbitrary, relative to a particular group and are socially determined.[9] Indeed, Durkheim endeavours to show how even the basic categories of thought as identified by Kant, have their origin in society.[10] In this framework, what gives symbolic forms their objectivity and meaning is the presupposition that they are upheld by a social consensus, or an agreement of the structuring subjectivities. This places the approach squarely within the idealist tradition.

Bourdieu concurs with the view that there is a correspondence between social structures and mental structures, and argues for and demonstrates the fruitfulness of extending this basic Durkheimian insight from the analysis of systems of classification in traditional communities to the study of those of 'advanced' societies. However, in place of social consensus, Bourdieu calls attention to variations in cognitive dispositions towards the world according to social positions and historical situations which he terms different kinds of 'world-making' that he suggests should be the subject matter of a differential anthropology of symbolic forms.[11] He further deconstructs the Durkheimian idea of social consensus and the related notion of a collective consciousness by showing how they conceal the crucial political role that symbolic systems play in relation to systems of social domination and subordination. This, symbolic systems do, for example, by enabling the naturalization of arbitraries, as happens when they are internalized by agents through socialization, and more generally, through the creation of a common sense, or 'doxa', as he terms it. Furthermore, as the existence of different kinds of 'world making' in conjunction with a cognizance of their political functions would suggest, systems of classification constitute a stake in the various struggles that oppose individuals and groups in society, leading to the emergence of orthodoxy that tries to formalize doxa and to heterodoxy that opposes it.

Bourdieu also critiques the notion of a collective consciousness for hypostasizing the social, thereby perpetuating the conventional dichotomy between the individual and the social. This, in turn, prevents Durkheimian sociology from being able to provide a sound causative mechanism for the social determination of classifications. What Bourdieu proposes is that social divisions and mental schemata are structurally homologous because they are genetically linked : the latter are nothing other than the embodiment of the former in subjective dispositions which he terms the habitus. Moreover, as the word embodiment suggests, these dispositions are embedded in bodies; and once we posit that the social (which includes the symbolically structured material environment in which social activity takes place) is instituted in biological individuals, the dichotomy between the material and the symbolic breaks down, as does the duality between mind and body. Furthermore, since the theory posits that the social is instituted in individuals, it implies that there is in each biological individual something of the collective or trans-individual valid for a whole class of agents. Thus the antinomy traditionally established between sociology and social psychology also disappears in it.[12]

Bourdieu's materialist theory of the symbolic marks a further rupture from Durkheim's idealism in the sense that while the latter makes conscious obedience to rules or the transcendental social norm via social constraint the determining principle of all practices (thus positing that the social world is governed by a symbolic system external to individual actors), Bourdieu sees this conception as an example of the error of misplaced concreteness and what he terms the fallacy of the rule; that is, of slipping from the model of reality to the reality of the model.[13] For it is an approach that projects the manner in which observed regularities are systematized and constructed into an explanatory system by the sociologist, that is, consciously and logically—into the content of its subject matter. Bourdieu's theory of the symbolic, as his theory of practice in general, in its search for the generative principles of practice, struggles against the distortions of such intellectualist and objectivist idealism. In contrast, it takes into account the role of unconscious and preconscious determinants, as well as the particular logic of practice which he terms practical logic, which is unlike abstract logic. Thus Bourdieu draws attention, for example, to the theoretical neutralization and falsification inherent in the use of synoptic diagrams of genealogies or of agrarian calendars and political structures of traditional societies (and, by extension, of 'advanced' societies) by structural functionalists of Durkheimian inspiration, purportedly to represent social reality more reliably than what native informants have to say. These according to Bourdieu, 'ignore the unceasing dynamism of units which are constantly forming and reforming, and the fuzziness which is an integral part of native notions in as much as it is at once the precondition and the product of their functioning.'[14] It may be noted here that attention to this aspect of social reality is a culmination of the movement in empirical social anthropology towards practice; a movement in which the works of J. Van Velsen and Max Gluckman using the method of situational analysis, and Victor Turner's work focusing on 'process', mark stages.

As the discussion above suggests, Bourdieu's theory of the symbolic shares with the neo-Kantian view of symbolic systems as structuring structures, a recognition of their cognitive functions, including the active aspect of cognition. It also finds a point of departure for a sociology of symbolic forms in Durkheim's postulate of a correspondence between mental structures and social structures. However, it moves away from the Durkheimian framework towards an alternative theoretical perspective in more ways than one. It critiques the notions of social consensus and of a collective consciousness by introducing the dimensions of differentiation and power; it rejects the dichotomy between the individual and the social; it transcends the idealist mind-body duality; and it reveals the objectivist errors of Durkheim's epistemology.

Symbolic Systems as Structured Structures

Bourdieu sees a continuity between the structuralist approach to the analysis of symbolic systems and the tradition discussed above in so far as the former seems to provide a methodological instrument to realize the neo-Kantian ambition of grasping the specific logic of each of the symbolic forms. However, unlike the neo-Kantian tradition which emphasizes the **modus operandi** or productive activity of consciousness, the structuralist tradition emphasizes the **opus operatum** or structured structures – that is, the structures of consciousness of the mind itself and of symbolic forms in general. In fact, the structuralist focus on the structure immanent in each symbolic production has affinities with the Hegelian search for their self-contained and self-sufficient essence.

However, Hegel's objectivist idealism views all particular symbolic forms, including those in the finite minds of human beings, in relation to the ultimate reality of the transcendental absolute idea, assessing the adequacy of various forms of art and religion, for example, as modes of comprehending it. The absolute idea is viewed as the logical culmination of a process of the development of the universal human mind through thesis, antithesis and synthesis, towards absolute knowledge or the self-knowing spirit. From this perspective, to arrive at a true analysis of particular symbolic forms, we need to abstract from them their real structure, that of a transcendent ultimate reality, which is an ideational reality, in the process of the conscious realization of which these forms constitute particular historical stages. But while the structuralist method, inaugurated by Saussure in linguistics and proposed as the basis for the science of semiology, does focus, like the Hegelian approach, on the immanent structures of symbolic forms, it does not view them as expressions of the evolving mind, but as primary phenomena.[15]

The structuralist approach to symbolic forms owes much to Saussure's distinction between 'langue' and 'parole' and to his analysis of the structure of 'langue' which is seen to provide an understanding of how language functions as an instrument of communication in society. By identifying 'langue' as the proper subject matter of linguistics, Saussure suggests that the essential nature of signifying systems is to be found, not in the substance of their empirical instantiations, but in their underlying structures, which are structured in accordance with the mechanism by which the mind performs the operation of signifying. This is an insight that Levi-Strauss incorporates into his study of human culture, in which various symbolic forms, ranging from kinship systems to religion are analysed as systems of communication (which subsumes their function as systems of logical classification and resolution of logical contradictions) and which in various permutations and combinations are structured in accordance with the collective unconscious of the human mind.[16] It follows that the meaning of symbolic forms lies in their internal structure, which is logical and coherent, and can be analysed independently of the social context in which they are found, even though they perform universal social functions—that is, those of logical classification, resolution of logical contradictions, and of communication.

Bourdieu's theory of the symbolic includes a critique of Saussurian linguistics as well as of Levi-Straussian structuralism. As regards Saussure, Bourdieu finds in his concept of langue the construction of a seemingly independent object domain which is in fact the idealization of a particular set of linguistic practices which have emerged historically and have certain social conditions of existence.[17] This undermines the basis of his method of analysis, and suggests an alternative which involves placing language as a symbolic form in the context of the social, historical and political conditions in which it is found. Once this is done, language is seen to perform a host of social functions of which communication is often, but not always, one, and which can be analysed in terms of the logic of the practice of which language forms a part. It follows that speaking cannot be adequately understood as the mere realization or 'execution' of a preexisting linguistic code (for that is found to be itself the product of variable socio-historical conditions), nor, by extension, can other symbolic works be seen as finished products to be deciphered by reference to a code which may be termed 'culture'.[18] In fact, this notion of conduct, including symbolic production and its products as execution, is an idealist construct, and as Bourdieu points out, is common to all modes of thought which he terms 'objectivist'. This includes the structural functionalism of Durkheim and Radcliffe Brown who view social practices as realizations of the workings of a system of norms embedded in a social structure, and of the structuralism of Levi-Strauss which views cultural phenomena as manifestations of the unconscious structures of the mind. It involves, Bourdieu argues, a viewpoint most easily adopted in elevated positions in the social space, where the social world presents itself as a spectacle seen from afar and from above, as a representation.[19] Thus, too, the error of misplaced concreteness and the fallacy of the rule, noted in the case of Durkheim's approach, are to be found in structuralism as well. For structuralism takes the intellectual process, by which it builds its models of reality to understand it, as constituting the content of that reality. In other words, the functions of logical integration and communication attributed to symbolic systems by this mode of thought (and as a corollary placed in the subjectivities of social agents) are a projection of the social scientist's relationship to his/her subject matter. Concomitantly, individuals or groups are portrayed as the passive supports of forces that mechanically work out their independent logic.[20]

However, it would be wrong to conclude from the above that Bourdieu's theory of the symbolic owes nothing to structuralism. To begin with, it credits structuralism with making possible a break with the substantialist mode of thought, which was current in the social sciences till well into the nineteen sixties, and informs the study of symbolic forms as well. The replacement of the idea that the meaning of each symbolic element in a symbolic system resides in it separately, by the insight that it is rather to be found in the structure by which other elements of the same class are related within a system, had revolutionary implications.[21] As we will discuss below, this mode of thought, which may be termed relational structuralism, is an intrinsic part of Bourdieu's sociological theory in general, and not just of his theory of the symbolic. What makes this relevant for an appreciation of his theory of the symbolic is that he uses the relational mode of thought in his analysis both of symbolic systems in particular, as well as of social systems in general, of which symbolic systems are a part. This provides his theory with a key to understanding how, as structured structures, symbolic systems are efficacious as structuring structures in relation to social reality, as well as enables him to make systematic comparisons between different systems. This includes the discernment of structural affinities and homologies between them, and even possible relations of transformations whereby one system of relations is changed into another, or is a subsystem of another.[22] The critical difference between Bourdieu's genetic structuralism and that of Levi-Strauss, however, is that in Bourdieu's theory, the coherence of symbolic structures emanates not from the universal structures of the human mind, but from the structures of the material and social environment that both engender human practice (which includes the practice of symbolization), and are constructed by it. The coherence of symbolic systems is therefore not a logical coherence (except or at least to a greater extent, where it is an explicit principle of practice, as in philosophy or science), but a practical coherence. This means that features of symbolic systems that deviate from logical logic, such as ambiguity and polythesis, are nevertheless comprehensible when they are seen in relation to their practical functions, in the context of which they obey what Bourdieu variously terms a logic of convenience, or a 'poor' logic, or an 'economical' logic.[23]

Symbolic Systems as Instruments of Domination

Though in neither is the social significance of symbolic systems conceptualized solely in terms of these functions, the Marxian framework highlights the role that symbolic systems play as ideologies, maintaining structures of economic domination and subordination in society, while Weber in his analysis of power, throws light on the importance of symbolic systems in legitimizing relations of power.

While there are strong affinities between the Marxist view of symbolic systems as supports of relations of power and Bourdieu's theory of the symbolic, there are major divergences as well.[24] For one, while the Marxist conceptualization of symbolic systems as forms of consciousness or embodiments and manifestations of such forms suggests that they are intellectual constructs involving conscious thought (hence the use of the term 'ideology' in the Marxist tradition), Bourdieu regards the knowledge construction that constitutes symbolic systems as having nothing in common with intellectual work, but as involving, preeminently, an activity of practical construction, even of practical reflection, as suggested by the discussion of practical logic above.[25] In fact, what makes symbolic systems efficacious in maintaining relations of domination is that they exert themselves, not in the pure logic of knowing consciousness, but in the obscurity of the dispositions of habitus, 'in which are embedded the schemes of perception and appreciation which, below the level of the decisions of the conscious mind and the controls of the will, are the basis of a relationship of practical knowledge and recognition that is profoundly obscure to itself.'[26]

Moreover, since the habitus are genetically linked to the social structure, and are, as we have noted earlier, embodied phenomena, it follows that the scholastic notion of false consciousness and the expectation that political liberation will come from the 'raising of consciousness' (a point on which certain versions of Marxist thought and feminism converge) neglects the extraordinary inertia, though not immutability, which results from the inscription of social structures in bodies. In this regard, Weber's insight into the significance of legitimizing discourses in maintaining systems of power, too, suffers from intellectualism, for it presupposes a free act of lucid consciousness underpinning the recognition of legitimacy.[27]

Bourdieu prefers to use the word 'belief', rather than 'ideology', for embodied symbolic systems; he, furthermore, coins the term 'symbolic violence' for describing the process by which arbitrary forms of domination are accepted as natural and inevitable by individuals and groups; and uses the term 'misrecognition' to designate the form of cognition that is involved in the process.[28]

The agreement between objective structures of the world and cognitive structures posited by Bourdieu also distinguishes his theory of symbolic violence from Gramsci's theory of hegemony, in the sense that the former requires none of the active 'manufacturing' of the work of 'conviction' entailed by the latter, and also from Althusser's theory of 'ideological state apparatuses', since the work of making domination accepted is largely done by the very logic of the functioning of symbolic systems in Bourdieu's framework of analysis.[29] To quote,

> Legitimation of the social order is not ... the product of a deliberate and purposive action of propaganda or symbolic imposition; it results, rather, from the fact that agents apply to the objective structures of the social world structures of perception and appreciation which are issued out of these very structures and which tend to picture the world as evident.[30]

More fundamentally, Bourdieu critiques certain versions of Marxism for reducing the social world to the economic field alone, resulting in the definition of social position with reference solely to the position within the relations of economic production. In its place, Bourdieu conceives of the social space as a multidimensional space of relatively autonomous fields, even as he concedes that these are more or less strongly and directly subordinate, in their functioning and their transformations, to the field of economic production.[31] While we will discuss the concept of field in detail in the next chapter, what is relevant here is that it follows that symbolic systems play a role in maintaining systems of domination and power defined by criteria other than economic class, such as, for example, sex and ethnicity. These, moreover, cannot always be reduced, even in the ultimate analysis, to refracted forms of economic relations. Further, in differentiated societies, virtually every field, according to Bourdieu, is characterized by the existence of its dominant and dominated, with symbolic forms and symbolic struggles, including processes of symbolic violence and misrecognition constituting elements of the field.

Bourdieu's theory of the symbolic also avoids what he terms the 'short-circuit' effect which is common in Marxist criticism, and consists of the reduction of ideological products to the interests of the classes which they serve.[32] This he does by noting that symbolic systems are fundamentally distinguishable according to whether they are produced and thereby appropriated by the group as a whole, as in simple, undifferentiated societies, and in the everyday symbolic struggles of groups in differentiated societies, or, on the contrary, produced by a body of specialists, and, more precisely, by a relatively autonomous field of production and circulation. Where they are produced by specialists, they owe their most specific characteristics not only to the interests of the classes or class fractions they express, but also to the specific interests of those who produce them and to the specific logic of the field of production.[33] Thus he also provides a corrective to the 'reflection' theory which relates works directly to the social characteristics of the authors, or of the groups to whom they are addressed or are assumed to be addressed, neglecting the fact of the existence of the field of cultural production as a relatively autonomous social universe.[34]

In conceptualizing the relative autonomy of the cultural field (while conceding that the Marxist tradition affirms this relative autonomy of ideologies and the producers of ideology, but without establishing the foundations and social effects of this autonomy), Bourdieu credits Weber's work on the sociology of religion for drawing his attention to the neglected area of the religious work carried out by specialist agents and their own interests. However, he moves away from the realist typology that informs Weber's discussion of the same, towards a construction of the religious field (as well as of all fields) as structures of objective relations which can account for concrete forms of the interactions to be found in them.[35]

Innovations by Synthesis

Symbolic systems exert a structuring power in so far as they are structured

The conceptions of symbolic systems as either structuring structures or as structured structures have conventionally been regarded as belonging to mutually exclusive intellectual traditions. However, as our discussion above shows, Bourdieu's theory of the symbolic draws upon both traditions, albeit with significant modifications. In other words, Bourdieu's theory synthesizes these viewpoints within an original framework of analysis. An important aspect of this synthesis is the insight that there is an essential link between these two perspectives, which is that while one key aspect of the social significance of symbolic systems is their structuring power, at the same time, what gives them this efficacy is the fact that they themselves are structured. For supposing 'moral' integration to be an important condition for the existence of social integration and the 'logical' integration of symbolic systems to be an important condition for their constitution, the contribution to social order made by symbolic systems involves both processes of the systematization of symbolic representations and of the inculcation of belief in individuals and groups in these representations. As our discussion above clarifies, this systematization, in the case of Bourdieu's theory of the symbolic, does not take place in a transcendental realm of ideas detached from social processes, or even via universal, transhistorical structures of the mind. So also, the inculcation of beliefs is neither the activity of a pure transcendental consciousness shaping the knowledge of reality, nor is it an external force, emanating from a hypostasized entity called 'society', acting upon passive social agents. Rather, both the coherence of symbolic systems and their constitution as systems of belief are part of a process which is critically shaped by and in turn shapes, the social and material environment in which human practice takes place.

Thus, in this *Outline of a Theory of Practice* Bourdieu defines symbolic systems as 'practical taxonomies, instruments of cognition and communication which are the preconditions for the establishment of meaning' and which 'exert their structuring efficacy only to the extent that they are themselves structured'.[36] But as he adds in his *The Logic of Practice,*

> This does not mean that they are amenable to a purely internal ('structural', componential', etc.) analysis which artificially isolates them from their conditions of production and use and so cannot understand their social functions. The coherence that is observed in all the products of the application of the same habitus has no other basis than the coherence that the generative principles constituting that habitus derive from the social structure (the structure of relations between the groups, the sexes or the generations, or between the social classes) of which they are the product and which they tend to reproduce in a transformed, misrecognizable form, by inserting them into the structure of a system of symbolic relations.[37]

To elaborate on the above, the fact that a social formation has a structure means that human practices are structured, and since human practices by definition involve symbolic practices as well, symbolic systems, too, are structured. However, the social structures and the structures of symbolic systems embodied in the habitus in the form of a system of dispositions that are the generative principles of the practices of individuals and groups, are not thereby identical in content, or even in the sense of the latter being a direct and true representation of the former, but are rather structurally isomorphic with each other. This enables the habitus to generate practices that are both objectively and subjectively compatible with the context in which they occur. This is so even as the symbolic component of the habitus may reproduce the principles of the social structure in a transformed and misrecognisable form, with this transformation and misrecognition playing a crucial role in the reproduction of the social order, and with symbolic systems sometimes, and to some extent, even overdetermining social structures with their specific symbolic effects. This underlines the fact that the structure of symbolic systems, as indeed the very fact that they are structured, is an important characteristic that makes them efficacious as structuring structures, capable of structuring human practices including the construction of reality and also thereby the social and material environment in which practice takes place. It also means that a proper analysis of their structures has to take into account the logic of the practices of which they form part, as well as of the social structures in which they are produced, and in which they circulate. And in all this, the process by which the system of dispositions termed the habitus is constituted clearly plays a key role, for it is the locus of the internalization of the external and the externalization of the internal.

While we will consider the relationship between Bourdieu's theory of the symbolic and the concept of habitus as part of his theory of practice in detail in the next chapter, here we will try and explain, with an illustration from Bourdieu's work, how the synthesis of the two approaches viewing symbolic systems as structuring structures and as structured structures discussed above actually works within the context of his particular framework.

Bourdieu's analysis of traditional Kabyle beliefs, values, myths, rituals and organization of domestic space provides a significant illustration of the fruitfulness of synthesizing the view of symbolic systems as structuring structures with that of them as structured structures. While we will look at his analysis of the Kabyle house here, it must be noted that it is in his essay called 'The Sense of Honour' that Bourdieu demonstrates how the moral system of a code of honour found among the Kabyle peasants, which, taken on its own, seems arbitrary, appears on the contrary to be necessary when reinserted into the Kabyle mythico—ritual system based on the opposition between the male and the female, of which the oppositions to be found between the sacred of the right hand, and that of the left hand, between the outside and the inside, between fire and water, the dry and the wet, at cetera were discovered to be particular modes.[38] Analysing the moral system in terms of the notion of the activation of a practical sense, rather than of the following of a system of rules, Bourdieu describes how it was inculcated among the Kabyle from a very early age in a way that makes it appropriate to regard the system of honour values as enacted rather than thought.

In the essay entitled 'The Kabyle House or the World Reversed' Bourdieu builds on the observation that the 'book' from which children learn their vision of the world is read with the body, in moving through space from parts of the house that are 'male' to others that are 'female' according to Kabyle cosmology.[39] As he does this, his description of the Kabyle house prises open the systematic structuring of the location and orientation of things and activities as parts of a symbolic system. Postulating that each of the phenomena observed—from the walls and placement of objects in the house to the social activities performed within it and outside it—derives its necessity and meaning from its relationship with all the others, Bourdieu's argument unfolds from a structural description of the interior of the house in terms of homologous oppositions between its different parts, to the system of oppositions which exists between the house as a whole and the rest of the universe—that is the symbolically qualified social and spatial external world. Thus the 'male' and 'female' components of the interior space, merge to form a 'female' unity opposed to the 'male' outside world, that is, a world of secrecy and intimacy, a nocturnal world, opposed to the male world of public life and farming, the diurnal world.

Significantly, what Bourdieu has introduced into this seemingly purely structuralist description of a symbolic system is not just the way it is linked to the process of the embodiment of a belief system, and that, too, in a very concretely material sense, but also the dimension of power. For he observes that the two opposite and symmetrical spaces in the structure of the Kabyle house, were not interchangeable but hierarchized. Thus in Kabylia (as in most patriarchal social structures) the male-female opposition, of which the public space-house opposition partook, also symbolized the better or higher or more valuable, versus the lesser, the lower, and the less desired. Indeed, in his later book, *Masculine Domination,* Bourdieu takes the example of Kabylia to analyse the processes by which historically, male domination has been structurally and symbolically reproduced.[40]

This takes us to a consideration of the second transformation through synthesis that informs Bourdieu's theory of the symbolic, which is that it is as structured and structuring instruments that symbolic systems fulfill their political function as instruments of domination. However, before we do so, we need to note Bourdieu's later observation that his article on the Kabyle house was perhaps the last work he wrote 'as a blissful structuralist'.[41] While we have already discussed above some of the ways in which his analysis differs from Levi-Strauss's structuralist analyses, this remark should be viewed in relation to our earlier discussion of how Bourdieu introduces the notion of 'practical logic' as often informing symbolic systems, in place of structuralism's logical logic. For, unlike the coherence observable in the structure of the Kabyle house ('which as a miniature version of the cosmos, constituted an object that was both complete and circumscribed'), Bourdieu writes that 'it was the ambiguities and contradictions which the very effort to push the application of the structural method to its furthermost conclusions constantly raised, that led me to question not so much the method itself as the anthropological thesis tacitly posited in the very fact of consistently applying it to practices.'[42] The important point thus, is that, in relating symbolic systems to human practice, Bourdieu's theory of the symbolic takes note of processes of the creation of structures and of structuring that involve practical logic, whose procedures `are rarely entirely coherent and rarely entirely incoherent.'[43]

It is as structured and structuring instruments that symbolic systems fulfill their political function as instruments of domination

While as Durkheim's structuring structures and Levi-Strauss's structured structures, symbolic systems remain unrelated to systems of power (except in the sense that social solidarity in the structural functionalist tradition is seen to rest on a shared symbolic system), Bourdieu's theory of the symbolic engages centrally with the relationship between the two, with the concept of symbolic power playing a crucial role in his sociological framework as a whole.[44] As we have seen, his critique of

Durkheim deconstructs the notion of a collective consciousness and consensus to reveal the political processes that they conceal, and his engagement with structuralism clarifies that relations of communication can simultaneously be conduits of power relations. Indeed, as our discussion of Bourdieu's work in relation to that of Marx and Weber shows, Bourdieu concurs with Marx in viewing symbolic systems as supports of systems of domination and subordination, and with Weber in seeing legitimization as an important part of the process of the maintenance of power.

But he differs from the Marxist tradition in that he does not view symbolic systems as direct, conscious, and intentional products of substantively constituted social classes maintaining their power. He also disagrees with the Marxist view that systems of economic domination and subordination are the only basis, even if only in the ultimate analysis, for the structuring of power in society. And while concurring with Weber in attributing to symbolic systems a role in legitimizing relations of power, and borrowing from him an insight into the social role of specialists in the religious domain and extending it to other fields of symbolic production and circulation, he does not view legitimation in terms of an act of lucid consciousness, and affects a methodological transformation by moving away from the realist typology that informs Weber's understanding of the religious field, to a notion of society and its subfields as systems of relationally structured social positions. This enables the conceptualization of the fields of symbolic production and circulation as both relatively autonomous from those where other forms of power are efficient, as well as of there being, among other possible relations between them, structural relations as well, such as those of isomorphism, homology, transformations, and so on.

The notion that symbolic systems are efficacious as instruments of domination because they are capable of structuring and are themselves structured, suggests the particular power of processes of symbolic construction and symbolic communication in maintaining systems of social domination—in other words, of the specific contribution of what

Bourdieu terms symbolic power, to any system of power. He brings to light the fact that, apart from what is obtained through force, whether physical or economic, the different classes and class fractions in society are engaged in a symbolic struggle properly speaking, aimed at imposing the definition of the social world that is best suited to their interests. Symbolic systems thus bring their own distinctive power to bear on the relations of power which underlie them, through the process of symbolic violence, that is, the creation of a belief in the legitimacy of relations of domination, which involves their structuring efficacy as structured systems. Moreover, as we have noted earlier, these symbolic struggles are engaged in by classes, either directly, in the symbolic conflicts of everyday life, or else via the struggle between the different specialists in symbolic production. And since the field of symbolic production is a relatively autonomous field, this means that even as the field of symbolic production is a microcosm of the symbolic struggle between classes, nevertheless, it is only by serving their own interests in the struggle within the field of production (and only to this extent) that producers serve the interests of groups outside the field of production. Thus, for instance, it is possible for ideologues of the dominant class—that is, of the economically dominant class, who are engaged in symbolic production including that of defining the principles of social hierarchization, to appropriate for their own benefit the power to define the social world that they hold by delegation, such as by tending, as they do, to set the specific capital to which they owe their position, which Bourdieu terms cultural capital, at the top of the hierarchy of the principles of hierarchization. Thus, it may be argued, for instance, with reference to the caste system in India, that the Brahmins, as ideologues of the dominant class, placed spiritual capital at the top of the caste hierarchy.

However, Bourdieu's analysis of symbolic systems as structuring and structured, and as capable of acting as instruments of domination, cannot be fully comprehended without seeing how it works within the context of his overall theoretical framework informed by the perspective of relational structuralism and by a critical appropriation of phenomenology.

While relational structuralism is used as a method to map the objective features of social reality, it is combined with phenomenology so as to encompass subjective realities as well, in order to arrive at a comprehensive understanding of social life. It is to these that we will turn next.

Innovations through Linkages

Relational Structuralism

Both as components of dispositional systems that consciously or unconsciously orient actions and shape perceptions, and as exteriorized symbolic products which are produced, consumed and circulated, symbolic systems, according to Bourdieu's theory of the symbolic, can be analysed sociologically by using relational structuralism, in conjunction and articulation with a more general framework of analysis that critically incorporates other theoretical modes as well. Thus, as we had noted, the fact that Bourdieu employs the relational mode of thought both in his analysis of symbolic systems in particular, as well as of social systems in general, of which symbolic systems are a part, enables him to make systematic comparisons between different systems (not just in a particular society or culture, but also in societies at different points of time in history, and between societies and cultures), including the discernment of structural affinities and even possible relations of transformation, whereby one system of relations is changed into another, or is a subsystem of another.[45] This has important consequences. For it enables us to understand, for example, how, while conceiving the cultural field as a relatively autonomous structure of objective relations, he can posit the possibility of homologies between it and the field of social classes, such that, for instance, the ideological systems that specialists produce in and for the struggle over the monopoly of legitimate ideological production, reproduce in a misrecognizable form, the structure of the field of social classes.[46] To understand this fully however, we need to note that what brings into being structural and functional homologies between fields, is the fact that there are shared properties between fields, which Bourdieu terms general laws of the functioning of fields, which are invariant across different fields.

While we will discuss the concept of fields in detail in Chapter 4, what is of significance here is that each field is conceived of by Bourdieu as a space of social positions, constructed on the basis of a principle of differentiation or distribution of a set of properties active within the field—that is capable of conferring strength or power within it (which Bourdieu terms various forms of capital). Each field, morever, is a field of struggle, with specific stakes and interests, irreducible to those of other fields. Generally speaking, the struggle for which a field is the site, has for stakes the monopoly of legitimate violence, or of the specific authority characteristic of the field under consideration, which is also a struggle for the conservation or subversion of the structure of the distribution of capital specific to the field. Indeed, 'the field as a whole is defined as a system of deviations on different levels and nothing, either in the institutions or in the agents, the acts or the discourses they produce, has meaning except relationally, by virtue of the interplay of oppositions and distinctions'.[47] As the above clarifies, the fact that there are homologies between the field of social class and that of ideological production, which make the latter efficacious in maintaining the system of class, can be understood by viewing the existence of invariants governing the structures of different fields, in conjunction with the existence of a logic specific to each field. This explains how the ideological function of the field of ideological production is performed almost automatically. In addition, the fact that the correspondence between social structures and systems of classification is effected only from system to system,

> conceals, both from the eyes of the producers themselves, and from the eyes of non-professional, the fact that the internal systems of classification reproduce overt political taxonomies in misrecognized form, as well as the fact that the axiomatics of each specialized field is the transformed form (in conformity with the laws specific to the field) of the fundamental principles of the division of labour.[48]

Incidentally, it should be noted that fields, in Bourdieu's conception, are products of history, and are subject to being transformed, with more or less difficulty, by history. Thus, the differentiation of the social world into different fields, and the growth and emergence of the relative autonomy of each field, including the field of economic production and the field of symbolic production, are historical processes. We may also note here that there is a somewhat bewildering prolixity of fields in Bourdieu's work, but also that, in each case, the term refers to the concept as outlined above.

However, the distance between Bourdieu's use of the method of relational structuralism and its use in natural sciences and in social science structuralism can clearly be seen in his observation that

> To give primacy to the study of the relations between objective relations rather than to the study of the relations between the agents and these relations, or to ignore the question of the relationship between these two types of relations, leads to the **realism of the structure** which, taking the place of the realism of the element, hypostasizes the systems of objective relations in already constructed totalities, outside the history of the individual or the group. Without falling into a naive subjectivism or 'personalism', one must remember that ultimately, objective relations do not exist and do not really realize themselves except in and through the **system of dispositions,** produced by the internalization of objective conditions.'[49]

Furthermore, and very pertinent from the point of view of his analysis of symbolic phenomena, Bourdieu attempts in his work to establish

> An adequate knowledge both of the space of objective relations between the different positions which constitute the field and of the necessary relations that are set up, through the mediation of the habitus of those who occupy them, between these positions and the points of view on that very space, which play a part in the reality and development of that space.[50]

Significantly, too, with reference both to individuals and to groups, habitus is the unifying principle of practices in different fields,

> the locus of practical realization of the 'articulation' of fields which objectivism from Parsons to the structuralist readers of Marx lays out side by side without securing the means of discovering the

> real principle of the structural homologies or relations of transformation objectively established between them (which is not to deny that the structures are objectivities irreducible to their manifestation in the habitus which they produce and which tend to reproduce them).[51]

Thus, for example, in his study of tastes entitled *Distinction: A Social Critique of the Judgement of Taste,* Bourdieu shows how to each class of positions in social space, there corresponds a class of habitus, including tastes, produced by the social conditioning associated with the corresponding condition and, through the mediation of the habitus and its generative capabilities, a systematic set of goods and properties, which are united by an affinity of style, across different fields.[52] What is very important is that since the habitus are not just generative principles of distinct and distinctive practices, but also classificatory schemes, differences in practices, in the goods possessed, or in the opinions expressed, become symbolic differences and constitute a veritable language, when they are perceived through them. As Bourdieu puts it 'Differences associated with different positions, that is, goods, practices, and especially manners, function, in each society in the same way as differences which constitute symbolic systems, such as the set of phonemes of a language, and of differential "ecarts" that constitute a mythical system, that is, as **distinctive signs**.'[53] The study thus also illustrates how the perception of the social world is the product of a double structuring. It is socially structured 'objectively' because the properties attached to agents or institutions are available to perception, not independently, but in combinations whose probability varies widely. It is, at the same time, structured 'subjectively' in the sense that the schemes of perception that make up the habitus, are a product of previous symbolic struggles, and in some way express the state of symbolic relations of power.[54]

The link between the systems of dispositions and fields is clear in the fact that the habitus, as a system of durable dispositions, exists as a potential for action in every individual, and determines, in the first instance, the inclination to take part in the struggles characterizing particular social fields, with the choice, usually unconscious, of these fields, being contingent on the existence of the pertinent capabilities within the habitus. The specific strategies of agents and the results of their actions, are, however, necessarily dependent on the individual skills of a player, and on the quantity and quality of the capital which an individual agent or group can mobilize in struggles, so that any given practice is the combined outcome of the activation of habitus and deployment of capital, within the parameters of the logic governing a field, which has its own specific structure.

Relational structuralism is also relevant for an understanding of how the relationship between the habitus of a class or a group, and the singular habitus of its different members, related to a specific social trajectory (organic individuality being defined in his theoretical framework by a social trajectory strictly speaking irreducible to any other) is conceptualized by Bourdieu, and what he means by referring to the habitus as a subjective, but not individual system.[55] As he clarifies, since the history of the individual is never anything other than a certain specification of the collective history of his/her group or class, each individual system of dispositions may be seen as a structural variant of all the other group or class habitus, expressing the difference between trajectories and positions inside or outside the class. Thus, the objective coordination and sharing of a worldview which the concept of a group or class habitus implies, are not founded on the perfect interchangeability of singular practices and views. In fact,

> it is in a relation of homology, of diversity within homogeneity reflecting the diversity within homogeneity characteristic of their social conditions of production, that the singular habitus of the different members of the same class are united; the homology of world views implies the systematic differences which separate singular world views, adopted from singular but concerted standpoints.[56]

Amplifying on the link between objective structures and the habitus, Bourdieu notes that 'between the system of objective regularities and the system of directly observable conducts a mediation always intervenes which is nothing else but the habitus, geometrical locus of determinisms and of an individual determination, of calculable probabilities and of lived through hopes, of objective future and subjective plans.[57] Moreover,

> The habitus of class as a system of organic and mental dispositions and of unconscious schemes of thought, perception and action is what allows the generation, with the well-founded illusion of the creation of unforeseeable novelty or free improvisation, of all thoughts, all perceptions and actions in conformity with objective regularities, because it has itself been generated within and by conditions objectively defined by these regularities.[58]

We should, however, remind ourselves here of the fact that while the structure of the symbolic systems constitutive of the habitus are generated by objective structures, the two may be identical in structure, but not necessarily in content, so that the former may reproduce the principles of the social structure in a transformed and misrecognizable form, thus contributing to the efficacy of symbolic systems in maintaining relations of domination and subordination.

But to understand some of the distinctive features of Bourdieu's conception of subjectivity contained in his notion of habitus, which plays such an important role in his theory of the symbolic, it may be useful next to see how his theory is linked to the tradition of phenomenology via a critical transformation.

However, before we do so, another extremely significant aspect of Bourdieu's use of the method of relational structuralism, with important implications for the analysis of the symbolic, must be noted. This is the way in which it allows Bourdieu to take into account empirical and historical specificities of social phenomena, without lapsing into essentialism or historical closure. For the relational mode of thought involves constructing the object of analysis 'as a "special case of what is possible", as Bachelard puts it, that is, as an exemplary case in a finite world of possible configurations'.[59] Thus, for example, in analysing the modern state in Western societies, Bourdieu notes that 'there is no more potent tool for rupture'—that is, rupture from the standpoint that accepts something as natural—'than the reconstruction of genesis'. This is so because 'by bringing back into view the conflicts and confrontations of the early beginnings and therefore all the discarded possibles, it retrieves the possibility that things could have been (and still could be) otherwise. And, through such a practical utopia, it questions the "possible" which, among all others, was actualized'.[60]

Phenomenology

As our discussion above of the articulation of Bourdieu's theory of the symbolic with relational structuralism shows, relational structuralism is part of the method used by Bourdieu to analyse the social significance of symbolic systems. But while acknowledging that relational structuralism facilitates the recognition of aspects of social reality which can be dealt with as a system with an immanent necessity independent of individuals' consciousness and will, and which can therefore be explored in the same way as are relationships among facts of the physical world, Bourdieu necessarily engages with certain traditions of analysis that explore the reality of subjective experience as well, for, as he clarifies, 'unlike natural science, a total anthropology cannot keep to a construction of objective relations because the experience of meanings is part and parcel of the total meaning of experience'[61] In fact, he insists that social science has to take account of the two kinds of properties that are attached to individuals and groups:

> On the one hand, material properties, starting with the body, that can be counted and measured like any other thing of the social world; and on the other hand, symbolic properties which are nothing other than material properties **when perceived and appreciated** in their mutual relationships, that is, as distinctive properties.[62]

Furthermore, and more specifically, he argues that

> The spurious alternatives of social physics and social phenomenology can only be superceded by grasping the principle of the relationship between the regularities of the material universe of properties and the classificatory schemes of the habitus, that product of the social world for which and through which there is a social world.[63]

From the point of view of method, the supercession of the

seemingly antagonistic paradigms of what Bourdieu terms a social physics, or a form of 'objectivism', and social phenomenology, which can be termed 'subjectivism', involves turning them into moments of a form of analysis capable of capturing the intrinsically double reality of the social world. As Loic Wacquant puts it, this means that first, common sense representations are pushed aside to construct objective structures, that is, the spaces of positions, including the distribution of socially efficient resources that define the external constraints bearing on interactions and representations. And second, the immediate, lived experience of agents is reintroduced, in order to explicate the categories of perception and appreciation—that is the dispositions—that structure their action from inside. Significantly, this also means that Bourdieu grants epistemological priority to objectivist rupture over subjectivist understanding, which is understandable not only because, in keeping with a basic tenet of classical sociology, Bourdieu lays stress on the need to systematically reject preconceptions regarding social reality as a first step in scientific research; but also because, as we have noted earlier, he posits that the viewpoints of agents vary systematically with the point they occupy in objective social space.[64]

As regards the phenomenological tradition, the central role of the dialectic between structures and habitus in Bourdieu's theoretical framework clearly implies that his analysis of subjectivity is at odds with the analysis of consciousness posited by the transcendental phenomenology of Husserl. For in Bourdieu's theory, the knowledge of wider and external causes and consequences of internal processes that are 'bracketed' in Husserl's philosophy, are among the very elements that contribute to the genesis and structure of subjective dispositions, and provide the context in which they function and shape experience. Moreover, as against the dualisms of mind and body, and of individual and society, which characterize, according to Bourdieu, the inclination towards 'mentalism' thematized in Husserl's theory of intentionality as noesis, an act of consciousness, containing noemata, the contents of consciousness, Bourdieu, as we have discussed earlier, posits the existence of transindividual schemes of perception, appreciation, and action, residing in bodies, which may not be wholly conscious, and which generate practices, but not always through the mediation of an intentional consciousness.[65] This is so even as Bourdieu includes Husserl among the phenomenologists who opened way for a non-intellectualist, non-mechanist analysis of the relations between agent and world, by giving a role to the notion of habitus in the analysis of antepredicative experience, and also acknowledges the usefulness of the distinction Husserl makes in *Ideen I* between protension as the practical aiming at a yet-to-come inscribed in the present, thus apprehended as already there and endowed with the doxic modality of the present, and the project as the position of a futurity constituted as such, that is, as capable of happening or not happening.[66]

Bourdieu also rejects Sartre's existentialism, which, as he puts it, describes practices as strategies explicitly oriented by reference to purposes, explicitly defined by a free project. In doing so, Sartre refuses to recognize anything resembling durable dispositions, making each action a sort of unprecedented confrontation between the subject and the world. Bourdieu refers instead to the dispositions of agents, which, in relation to, and adapted to, objective conditions, generally incline agents to 'cut their coats according to their cloth', thus invoking Marx's concept of 'effective demand' (as opposed to 'demand without effect' based on need and desire), elucidated in his *Economic and Philosophical Manuscripts*, making for a realistic relation to what is possible, founded on and therefore limited by power.[67] A related problem is existentialism's projection and universalisation of what Bourdieu terms the intellectual's illusion of himself or herself as a subject—that of being distant from all positions—on to those whom he/she purports to understand—a form of intellectualism very cogently illustrated by Sartre's description of a café-waiter in *Being and Nothingness*. As Bourdieu writes, 'One surely has to have the freedom to stay in bed without being fired in order to find that someone who gets up at five to sweep the café and start the percolator before the customers arrive is (freely?) freeing himself from the freedom to stay in bed even if it means being fired'.[68] Furthermore, even as Sartre in his *Critique of Dialectical Reason* recognizes the existence of 'agentless actions, totalizer-less productions, counter finalities and internal circularities,' thus tempering the voluntarism of *Being and Nothingness*, he leaves no room for blurring 'the sharp line his vigorous dualism seeks to maintain between the pure transparency of the subject and the mineral opacity of the thing.' In contrast, in Bourdieu's theory, the social world is one in which thing and meaning interpellate, with the possibility of conceptualizing 'objective meaning' or meaning—made—thing, and dispositions, as meaning—made—body. The theory is a materialist theory, opposed to subjectivist idealism, and thus 'a challenge to someone who can only live in the pure, transparent universe of consciousness or individual "praxis"'.[69]

As regards various forms of social phenomenology, Bourdieu concedes that they do provide rich descriptions of the subjective experience of the social world as self-evident which social theory has to take account of, and that they are quite right in recognizing that mundane knowledge, subjective meaning, and practical competency play a part in the continual production of society. But they fail to explain the feeling of self-evidence, and also cannot fully understand practical understanding.

According to Bourdieu, the feeling of self evidence that characterizes the subjective experience of being in the world, can only be understood in terms of the notion of habitus, since the immediate understanding that agents obtain of the world, is the result of applying to it forms of knowledge derived from the history and structure of the very world to which they apply them. Moreover, phenomenologists ignore the political dimension of the perception of the world as self-evident which Bourdieu incorporates into his analysis through the notion of misrecognition. He points out that while the political function of classifications is likely to pass unnoticed in the case of relatively undifferentiated social formations, in which the prevailing classificatory system encounters no rival or antagonistic principle, in situations of crisis, the adjustment between the order of things and the order of bodies which characterizes the doxic mode of existence, forms the basis of the political action of legitimation, with guardians of the symbolic order, whose interests are bound up with commonsense, trying to restore the initial self evidences of doxa, and the political action of subversion trying to liberate the potential capacity for refusal, which is neutralized by misrecognition, by performing a critical unveiling of the founding violence masked by the feeling of self-evidence.[70]

As regards practical understanding, Bourdieu points out that phenomenologists are unable to see that the principle of practical comprehension is not a knowing consciousness but the practical sense of a habitus, which, as we have noted earlier, is constituted by schemes of perception, appreciation and action that are often not conscious and are properties of the socialized body. Indeed, as in the case of ethnomethodology, they attribute unjustified autonomy and importance to linguistic schemes, which are only one aspect of the system of habitus.[71] Moreover, tending to be ahistorical and antigenetic, phenomenology does not perceive the social classifications and social meanings it draws attention to, in relation to the social experiences in the course of which they are acquired, and which, as Bourdieu points out, are always situated and dated.[72] In fact, being the product of incorporation of the structures and tendencies of the world, the schemes of habitus that inform practical knowledge, make it possible for them to adapt endlessly to partially modified contexts, and to construct the situation as a complex whole endowed with meaning, including a quasi-bodily anticipation of the immanent tendencies of the field, and also of other behaviours engendered by isomorphic habitus.[73] Thus, subjective hopes and even emotional experiences, can be analyzed in terms of the dialectic of habitus and structures. Clearly, such a mode of understanding is far removed from the Schutzian mode, in which the adequacy of explanatory models is validated in terms of the consistency of the constructs of the social scientist with the constructs of common sense experience of the social reality.[74]

Insofar as Bourdieu's conceptualization of subjective

experience in terms of the dialectic of habitus and field rejects the dualism of mind and body, and of conscious intentionality as the sole basis of meaningful practice, it has a certain link with the phenomenological perspective of Merleau Ponty. As Bourdieu writes, 'The agent engaged in practice knows the world but with a knowledge which, as Merleau Ponty showed, is not set up in the relation of externality of a knowing consciousness.'[75] In particular, the notion that the practical comprehension of the world involves corporeal knowledge, can be seen to be based, in part, on Merleau Ponty's idea of the intrinsic corporeality of the preobjective contact between subject and world.[76] Furthermore, the description of the practical, non-thetic intentionality characterizing the habitus, and of the habitus constructing the world by a certain way of orienting itself towards it, 'of bringing to bear on it an attention which, like that of a jumper preparing to jump, is an active, constructive bodily tension towards the imminent forthcoming,' is very much like Merleau Ponty's account of consciousness as a dialectic of milieu and action, illustrated by the example of a soccer player, who,' caught in the heat of the action, instantaneously inituits the moves of his opponents and teammates, acts and reacts in an "inspired" manner without the benefit of hindsight and calculative reason.'[77]

However, unlike the milieu that Merleau Ponty posits, which is viewed strictly from the standpoint of the acting agent, Bourdieu relates practical comprehension to the habitus as well as to the objective structures of the fields in which the habitus is formed, and in which agents act. This he does even while maintaining that there is a relation of 'ontological complicity' between habitus and the social world, for as we have noted earlier, this complicity is itself, according to Bourdieu, the product of situated and dated social experiences. Significantly, this also means that unlike the relationship between the body of Merleau Ponty's subject and the milieu in which he/she acts, the body of Bourdieu's agent is included in the world in a mode of inclusion not only irreducible to simple material and spatial inclusion, but in a way that is affected by 'something very distant, even absent,' which is linked to his or her participation in the structure of a field, with its own logic, which does not always involve physical interaction or proximity with other participants.[78]

As the above would lead us to expect, even though Bourdieu is an admirer of the work of Goffman, who, as he writes, 'Through the subtlest, most fugitive indices of social interaction, grasped the logic of the **work of representation**; that is to say, the whole set of strategies with which social subjects strive to construct their **identity**, to shape their social image, in a word, to produce a show,' he has serious reservations about symbolic interactionism as a method of social analysis in general.[79] This is so, even as he asserts that

> the most resolutely objectivist theory must take account of agents' representation of the social world and, more precisely, of the contribution they make to the construction of the vision of this world, via the labour of representation (in all senses of the term) that they continually perform in order to impose their own vision of the world or the vision of their own position in this world, that is, their social identity.[80]

For by describing practices as strategies explicitly oriented by reference to the anticipated cues as to the reaction to practices in situations of interaction, symbolic interactionism not only ignores the role of pre-cognitive or corporeal knowledge in processes of interaction, including the sensing of imperceptible cues of bodily hexis via a habitus which is a product of past social experiences and which, as a shared system of dispositions, orchestrates collective action, without conscious intervention, in the first instance; but also, more generally, the fact that 'interpersonal' relations are never, except in appearance, individual to individual relationships; that the truth of the interaction is never entirely contained in the interaction. It is to forget, as Bourdieu clarifies, that interaction owes its form to the objective structures which have produced the dispositions of the interacting agents, which, moreover, allot them their relative positions in the interaction and elsewhere.[81]

It follows that the construction of social reality which symbolic interactionists (as well as ethnomethodologists) try to describe and analyse by referring solely to what occurs within the conjunctural structure of interaction, such as the relative spatial positions of the participants, or the nature of channels used in communication, cannot really be understood without taking into account the fact that every confrontation between agents brings together, in an interaction defined by the objective structure of the relation between the groups they belong to, systems of dispositions, and through these habitus, all the objective structures of which they are the product, structures which are active only when *embodied* in a competence acquired in the course of a particular history. Thus, for example, dispositions, as so many marks of social position, are reminders of the social distance between objective positions and of the conduct required

> in order to 'keep one's distance' or to manipulate it strategically whether symbolically or actually, to reduce it (easier for the dominant than for the dominated), increase it, or simply maintain it (by not 'letting oneself go', not 'becoming familiar', in short, 'standing on one's dignity,' or on the other hand, refusing to 'take liberties' and 'putting oneself, forward,' in short, 'knowing ones place and staying there)'.[82]

Indeed, 'the sense of one's place', as Goffman puts it, is, according to Bourdieu, part of each agent's practical, bodily knowledge of her present and potential position in the social space, and is 'converted into a **sense of placement** which governs her experience of the place occupied, defined absolutely and above all relationally as a rank, and the way to behave in order to keep it and to keep within it.'[83] It is this practical knowledge that orients interventions in the symbolic struggles of everyday life which contribute to the construction of the social world, 'less visibly but just as effectively as the theoretical struggles that take place within the specialized fields, especially the political, bureaucratic, juridical and scientific ones, that is, in the order of symbolic, mostly discursive, representations.'[84]

Nevertheless, Bourdieu does take into account discursive forms of knowledge as well, including the fact that practical sense itself is capable of being made explicit in several ways. This, significantly, leads to the relative independence, with respect to position, of explicit position taking, or verbally stated opinion, and opens the way for the specifically political action of representation.[85] As this suggests, by focussing on processes of the construction of meaning in situations of person-to-person interaction alone, not only is symbolic interactionism unable to fully explain the situation of interaction itself; it is also unable to bring within its purview other contexts of the creation of meaning, such as the field of politics and the specialized fields of symbolic and cultural production, which, independently and in articulation with the world of everyday symbolic struggles, play an important role in shaping the subjective experience of the social world. Thus, for example, to understand the subjective experience of the appreciation of a work of art, we need to take into account the structures of all the fields through participation in which the subjective disposition to understand art have been formed, including that of the artistic field, in which, through symbolic labour, belief in the work of art as art has been produced. As Bourdieu puts it.

> The quasi-magical potency of the signature is nothing other than power, bestowed on certain individuals, to mobilize the symbolic energy produced by the functioning of the whole field, i.e. faith in the game and its stakes that is produced by the game itself. As Marcel Mauss observed, the problem with magic is not so much to know what are the specific properties of the magician, or even the magical operations and representations, but rather to discover the bases of the collective belief, or more precisely, the **collective misrecognition**, collectively produced and maintained, which is the source of the power the magician appropriates.[86]

In other words, the fact that the perception of the social world is not just the product of a spontaneous taken-for-granted subjective adherence to perceived reality, but requires an account of the basis of the belief in the self evidence of the world, which, as we have discussed earlier, Bourdieu explains in terms of the genetic link between social divisions and mental schemata, needs further elaboration in the case of differentiated societies, to account for the creation of belief within a differentiated habitus, underpinning the participation of agents in various relatively autonomous fields. For the 'illusio', as Bourdieu terms it, understood as immediate adherence to the necessity of the field, involves an acceptance of the arbitrary 'nomos' or principle of vision and division of the field, and is the basis of all fields, even the 'purest' ones, like the world of art or science.[87] What is significant is Bourdieu's observation, that paradoxically, while unlike undifferentiated societies, in class societies, the definition of the social world is at stake in overt or latent class struggle, and in each field too, there is a struggle between doxa, orthodoxy, and heresy; yet since these struggles operate within the bounds of a basic belief in the value of participation in the field, they contribute to the process of misrecognition whereby the 'illusio' masking the arbitrariness of the 'nomos' of the field is maintained. Thus this 'illusio' is once again a product of the embodiment of the social structure, albeit one differentiated into various fields, with a number of agents and institutions contributing to the creation of belief.

It may be noted that according to Bourdieu's theory, in the struggle for the imposition of the legitimate vision of the social world, in which science itself is inevitably involved, agents wield a power proportional to what he terms their symbolic capital : that is, to the recognition they receive from a group. 'The authority which underlies the performative effectiveness of discourse about the social world, the symbolic force of visions and pre-visions aimed at imposing the principles of vision and division of this world, is a *percipi*, a being known and recognized (nobilis), which allows a *percipere* to be imposed.' Thus,

> all the symbolic strategies through which agents aim to impose their vision of the divisions of the social world can be located between two extremes: the insult, that *idios logos* through which an ordinary individual attempts to impose his/her point of view by taking the risk that a reciprocal insult may ensue, and the official naming, a symbolic act of imposition which has on its side all the strength of the collective, of the consensus, of common sense, because it is performed by a delegated agent of the state, that is, the holder of the monopoly of legitimate symbolic violence.

Moreover, 'It is the most visible agents, from the point of view of the prevailing categories of perception, who are best placed to change the vision by changing the categories of perception. But they are also, with a few exceptions, the least inclined to do so.'[88]

As the discussion above shows, Bourdieu's theory of the symbolic does not negate the value of phenomenological descriptions of subjective experience, and even builds on certain insights it provides, such as Merleau Ponty's notion of bodily experience as part of the process of the construction of meaning. However, it relates subjectivity (which is not defined purely in terms of consciousness) to objective social structures, in a dialectic that goes beyond the immediate context of subjective experience in time and in space, but is at the same time materially and historically grounded. This also includes a focus on how structures of subjectivity play a role in power struggles in general, through the embodiment and effect of the differentially distributed power of symbolic capital.

Conclusion

The discussion in this chapter of the points of convergence and divergence between Bourdieu's theory of the symbolic and the other traditions of analysis that he engages with and critically incorporates in his theory is not an attempt to reconstruct the process by which the theory has been constructed, but a step towards an appreciation of some of its distinctive features in relation to the theoretical trends that have influenced it. Thus, we have seen that in contrast to the idealism of the neo-Kantian tradition, including its sociological version in the work of Durkheim and Mauss, Bourdieu's theory of the symbolic, even while recognizing the cognitive function of symbolic systems, and finding in the work of Durkheim and Mauss the beginnings of a properly sociological approach to symbolic phenomena, is a materialist theory, linked to a sociological perspective that is critical of structural functionalism. Furthermore, it is a theory that views symbolic systems as cognitive instruments that are themselves structured and thus finds in the structuralist tradition some useful tools for the internal analysis of these forms. However, it transforms the internalist readings structuralism offers by opening them up to relate symbolic forms to the practices of which they form a part and the social and material environments in which they exist. Thus, even as Bourdieu accepts the idea that as structured structures, symbolic systems are effective instruments of communication, he rejects the idealist postulate of structuralism that relates symbolic systems to universal structures of the human mind.

We have also seen that Bourdieu's is a theory that recognizes the political functions of symbolic systems, which the Durkheimian and structuralist traditions do not take into account, but which are part of the Marxist and Weberian perspectives. However, while it incorporates some of the insights of these two thinkers, Bourdieu's theory rejects certain basic features, both of their conceptualizations of symbolic systems, as well as of their analyses of social reality in general. Thus the fact that by recognizing the cognitive, communicative, and ideological aspects of symbolic systems, Bourdieu synthesizes disparate perspectives, is a feature of his theory of the symbolic whose distinctiveness is related to the distinctiveness of his overall sociological approach.

Indeed, an important feature of Bourdieu's sociology is the attempt to transcend the opposition between objectivist and subjectivist modes of analysis. Our discussion of Bourdieu's theory of the symbolic in relation to the method of relational structuralism (conventionally part of 'objectivist' analyses), and in relation to phenomenology (a typically 'subjectivist' approach), apart from taking us closer to some characteristic features of his theory, brings to the fore the rationale for Bourdieu's refusal to accept this dichotomy, and some key aspects of the manner in which he overcomes it.

In concluding this chapter, it seems pertinent to raise the question of how valid it is to view all symbolic systems as being in the service of relations of dominance. As we will have occasion to discuss in later chapters, Bourdieu himself takes into consideration the existence of forces of resistance and subversion in different fields. However, there does seem to be a neglect of the possibility of non-temporal power of the kind described by Louis Dumont in *Homo Hierarchicus*, or of a form of power which, as the conceptualizations of Anthony Giddens and Michel Foucault lead us to expect, is a form of power other than power as domination.[89]

In our discussion of the link between Bourdieu's theory of the symbolic and other traditions, certain concepts that constitute part of Bourdieu's theory of the symbolic and his theory of practice in general have been introduced in a preliminary way. These are the concepts of habitus, of fields, symbolic violence, misrecognition, symbolic capital, symbolic power, symbolic labour, doxa, orthodoxy, heterodoxy, practical logic, and illusio. We will analyse and evaluate their strengths and limitations in the context of his overall theory of practice, with special reference to his theory of the symbolic, in the following chapters.

ENDNOTES

1. Pierre Bourdieu, 'The Genesis of the Concepts of *Habitus* and of *Field'*, *Sociocriticism: Theories and Perspectives,* Vol. 11, No. 2, December 1985, p. 15. See also Pierre Bourdieu, *Rules of Art,* Cambridge, Polity Press, 1996, p. 180.
2. See Pierre Bourdieu, *Practical Reason: On the Theory of Action,* Cambridge, Polity Press, 1998, pp. 40, 46, 53-4, 56, 121.
3. Pierre Bourdieu (edited and introduced by John B. Thompson), *Language and Symbolic Power,* Cambridge, Polity Press, 1991, pp. 163–70.
4. Ernst Cassirer, *The Philosophy of Symbolic Forms,* New Haven, Connecticut, Yale University Press, 1953, and John B. Carroll (ed), *Language, Thought and Society: Selected Writings of Benjamin Lee Whorf,* New York, John Wiley and Sons, 1956.
5. Karl Marx and Frederick Engels, *The German Ideology*. Moscow, Progress Publishers, 1976.
6. Erwin Panofsky, *Perspective as Symbolic Form,* New York, Zone Books, 1991.
7. Pierre Bourdieu, *Language and Symbolic Power,* p. 164, and Pierre Bourdieu, *Outline of a Theory of Practice,* Cambridge, Cambridge University Press, 1986, p. 218, note 2.
8. Emile Durkheim, *The Elementary Forms of the Religious Life,* New York, The Free Press, 1965, and Emile Durkheim and Marcel Mauss, *Primitive Classification,* Chicago, The University of Chicago Press, 1963.
9. For a discussion of the meaning of arbitrary in Bourdieu's theory, see Edward LiPuma, 'Culture and the Concept of Culture in a Theory of Practice' in Craig Calhoun, Edward LiPuma and

Moishe Postone (ed) *Bourdieu: Critical Perspectives*, Cambridge, Polity Press, 1993, pp. 17–8.
LiPuma explains here that the notion of the arbitrariness of symbols appears in three senses in Bourdieu's work. The first is that a particular, specific cultural form is arbitrary from a cross-cultural standpoint. Secondly, that there is a formal arbitrariness within a culture. For instance, inequality in wealth leads to relations of domination and hierarchy, symbolically expressed and socially reproduced through the high, but arbitrary, valuation of upper class culture. The third is an absolute substantive theory of arbitrariness. The claim is that cultural contents and practices are *historically* arbitrary. Thus a 'relational analysis' of social fields need not analyse the structural history of symbolic valuation or the cultural order. LiPuma points out that on this last point there is a telling difference between *Outline of a Theory of Practice* and Bourdieu's studies on France, insofar as *Outline* gave a structural and cultural account of the categories and oppositions of Kabyle society.

10. Anthony Giddens, *Durkheim*, Glasgow, Fontana Press, 1978.
11. Pierre Bourdieu, *Pascalian Meditations*, Cambridge, Polity Press, 2000, p. 16.
12. Ibid., pp. 156–7, and Pierre Bourdieu and Loic J.D. Wacquant, *An Invitation to Reflexive Sociology*, Cambridge, Polity Press, 1992, pp. 12-3.
13. Pierre Bourdieu, *Outline of a Theory of Practice*, p. 29.
14. Ibid., p. 109.
15. F. de Saussure, *Course in General Linguistics*, Glasgow, Collins, 1974.
16. Claude Levi-Strauss, *Structural Anthropology*, Vol. 1, New York, Anchor Books, 1967.
17. Pierre Bourdieu, *Language and Symbolic Power*, p. 5.
18. Pierre Bourdieu, *Outline of a Theory of Practice*, p. 23.
19. Pierre Bourdieu, *The Logic of Practice*, Cambridge, Polity Press, 1990, p. 27.
20. Pierre Bourdieu and Loic J.D. Wacquant, *An Invitation to Reflexive Sociology*, p. 8.
21. Pierre Bourdieu, 'Structuralism and the Theory of Sociological Knowledge', *Social Research*, Vol. No. 35, Part 4, 1968, Winter, pp. 684–5.
22. Ibid., p. 700.
23. Pierre Bourdieu, *Outline of a Theory of Practice*, p. 109.
Polythesis refers to the form of relations (between terms etc.)

produced and used in different situations, and never brought face to face in practice, which are practically compatible though logically contradictory, involving what logicians call 'the confusion of spheres'. Their meanings are produced and used polythetically, that is to say, one after another and one by one, or step by step. See Ibid, p. 107 and p. 110.

24. For the Marxian view, see Cary Nelson and Lawrence Grossberg (ed) *Marxism and the Interpretation of Culture*, Urbana, University of Illinois Press, 1988.
25. Pierre Bourdieu and Loic J.D.Wacquant, *An Invitation to Reflexive Sociology*, p. 121.
26. Pierre Bourdieu, *Pascalian Meditations*, p. 171.
27. Ibid., p. 177.
28. For a clarification of the meaning of the notion of arbitrary in Bourdieu, see footnote 8 above.
29. Pierre Bourdieu and Loic J.D. Wacquant, *An Invitation to Reflexive Sociology*, p. 168, fn. 123
30. Pierre Bourdieu, 'Social Space and Symbolic Power', *Sociological Theory*, 7, No. 1 (June) 1989, p. 21.
31. Pierre Bourdieu, *Language and Symbolic Power*, p. 244.
32. Ibid., p. 169.
33. Ibid., p. 168.
34. Pierre Bourdieu, *Rules of Art*, p. 202.
35. Ibid., p. 182.
36. Pierre Bourdieu, *Outline of a Theory of Practice*, p. 97.
37. Ibid., p. 95.
38. Pierre Bourdieu, 'The Sense of Honour', in *Algeria 1960*, Cambridge, Cambridge University Press, 1979.
39. Pierre Bourdieu, 'The Kabyle House or the World Reversed', in *Algeria 1960*, Cambridge, Cambridge University Press, 1979.
40. Pierre Bourdieu, *Masculine Domination*, Cambridge, Polity Press, 2001.
41. Pierre Bourdieu, *The Logic of Practice*, p. 10
42. Ibid.
43. Ibid., p. 12.
44. Bourdieu defines symbolic power as the power of constructing reality. See Pierre Bourdieu, *Language and Symbolic Power*, p. 166.
45. Bourdieu discusses how his model aspires to a universal validity in 'Social Space and Symbolic Power' in Pierre Bourdieu, *Practical Reason: On the Theory of Action*, Cambridge, Polity Press, 1998, pp. 2–3.
46. It should be noted, however, that according to Bourdieu, the

relations of the other fields to the field of economic production are both relations of structural homology and relations of causal dependence, the form of causal determinations being defined by structural relations and the form of domination being greater when the relations in which it is exercised are closer to the relations of economic production. See Pierre Bourdieu, *Language and Symbolic Power*, p. 246.

47. Ibid., p. 185.
48. Ibid., p. 169. A clarification may be in order here, which is, that as I understand it, by division of labour Bourdieu means the division of social labour, which in turn refers to the division into classes. See *Language and Symbolic Power*, p. 168.
49. Pierre Bourdieu, 'Structuralism and the Theory of Sociological Knowledge', *Social Research*, Vol. No. 35, Part 4, 1968, Winter, p. 705.
50. Pierre Bourdieu, *Language and Symbolic Power*, p. 242.
51. Pierre Bourdieu, *Outline of a Theory of Practice*, pp. 83–4.
52. Pierre Bourdieu, *Distinction: A Social Critique of the Judgement of Taste*, London, Routledge and Kegan Paul, 1979.
53. Pierre Bourdieu, *Practical Reason: On the Theory of Action*, pp. 8–9.
54. Pierre Bourdieu, *Language and Symbolic Power*, p. 234
55. Pierre Bourdieu, *Outline of a Theory of Practice*, p. 86.
56. Ibid.
57. Pierre Bourdieu, 'Structuralism and the Theory of Sociological Knowledge', *Social Research*, Vol. No. 35, Part No. 4, 1968, Winter, p. 705.
58. Ibid., p. 706.
59. Pierre Bourdieu, *Practical Reason*, p. 2.
60. Ibid., p. 40.
61. Pierre Bourdieu et. al. 1965, p. 20, quoted in Pierre Bourdieu and Loic J.D.Wacquant, *An Invitation to Reflexive Sociology*, p. 9.
62. Pierre Bourdieu, *The Logic of Practice*, p. 135, Emphasis mine.
63. Ibid., p. 40.
64. Pierre Bourdieu and Loic J.D. Wacquant, *An Invitation to Reflexive Sociology*, p. 11.
65. Pierre Bourdieu, *Pascalian Meditations*, pp. 131–3.
66. Pierre Bourdieu, *In Other Words*, pp. 10, 12.
67. Pierre Bourdieu, *The Logic of Practice*, pp. 64–5. It should be noted, however, that this is a qualified appropriation of Marx's statement, since for Bourdieu, power refers not just to the effects of the power of money in bourgeoise society, but to the power

of what he terms various forms of capital, in all forms of society, the relevant quote from Marx being: 'If I have no money for travel, I have no *need* – that is, no real and realizable need to travel. If I have the *vocation* for study but no money for it, I have *no* vocation for study – that is, no *effective*, no *true* vocation.' In Karl Marx, *Economic and Philosophical Manuscripts of 1844*, Moscow, Progress Publishers, 1974, p. 122.
68. Pierre Bourdieu in 'Men and Machines' in Cetina, K. Knorr and Cicourel, A.V. (ed) *Advances in Social Theory and Methodology*, London, R.K.P., 1981, p. 310.
69. Pierre Bourdieu, *Outline of a Theory of Practice*, pp. 74–5.
70. Pierre Bourdieu, *Pascalian Meditations*, p. 187.
71. Pierre Bourdieu, *Outline of a Theory of Practice*, pp. 123–4.
72. Pierre Bourdieu, *Pascalian Meditations*, p. 136.
73. Ibid., p. 139.
74. Richard J. Bernstein, *The Restructuring of Social and Political Theory*, Oxford, Methuen & Co. Ltd., 1985, p. 156.
75. Pierre Bourdieu, *Pascalian Meditations*, p. 142.
76. Ibid., p. 135, and Pierre Bourdieu and Loic J.D. Wacquant, *An Invitation to Reflexive Sociology*, p. 20.
77. Pierre Bourdieu, *Pascalian Meditations*, p. 143, and Pierre Bourdieu and Loic J.D. Wacquant, *An Invitation to Reflexive Sociology*, p. 21.
78. Pierre Bourdieu, *Pascalian Meditations*, p. 135.
79. Pierre Bourdieu, 'Erving Goffman, Discoverer of the Infinitely Small' in *Theory: Culture & Society*, Vol. 2, No. 1, 1983, pp. 112–3.
80. Pierre Bourdieu, *Language and Symbolic Power*, pp. 234–5.
81. Pierre Bourdieu, *Outline of a Theory of Practice*, pp. 81–2.
82. Ibid.
83. Pierre Bourdieu, *Pascalian Meditations*, p. 184; Erving Goffman, *Asylums: Essays on the Social Situation of Mental Patients and Other Inmates*, Harmondsworth, Penguin Books, 1961.
84. Pierre Bourdieu, *Pascalian Meditations*, p. 146.
85. Ibid.
86. Pierre Bourdieu, *The Field of Cultural Production: Essays on Art and Literature*, Cambridge, Polity Press, 1993, p. 81.
87. Pierre Bourdieu, *Pascalian Meditations*, pp. 96–7.
88. Pierre Bourdieu, *Language and Symbolic Power*, pp. 238–9.
89. Louis Dumont, *Homo Hierarchicus: The Caste System and Its Implications*, London, Weidenfeld and Nicolson, 1970, Anthony Giddens, *The Constitution of Society, Outline of the Theory of Structuration*, Cambridge, Polity Press, 1984, and Michel Foucault, *Power/Knowledge*, Sussex, The Harvester Press, 1980.

3

The Symbolic in Relation to Practice, Habitus, and Capital

Introduction

In this chapter, I will begin a discussion of Bourdieu's theory of practice in terms of the interrelated concepts of habitus, capital and fields, to identify how his theory of the symbolic forms part of it. I will deal with these and related concepts in two parts: the concept of practice itself and those of habitus and capital in Chapter 3, and the concept of fields and the notion of an economy of practice in Chapter 4.

The term 'theory of the symbolic' is being used to refer to Bourdieu's conceptual framework for the analysis of mental structures, including schemes and categories of perception, thought, evaluation, and action, both conscious and unconscious, as well as to activities, institutions, and objects pertaining to such schemes and categories. By subsuming mental structures as well as related activities, institutions, and objects under its rubric, the theory partakes of what might be termed a post-Foucauldian trend of viewing social practices as being constituted by both material and discursive practices and of analysing the complex interrelationship between them. Thus, Valentine Daniel and Jan Breman, in their work on the identity of a labourer as a coolie, write that 'In the various work regimes in colonial Asia as seen, material practices colluded with discursive practices to sustain the image of the coolie as shifty'.[1]

Then again, Brian Keith Axel in his study of the interrelationship between the Sikh diaspora, colonialism and the nation state, writes that 'What an ethnographic approach may add to understanding these problems is a detailed attention to material practices and discursive formations...'[2] A similar inclusiveness marks Anthony Giddens' structuration theory where the symbolic orders and modes of discourse are conceptualized as intrinsic parts of social systems, constituting their 'cultural' aspects.[3] Thus in what follows we will see precisely how in Bourdieu's framework of analysis, symbolic practices mesh with other practices.

Since Bourdieu has analysed symbolic phenomena in very disparate types of social formations, ranging from precapitalist and colonial Algeria, to capitalist France and the international order of globalized capital, in the discussion to follow, I will draw upon examples from his analyses from varied contexts, noting how exactly they are related to his theory of the symbolic. It is pertinent to note here that even as Bourdieu's method of analysis is keenly attuned to empirical and historical specificities, his theory of practice aspires to a universal validity. But this is not to overlook the fact that theory for Bourdieu is not a set of immutable propositions about reality but a set of modifiable and even discardable/replaceable tools to understand it. Moreover, in his practice of theory, the notion of universality, including that of theoretical constructs, is not opposed to historicity, but involves viewing a phenomenon as a particular case (that is, the historically specific) of the possible (that is, of the universal, or more precisely, what is derived from a universal model).[4]

Bourdieu's theory of Practice

The Concept of Practice

While in general practice refers to anything people do, when it is thought of with the intention of understanding or explaining people's activities, we must look for its conceptual construction in relation to the theoretical tools devised to realize such an aim. Also, and most emphatically in the context of Bourdieu's work (since this is an aspect he is explicitly concerned with himself), we need to be aware that the construction of a theory of practice is itself a practice which the theory must take into account, including a cognisance of the scope and limits of theoretical practice in relation to the aim of explaining or understanding practice. Thus Bourdieu's theory of practice includes reflections on the practice of theory, which can help avoid what he calls a theoreticist or intellectualist bias 'which consists in forgetting to inscribe into the theory we build of the social world, the fact that it is a product of a theoretical gaze, a 'contemplative eye".[5] This is the problem, for example, with Geertz's 'thick description' which leads to the conclusion that the social world and the whole set of social relations and realities are simply 'texts'. Rational Actor Theory, similarly, imputes to its objects what belongs in fact to the way of looking at it, and projects into practice an unexamined social relation 'which is none other than the scholastic relation to the world'.[6]

This projection of the aims of analysis on to the practices examined also leads to a neglect of the temporal dimension of both the practice of theory and of the practices analysed. Thus, we have Bourdieu's critique of structuralism exemplified very clearly by his alternative analysis of gift exchange as practised in relatively simple societies such as Kabyle society.[7] To consider this example, Levi-Strauss interprets such exchange in terms of a model of reciprocity which, Bourdieu points out, projects the countergift into the project of the gift. This interpretation is criticized for overlooking completely the real social processes involved in gift exchange—in particular the play on time or tempo by the agents concerned and the complex and far from mechanical ways in which it reproduces the structure of social relations—including its capacity to modify the same within limits. Moreover, by constructing a reversible model of gift exchange, it not only eliminates the time dimension, but also misrepresents the fact that a gift is not only potentially capable of not being returned, but also that the institution exists within an ideological frame of reference which actively renders the return gift as response to the inaugural gift misrecognisable as such—a misrecognition as essential to the institution as is the actual giving and receiving of gifts. Importantly, it is elapsed time which enables the gift or countergift to be seen as an inaugural act of generosity without a past or a future; an act which like visits or courtesies and marriage in particular, 'tends or pretends to put the law of self interest into abeyance'.[8] The structuralist model which telescopes exchanges that take place over a period of time into an instant is incapable of actually perceiving their social truth as interested action in a misrecognisable form.

Attention to the temporal dimension of practice is central also to Bourdieu's critique of the notions of pre-logical thought and the 'savage mind', to which he counterposes the concept of 'practical logic'. The partial or discontinuous character of this logic is, according to Bourdieu, primarily explicable by the saving in time demanded by the urgency of practice that it makes possible and which, as he clarifies along the way, is not peculiar to 'primitive societies'. This notion draws attention to the truth of practice as a blindness to its own truth, for it refers to a logic in which reflexive attention to action remains subordinate to the pursuit of the result, excluding distance, perspective, detachment, and reflection. In short, most of what characterizes the logician's logic and defines the time of science is absent in 'practical logic'.

Bourdieu first discusses his concept of practice in *Outline of a Theory of Practice* (French publication in 1972) where he describes it, in terms specific to his theory, as the site of the dialectic between structures and habitus.[9] While Bourdieu discusses some of the major theoretical underpinnings and ramifications of this concept in *Outline* itself, they are further clarified in subsequent writings, particularly in *The Logic of Practice* (French publication in 1980). However, following the development of the concepts of forms of capital and of fields (the latter denoting a feature virtually absent in certain archaic societies), Bourdieu in his *Distinction* (French publication in 1979) introduces the formula: [(habitus) (capital)]+field = practice.[10]

What both the definitions of practice identified above have in common is the concept of habitus, in relation to structures, which are conceptualized as fields in the second definition. In addition, in the second definition, it is the interaction of habitus with capital, in the context of field, that is seen to result in particular practices. In other words, what people do can be explained and understood by analysing the interaction between their system of dispositions (for that is what, in a preliminary way, habitus can be described as consisting of) and the forms of power and resources at their disposal (a preliminary definition of capital) in the context of the particular structuring of social positions in terms of the distribution of power and resources, animated by struggles for the conservation or transformation of the structure of this distribution (a preliminary definition of field).

However, to grasp the precise way in which the above formulation can lead to an explanation of practice, and how it subsumes a framework for the analysis of symbolic phenomena, requires that we examine the concepts of habitus, of capital, and of fields, and their interrelationship, in some detail. Since they have been extensively discussed by Bourdieu himself, and have also been the subject of numerous exegeses, I will delineate them in what follows with specific reference to these aspects. As we do so, we will find that the formula of practice in *Distinction* is only a useful starting point, and should not be taken as a wholly accurate representation of Bourdieu's theory of practice.

Habitus

The concept of habitus in Bourdieu's theory of practice is critical both for an understanding of how it is a materialist theory as well as for discerning the role of symbolic phenomena in his overall framework. For it refers to systematic propensities to perceive, think, evaluate, and act in certain ways, embodied in individuals, but shared by all those living in similar social and material conditions. Indeed, Bourdieu analyses the habitus as being products of these conditions, and as belonging in part to the symbolic realm, since they include schemes of perception, thought, evaluation, and action.

Significantly, the schemes of the habitus are not symbolic in the sense of always being coherent, logical, and explicit representations. Rather, they exist in the mode of schemes for practice, including the practices of perceiving, thinking, evaluating, feeling, and acting, whose coherence, logic, and explicitness are limited to what is needed for practice to be possible.[11] Thus, the range of dispositions subsumed by the concept of habitus is very wide, and includes within its ambit phenomena such as involuntary body postures and gestures (ways of standing, sitting, walking, speaking, et cetera), as well as likes and dislikes, from the visceral to the consciously articulated. It also includes forms of practical knowledge and practical mastery which may not be transmitted through formal instruction and be reflexively perceived, except in the mode of what Bourdieu terms practical reflection, as well as ways of thinking and doing things which are products of specialized learning and explicit transmission. It can, arguably, even include systems of reflexive symbolic mastery of previously obscure schemes of the habitus—that is conscious recognition and verbal expression of processes practically applied, insofar as they are socially acquired and incorporated in the body. It may be worth noting here that the concept of habitus allows one to place in the same category, phenomena which are conventionally classified as either conscious or unconscious, so that within it, particular forms may be seen as lying along a continuum from the precognitive to the reflexive, thus providing access to a wide spectrum of kinds of phenomena, unlike a dichotomous view.

To understand the concept of habitus and the role it plays in his theory of practice, we have to be clear about what Bourdieu means when he describes them as structured structures predisposed to function as structuring structures.[12] And if we begin with a consideration of how they are structured, we are lead to certain basic postulates regarding social existence that underpin Bourdieu's theory of practice. For what makes social life possible, according to him, is the fact that people have an interest in participating in it, and this interest is ensured by their mutual dependence as well as competition for gaining access to whatever it is that they value.

To take up the process of the structuring of what Bourdieu terms the primary habitus first. This is the system of dispositions that is acquired in the early years of life, through the effect, on agents, of economic and social necessities, mediated by the relatively autonomous world of the domestic economy and family relations, and more specifically, through the familial manifestations of these external necessities (forms of division of labour between the sexes, household objects, modes of consumption, parent-child relations et cetera).[13] Thus, the characteristic structures of determinate conditions of existence produce the structures of the habitus. And these structures of the habitus in turn form the basis of the perception and appreciation of all subsequent experience. Analysed in some detail with reference to the traditional Kabyle peasant in precolonial Algeria, Bourdieu notes that in fact, the domestic space is always the initial site of an interest in and adherence to immediate reality leading to what he terms investments, 'the principle of all truly social energy.'[14] Though the analysis of its genesis he offers is provisional, pending a combined effort by sociology and psychology, he draws upon Freud to highlight the significance of the transition from the child's narcissistic organisation of libido to a state in which 'self love' is sacrificed for other object relations. He suggests that the search for recognition may be posited as one of the motors that makes the transition possible, whereby the child discovers others who take him/her as an object, leading to its own discovery of itself as a subject. Bourdieu subsumes this search for recognition under the category of the search for symbolic capital, that is, for social importance, which can later take the forms of a search for glory, honour, credit, reputation, and fame, and more fundamentally, for reasons for living. Significantly, Bourdieu points out an ambiguity at the root of symbolic capital, implying as it does both dominance and dependence, for 'Symbolic capital enables forms of domination which imply dependence on those who can be dominated by it, since it only exists through the esteem, recognition, belief, credit, confidence of others, and can only be perpetuated so long as it succeeds in obtaining belief in its existence.'[15] Thus it is that an original relationship of symbolic dependence underlies the creation of the primary habitus. It involves the socialization of drives, and the inculcation of the moral order, which takes place via silent and not so silent censures and injunctions in the domestic sphere. This process also involves a repression of desires, thereafter buried at the deepest level of the body in the form of passion, and exchanged for testimonials of recognition, consideration, and admiration. It is thus also the beginning of the inculcation and naturalization of cultural arbitraries.

We should be clear, however, that even as the process of the acquisition of habitus proceeds, the habitus are both structured and structuring. For it is because dispositions incline towards certain practices, and because that inclination stems from the structures in which practice occurs, that they tend to reinforce by the practices they are likely to result in, those very structures and the related dispositions. Thus, rather than being a mechanical imprint of the conditions in which they are created, the habitus are also structured by the responses they elicit, and therefore by the environment which they themselves contribute to the creation of. The creation of the habitus is also therefore not a process that gets completed once and for all, but goes on throughout the biographical trajectory of an agent's life, from restructuring to restructuring. This means, moreover, that the structuring of the habitus varies according to whether the conditions in which it is formed are continued in the context in which it structures practices, or are modified, with the habitus, too, undergoing transformation in the latter case, even though the primary habitus always has a certain inertia, and is the base on which changes are affected.

It is also significant that according to Bourdieu, while the schemes of the habitus are acquired through practice, and are also applied in their practical state without acceding to explicit representation, they are nevertheless structured and coherent because of the coherence of the social structures—such as structures of relations between groups—the sexes or age-classes—or between social classes—of which they are the product.[16] However, being a product of social conditionings, it follows that the habitus can, in certain instances, be built upon contradiction and tension, and even instability, such that they too are divided and contradictory, rather than systematic and constant. In fact, the particular form of a habitus can only be measured and explained empirically, according to Bourdieu, as for example in the case of the habitus of the Algerian subproletariat, analysed by him, which has inscribed upon it the instability of their living conditions, and who are doomed to insecurity in their conditions of employment and housing, and thereby of existence.[17] Significantly, it was in the context of his study of the Algerian subproletariat, where there was a radical disjuncture between their initial dispositions and the conditions of their existence, that the concept of habitus was forged as part of Bourdieu's conceptual vocabulary. Bourdieu uses the term 'hysterisis effect' to refer to the action of a habitus produced in an earlier condition, which has changed in the present conjuncture, resulting in practices which are maladjusted and out of sync. with the current situation.[18] At the same time, though he does not go into this aspect in detail, Bourdieu does point out that because they are incorporated in the body, which is an organism based on the integration of increasingly complex levels of organisation, the habitus do tend towards the generalization and systematicity of their dispositions.[19]

Another significant aspect of the habitus related to the fact that its dispositions are embodied is that their analysis belies the distinction between mind and matter, between morality and bodily hexis, and between logical schemes and practical axiological schemes. For as Bourdieu writes, the notion of habitus encompasses the notion of ethos, the latter being a morality made flesh, with values being postures, gestures, ways of standing, walking, speaking.[20] Thus for instance one associates the term 'uprightness' with a quality of character and a bodily stance; one speaks of the head hung in shame; one understands modesty as a particular way of carrying oneself, including ones' bodily comportment, etc. Moreover, it requires one to abandon the distinction between *eidos* as a system of logical schemes and *ethos* as a system of practical, axiological schemes, because the practical principles of classification which constitute the habitus are inseparably logical and axiological.[21] Thus, in the context of a particular habitus, good may be opposed to bad, as brightness to dullness, as more to less, and so on. This is an important point also because compartmentalizing different dimensions of the habitus needlessly reinforces a realist position that posits the existence of separate faculties.[22]

The habitus, moreover, is the product of what Bourdieu terms a double historicity.[23] By this he means that it is issued out of the embodiment through socialization or ontogenesis, of social structures, which themselves are products of the historical work of succeeding generations, or phylogenesis. Thus Bourdieu's theory of practice takes into account the historicity, and thus the relativity, of the habitus, while recording the fact that agents universally put them to work. Indeed habitus is described by Bourdieu as embodied history, and field—a concept we will discuss below—as objectified history. Also, in so far as the habitus refers to a socialized subjectivity, it means that the subject is not conceptualized by Bourdieu as an ego of a sort of singular cogito, but the individual trace of an entire collective history.

In a differentiated society, what follows the creation of the primary habitus, is the acquisition of the specific dispositions demanded by particular fields. However, according to Bourdieu, the dispositions of the original habitus are more or less adjusted to the requirements of the field an agent later participates in. This is in so far as the very inclination to invest in a particular field is a kind of self selection, experienced as a 'vocation', or it may be the product of occupational heredity. And once more,

> it is only through a whole series of imperceptible transactions, half conscious compromises, and psychological operations (projection, identification, transference, sublimation, etc.), socially encouraged, supported, channeled and even organised that these [primary] dispositions are little by little transformed into specific dispositions, after all the infinitesimal adjustments needed in order either to 'rise to the challenge' or to 'back down', which accompany the infinitesimal or abrupt redirections of a social trajectory.[24]

Above all, the creation of every specific disposition involves what Bourdieu terms 'illusio' or immediate adherence to the necessity of a field and acceptance of its value and presuppositions, or what Bourdieu calls its 'doxa'. Thus, for example, participation in the scientific field may be based on an unquestioning belief in the value of science, and practice within it would proceed from an acceptance of the debates current in it, whatever particular stance one may take vis a vis specific issues.

As the above suggests, to understand how habitus structures practices, and can even be a principle of the generation of practices, we need to view it in relation to the structure of the context in which it is active, which Bourdieu terms a field. Thus there may be situations where the objective conditions the habitus is confronted with are identical with or similar to those of which it is the product. In such a situation, the habitus perceives the field immediately, as endowed with meaning and interest, and the agents' practices, virtually perfectly adapted to the field, are not posed explicitly as a goal, but are activated below the level of calculation and consciousness, and beneath discourse and representation. Indeed, interest in the field, or acceptance of its *illusio*, which is a condition for participation in a field, and constitutes part of the habitus as a motivating structure, may be sufficient to ensure the production of practices in conformity with what the field demands. The sense of the objective structures of the field is immediately given where the habitus and the field are in harmony, and practices then are the result of a practical sense, which reactivates the sense objectified in the institutions of the field, pulling them out from the state of dead letters, while at the same time imposing the revisions and transformations that reactivation entails. This practical sense is both subjective and objective. The former in that it is what gives participation in the field a meaning and a raison d'etre and a direction in the sense of an impending outcome or anticipation of the future inscribed in the situation, the latter in that being adjusted to the situation and probable future, its practices are sensible—'Linked intelligibly to the conditions of their enactment, and also among themselves, and therefore immediately filled with sense and rationality for every individual who has the feel for the game.'[25] This relation to the imminent future, which seems in retrospect to be the product of a calculation of probabilities, is actually the activation of the habitus, which, given the fact that practice is inseparable from temporality and the fact that habitus is a product of past experiences of practice, unconsciously adapts to possibilities that objective statistical analysis may confirm.

However, by relating practices to the practical sense of the habitus, Bourdieu does not mean to suggest that practices are entirely predictable. Even where the same conditions mark the field as have produced the habitus, a particular conjuncture would represent a particular state of the field, which is never a static, but a dynamic structure, and the agents as individuals would have varying levels of skill and mastery of practical sense, leading to varied practices. They may even adopt strategies to avoid the most likely outcome. For in their interactions as agents with a common habitus, people nevertheless exercise their ability to improvise and implement strategies dictated by their social positions, particular biographical trajectories, and corresponding interests, resulting in practices which may or may not be as anticipated. More generally, in so far as practices are the combined outcome of habitus and field, depending on the stimuli and structure of the field, the very same habitus can generate different, even opposite, outcomes. Thus the habitus is described by Bourdieu not as a monolithic, immutable, inexorable, and exclusive principle of practice, but as being among the principles of the generation of practices and representations; the basis for the intentionless invention of regulated improvisation; of the unintended objective harmonisation of the practices of a group or class even in the absence of any direct interaction; and as a strategy generating principle, which makes possible the achievement of infinitely diversified tasks.

What makes possible the achievement of diverse tasks in diverse fields by the habitus, according to Bourdieu, is what he terms a kind of practical generalization—that is, the analogical transfer of schemes from an initial situation eliciting a particular reaction, to all similar situations, however new, in which one behaviour is made substitutable for and is substituted for another, in so far as the form of the problem is the same. The operation of this system of acquired equivalences is part of what

Bourdieu calls practical logic which he has analysed in detail with reference to the Kabyle mythico-ritual system. However, the economical use of polysemy, fuzzy logic, vagueness, approximation and the art of sequencing practices linked by a more or less observable 'family likeness' that it involves, is not limited to archaic societies, and as Bourdieu clarifies, is to be found, among other realms, in the field of politics in contemporary society. There it brings into play imprecise and approximate metaphors such as, for example, liberalism, liberation, liberalization, flexibility, free enterprise, deregulation, et cetera.[26]

The above example of the similar workings of practical logic in otherwise dissimilar societies illustrates what Bourdieu terms the *universal logic of practice*, and is arrived at by the use of what he calls the method of 'participant objectivation'.[27] This method involves the objectivation of the subject of objectivation, that is, of the researcher herself, and has the capacity to reveal in other cultures studied, processes analogous to those found in ones' own society, and vice versa. It is something other than either putting the primitive at a distance because the researcher does not recognise the primitive, prelogical thought within himself, a la Frazer, or the attempt at participant observation with its inherently difficult posture of immersion in a foreign universe while simultaneously observing it. Indeed, as Bourdieu puts it, from this point of view, nothing is more false 'than the maxim almost universally accepted in the social sciences according to which the researcher must put nothing of himself into his research. He should on the contrary refer continually to his own experience but not, as is often the case, even among the best researchers, in a guilty, unconscious, or uncontrolled manner'. Infact, 'keeping firmly in mind the irreducible specificity of the logic of practice, we must avoid depriving ourselves of that quite irreplaceable scientific resource that is *social experience previously subjected to sociological critique*.'[28] In Bourdieu's work, particpant objectivation has led to the mutual illumination of practices in societies otherwise distinguished by him into those which are undifferentiated and those which are differentiated, ranging from precolonial and colonial Algeria to contemporary France.

This, in turn, has led to a rejection of the distinction between sociology and social anthropology. However, what makes the universal logic of practice discernible is the particular historical and empirical prism through which it is refracted, and to conceptualise that, we need to consider the structures in which habitus is located. Thus we will turn to the concepts of capital and of fields next. For in Bourdieu's theory of practice, it is a combination of habitus and capital, in the context of a field, that leads to specific practices.

Capital

Bourdieu uses the concept of capital in a wider sense than is used in economics where it generally refers to a material resource. For Bourdieu, there are various forms of capital, though he distinguishes at least four major kinds. These are: economic capital, social capital, cultural capital, and symbolic capital.

Before we look at these different forms, we need to be clear that capital itself has been defined by Bourdieu as 'all goods, material and symbolic, that present themselves as rare and worthy of being sought after in a particular social formation,'[29] and also as 'accumulated labour [in its materialized forms, or in its 'incorporated', embodied form] which, when appropriated on a private, i.e., exclusive, basis by agents or groups of agents, enables them to appropriate social energy in the form of reified or living labour.'[30] Thus, in relation to the notion of interest, capital refers to the material and symbolic goods that interests are directed towards, as well as to the resources possessed by an individual or group—that is, forms of accumulated labour—which allow them to enter struggles within fields for the reproduction and expansion of the relevant form of capital, a characteristic of fields we will discuss when we examine the concept in the following chapter. In this sense, the investments in social fields that Bourdieu refers to are investments of capital, and the returns or profits on these investments too, are in the form of capital. However, apart from the above, another referent for the concept of capital that appears in Bourdieu's work is power. While describing his idea of a general science of the economy of practices, he writes that it must try 'to grasp capital and profit in all their forms and establish the laws whereby the different types of capital (or power, which amounts to the same thing) change into one another'.[31] One can thus conclude that the concept of capital refers to rare and valuable material and symbolic goods, which are composed of accumulated labour, that enable appropriation of social energy in the form of reified or living labour, and constitute forms of power. So we need to understand what exactly Bourdieu means by referring to capital as accumulated labour in its materialized or embodied form which enables the appropriation of social energy in the form of reified or living labour—labour which, incidentally, Bourdieu clarifies, may be physical or symbolic; and what he means by referring to it as power.

As regards the first, it seems he is referring to the fact that labour goes into the production of both material objects (i.e. tools, foodstuff, paintings, et cetera), as well as the habitus, which are an incorporation of external structures in the form of subjective tendencies (for example, practical sense, tastes, et cetera). However, while it is easy to understand the sense in which the former category of goods are a product of labour, it is not so easy with reference to the second category. In the latter case, it would seem that Bourdieu is drawing our attention to the fact that dispositions involve a process of learning, which in turn requires expenditure of energy and therefore inputs of labour, or more simply of energy and time.

However, not all such embodiments and objectifications of labour are capital. They are capital only when their appropriation results, or potentially results, in the appropriation of reified or living labour—physical or symbolic. In other words, they are capital only when they are accorded value, and are able to command human labour. Thus, capital is what is desirable within the context of a field where it is invested with the result that it brings its owner into a struggle with other agents or groups of agents, for its expansion and reproduction, through its ability to command human labour, and thereby to satisfy human desires. However, the capacity to command labour is realized in a more or less circuitous form, depending on the particular species of capital being considered, and the overall relations of dominance and power within a given field. In the process, capital may have to be transformed from one form into another. Thus, it may be useful to consider the forms of capital identified by Bourdieu, noting how each enables the appropriation of labour. While doing so, it is important to keep in mind that according to Bourdieu, the measure of all equivalences of capital is labour time, and the conservation of social energy through all its conversions is verified if in each case one takes into account both the labour time accumulated in the form of capital and the labour time needed to transform it from one type to another.[32] But before we do so, we need to be clear about the sense in which capital is power.

Since power is defined by Bourdieu as a relation to what is possible,[33] it follows that the existence of possibilities in social life, which implies the ability to realize them, is seen by him to depend upon the appropriation of social energy in the form of reified on living labour, so that capital is the concept that describes these possibilities with reference to individuals or groups who possess it. This understanding of Bourdieu's concept of capital also clarifies the conceptual value of Bourdieu's notion of social space which is basic to his sociology. Social space refers to a space of positions in which agents are distributed, in the first dimension, according to the overall volume of the capital they possess and, in the second dimension, according to the structure of capital, that is, the relative weight of the different species of capital in the total volume of their assets. From this synchronic perspective, the structure of distribution of capital at a particular point of time is the structure of society in suspended animation, for it maps the various possibilities and impossibilities that are the bases of social action. Viewed diachronically, however, social space is a three dimensional space, for the strategies of an agent and everything that defines the manner of his/her participation in a field are a function not only of the volume and structure of her capital at the moment under consideration and of her chances of success, but also of the evolution over time of the volume and structure of this capital, that is, of her social trajectory and of the dispositions or habitus constituted in the prolonged relation to a definite distribution of objective chances.[34] Thus the significance, in combination with their habitus, of an agent or group's possession of forms of capital, and their relative position in the structure of the distribution of capital in social space generally, and in a particular field, more specifically, for an understanding of their practices.

As regards forms of capital, Bourdieu broadly classifies capital into three types, including a fourth type which defines a quality shared by all forms of capital, although he also distinguishes multifarious subtypes. Indeed, in his conception, there are as many forms of capital as there are fields. In his essay called 'Forms of Capital', he distinguishes between economic capital; cultural capital, which may in turn be classified into cultural capital in the embodied state [e.g. dispositions of mind and body], cultural capital in the objectified state, and cultural capital in the institutionalized state; social capital; and symbolic capital.

As regards economic capital, it refers to that which is immediately and directly convertible into money and may be institutionalised in the form of property in the form of property rights. It assumes the existence of an economic field, and, in particular, the appearance of a monetary economy, in turn implying the existence of a market economy. In his analysis of Kabylia, for example, Bourdieu analyses the gradation of values as one moves from the processes of the economy of honour, exemplified, among other things, by the gift economy, to the economy of the distant market place, where monetary transactions are the norm. Thus, all commodities which can be sold, including labour power, are forms and examples of economic capital. To give a summary account of examples of economic capital, we can take a cue from John Thompson, according to whom, 'economic capital' 'includes property, wealth and financial assets of various kinds.'[35]

However, it would be wrong to treat each form of capital identified by Bourdieu in isolation. This is because in the actual process of the functioning of an economy of practice, there are numerous ways in which the various forms of capital are linked to one another, as well as there are, as already noted, significant processes of the transformation of one form of capital into another. Thus, talking of capitalist society, Bourdieu maintains that economic capital is the dominant form of capital, while at the same time pointing out the numerous ways in which economic capital is unable to work effectively, unless it is transformed into symbolic capital. While we will discuss the concept of symbolic capital later below, it refers, generally speaking, to a belief in the value of a thing or person. For example, for the possession of a commodity to lead up to the appropriation of money, one may require the labour of advertising to turn it into a desirable object, for which partly, the possession of economic capital is relevant only if it is also capable of mobilising cultural capital—in other words, only if some part of economic capital can be transformed into cultural capital—another concept we will discuss in detail below.

Considering the process of conversion with regard to economic capital, it is worth nothing here that according to Bourdieu, the different types of capital can be derived from economic capital, but only at the cost of a more or less great effort of transformation which is needed to produce the type of power effective in the field in question. Indeed, it is posited that economic capital is at the root of all other types of capital, but that as transformed, disguised forms of economic capital, they are never entirely reducible to that definition. In fact, they 'produce their most specific effects only to the extent that they conceal (not least from their possessors) the fact that economic capital is at their root, in other words, but only in the last analysis —at the root of their effects.'[36]

However, it is essential to note some of the limitations of Bourdieu's definition of economic capital as that which is directly convertible into money. Talking of the economy of practice in traditional Kabylia, for instance, Bourdieu tells us that it was a social formation which was still to be characterized by the emergence of an autonomous economic field, and thus that we must be wary of applying the categories of, for instance, a capitalist social formation to understand what happens in Kabylia. Significantly, the market economy is a presence, albeit peripheral, whose transactions are to a large extent governed by the logic and interests of the economy of honour. Given the marginal role of monetization, the question that arises is of the meaningfulness of using the notion of economic capital for any one of the forms of accumulated labour in Kabyle society. Bourdieu would appear to be justified in using this notion, as he does, only if the definition of economic capital as that which is directly convertible into money is not literally adhered to, and indeed, Bourdieu's reference to economic capital and physical, material capital as interchangeable terms, seems to create room for a less rigid definition of economic capital.

Moving next to the concept of cultural capital, it may be noted at the outset that it refers again to a category inapplicable to traditional social formations like Kabylia, which, though characterized by some differentiation in the possession of knowledge about and proficiency in various aspects of its cultural heritage, is not differentiated enough to be regarded as a society with an autonomous cultural field. It is thus characterized by an absence of cultural capital, though not of culture.

The genesis of the concept of cultural capital in Bourdieu's work lies in his attempt to account for differences in scholastic performance of school children, differences which were understandable once the cultural context of their social backgrounds was taken into consideration. Cultural capital referred, then, in its originary form, to 'the cultural goods transmitted by the different family PAs (pedagogical actions), whose value qua cultural capital varies with the distance between the cultural arbitrary imposed by the dominant PA and the cultural arbitrary inculcated by the family PA within the different groups or classes.'[37] Thus, cultural capital exists generally in the form of what is called culture, and is accumulated in the embodied state, and may also exist in an objectified state, including in the form of academic qualifications. However, drawing upon the study *Distinction*, and the discussion in 'Forms of Capital', we can arrive at a more general definition of the concept, which is that cultural capital is a form of knowledge, an internalised code or a cognitive acquisition which equips the social agent with empathy towards, appreciation for or competence in deciphering cultural relations and cultural artifacts, and which exists either in the embodied state, or in an objectified state, including in the form of cultural goods, or in the form of academic qualifications, that is in an objectified form which is institutionalized.

As regards cultural capital in an embodied form, its inculcation costs time, as well as an investment of what Bourdieu calls a socially constituted form of libido, '*libido sciendi* with all the privation, renunciation, and sacrifice that it may entail'.[38] Thus, it is accumulated labour which is embodied in the sense that it forms an integral part of a person, which cannot be transmitted instantaneously by gift or bequest, purchase or exchange.

According to Bourdieu, the least inexact of all the measurements of cultural capital are those which take as their standard the length of acquisition, whether in the family, in schools, or elsewhere. However, the role of early socialization is paramount, and it is the most disguised as capital. The hereditary transmission of cultural capital is misrecognized later as individual achievement or inherent capability. Indeed, such capital manages to combine the prestige of innate property with the merits of acquisition. All in all, the Arrow effect of inculcation, that is, of learning by doing, via the family, is a strong component of the process of the initial accumulation of cultural capital, and is crucial to social reproduction.

The fact that cultural capital is misrecognised means that it usually exists in the form of symbolic capital—that is, there is usually a legitimation of the possession of cultural capital in terms of an explanation or a belief which disguises the fact that it is capital.

Moreover, the link between economic and cultural capital tends to be disguised, even though it is very clearly present. As Bourdieu points out, it is established through the mediation of the time needed for acquisition. Thus, for example, depending on the differences in the cultural capital possessed by the family, there are variations, first, in the age at which the work of accumulation and transmission begins, and secondly, the length of time for which a given individual can prolong his or her acquisition process depends on the length of time for which his or her family can provide him or her with the free time that is time free from economic necessity, which is the precondition for the initial accumulation.

What also needs to be clarified, however, is how the private appropriation of embodied cultural capital enables agents to appropriate social energy in the form of reified or living labour. Numerous examples can be cited from Bourdieu's work to establish this point. To turn to his analysis in *Distinction*, for example, we are led to the understanding that cultivated artistic taste enables the 'consumption' of works of art, that is, of objects which are embodiments of living and reified physical and symbolic labour. In every instance examined, however, it is essential to take into account the historical structure of the relevant field: in this example, the field of cultural consumption, —to identify the value of a particular form of capital, —in this example, that of artistic capital. Thus, cultural capital is both a product of labour, for it involves a process of learning, and also a medium for the appropriation of labour.

Moving to the next category of cultural capital, that is such capital in the objectified state: the realm of cultural goods in which culture is objectified, presents itself, according to Bourdieu, with all the appearances of an autonomous coherent universe which, although the product of historical action, has its own laws, transcending individual wills, 'and which, as the example of language well illustrates, therefore remains irreducible to that which each agent, or even the aggregate of the agent, can appropriate (that is to the cultural capital embodied in each agent or even in the aggregate of agents)'.[39] However, cultural capital objectified, has many properties which are only defined in the relationship with cultural capital in its embodied form. For while cultural goods can often be appropriated materially—which presupposes economic capital—what constitutes the precondition for specific appropriation, is embodied capital. Thus, while material objects may be transmissible as regards their legal ownership, their transmission as cultural capital is subject to the same laws of transmission as embodied capital. In other words, the symbolic appropriation of cultural goods is presupposed by cultural capital.

It follows that the appropriation of objectified cultural capital by those who have economic or political capital, is a complicated process, in which the relationship between the holders of different types of capital is sometimes weighted, in terms of dominance, towards those endowed with cultural capital, and sometimes toward those who use other forms of capital to have access to cultural capital embodied by other social agents. However, Bourdieu, remarks that everything suggests that as the cultural capital incorporated in the means of production increases (and with it the period of embodiment needed to acquire the means of appropriating it), so the collective strength of the holders of cultural capital would tend to increase —but for the fact that holders of economic capital are often able to set the holders of cultural capital in competition with one another.

Finally, Bourdieu reminds us that objectified cultural capital exists as symbolically and materially active, effective capital only in so far as it is appropriated by agents and implemented and invested as a weapon and a stake in the struggles which go on in the fields of cultural production and, 'beyond them, in the field of the social classes—struggles in which the agents wield strengths and obtain profits proportionate to their mastery of this objectified capital, and therefore to the extent of their embodied capital.'[40] This, however, does not obliterate the fact that objectified cultural capital is a form of accumulated labour, whose private appropriation, when facilitated by the possession of embodied cultural capital, gives access to living and reified labour, as is very clear in the case of machines and other technological products, but also in the case of other cultural artifacts, since it can initiate the process of expanding one's embodied cultural capital, giving access to more cultural artifacts, et cetera.

As for cultural capital in its institutionalized state, by this, Bourdieu is referring to the objectification of cultural capital in the form of academic qualifications. Unlike the general category of embodied capital, cultural capital academically sanctioned by legally guaranteed qualifications, is formally independent of the person of its bearer. This capital confers on its holder a conventional, constant, legally guaranteed value with respect to culture , and is a product of what Bourdieu terms the performative magic of the power of instituting that secures a belief in the possession of certain attributes by those on whom a title is conferred.

That this capital is independent of the person of its bearer, means that it is possible to compare qualification holders and even to exchange them. It also makes possible the establishment of conversion rates between cultural capital and economic capital, which is the monetary value for which it can be exchanged on the labour market. The profitability of this form of investment is changeable, however, mainly because it depends on the scarcity of academic qualifications.

That this form of capital enables the appropriation of social energy in the form of reified or living labour, is manifest in the monetary returns on academic qualifications, as well as in the fact that they provide access to various cultural goods, themselves embodiments of physical and symbolic labour—whose consumption requires properly academic capital. Moreover, there is the profit of distinction linked to scarcity, which enables the appropriation of living labour in the form of acts of deference and importance, including the authority to be taken seriously, once the alchemy of instutionalization begins to work.

According to the empirical work conducted by Bourdieu, capital can also exist in a third form, which he terms social capital, that is, as 'the aggregate of the actual or potential resources which are linked to possession of a durable network of more or less institutionalized relationships of mutual acquaintance and recognition—or in other words, to membership in a group—which provides each of its members with the backing of collectively owned capital, a 'credential' which entitles them to credit, in the various senses of the word.'[41] The volume of the social capital possessed by a given agent thus depends on the size of the network of connections he or she can mobilize and on the volume of the capital (economic, cultural or symbolic) possessed in his or her own right by each of those to whom he is connected.

That via social capital, a person has access to the capital of those to whom one is connected, is a fact that lies at the genesis of this concept of capital, for, as Bourdieu notes, 'It arose from the need to identify the principle of social effects which, although they can be clearly seen at the level of singular agents—where statistical inquiry inevitably operates—cannot be reduced to the set of properties individually possessed by a given agent.' Furthermore,

> these effects, in which spontaneous sociology readily perceives the work of 'connections', are particularly visible in all cases in which different individuals obtain very unequal profits from virtually equivalent (economic or cultural) capital, depending on the extent to which they can mobilise by proxy the capital of a group (a family, the alumni of an elite school, a select club, the aristocracy, etc.) that is more or less constituted as such and more or less rich in capital.[42]

Social capital is based on indissolubly material and symbolic exchanges, which may also be socially instituted and guaranteed by the application of a common name—for example of a family, a class or a tribe, of a school, party, et cetera—and by a whole set of instituting acts. Thus, they are neither a natural, nor a social given. It is the product of investment strategies, individual or collective, consciously or unconsciously aimed at establishing or reproducing social relationships that are directly useable in the short term or long term, that is, 'at transforming contingent relations such as those of neighbourhood, the work place, or even kinship, into relations that are at once necessary and elective, implying durable obligations subjectively felt (feelings of gratitude, respect, friendship, etc. or institutionally guaranteed rights).'[43] Once more according to Bourdieu, it is the social alchemy of institution which is at work, the symbolic constitution produced by social institution (institution as a relative—brother, sister, cousin etc.—or as a knight, an heir, an elder, et cetera) being endlessly reproduced in and through the exchange of gifts, words, women, et cetera, which presupposes and produces mutual knowledge and recognition. Exchange transforms the things exchanged into signs of recognition, and reproduces the group. As a consequence, it also reaffirms the limits of the group, that is the limits beyond which the constitutive exchange—trade, commensality, or marriage—cannot take place. Thus each member of the group is a custodian of the limits of the group, and can modify the limits of legitimate exchange through some form of misalliance.

The reproduction of social capital through exchanges is work which implies investments of time and energy, and so, directly or indirectly, of economic capital. However, it is not profitable or even conceivable unless one invests in it a specific competence, such as knowledge of genealogical relationships and of real connections and skill at using them, et cetera, and an acquired disposition to acquire and maintain this competence, which are themselves integral parts of social capital. This is one of the reasons why the profitability of this labour of maintaining and accumulating social capital rises in proportion to the size of the capital.

That this form of capital is accumulated labour, is evident in the fact that it involves a continuous work of exchange. This fact, moreover, also demonstrates how this capital gives access to reified and living labour. For in the process of exchange, a fair amount of physical and symbolic labour is mobilized, and potentially available to those who benefit from the exchange.

Bourdieu also draws our attention to the more or less institutionalized forms of delegation that every group has, which enables it to concentrate the totality of the social capital in the hands of a single agent or a small group of agents. Thus a mandated plenipotentiary may be changed with full power to act and speak, to represent the group, to speak and act in its name and so, with the aid of this collectively owned capital, to exercise a power incommensurate with the agent's personal contribution. Consequently, one of the paradoxes of delegation is that the mandated agent can exert on (and up to a point, against) the group the power which the group enables him to concentrate.

> The mechanisms of delegation and representation (in both the theatrical and legal senses) which fall into place—that much more

> strongly no doubt, when the group is large and its members weak —as one of the conditions for the concentration of social capital (among other reasons, because it enables numerous, varied, scattered agents to act as one man and to overcome the limitations of space and time) also contain the seeds of an embezzlement or misappropriation of the capital they assemble.[44]

Incidentally, it is also worthwhile to note here, that in his later work Bourdieu draws attention to a 'peculiar form of social capital constituted by political capital' in some differentiated societies. Referring in particular to Sweden and Soviet-type societies, Bourdieu draws our attention to the fact that in them, such capital 'has the capacity to yield considerable profits and privileges, in a manner similar to economic capital in other social fields, by operating a 'patrimonialisation' of collective resources (through unions and the Labour Party in the one case, the Communist party in the other).'[45]

It is important to note, as we move on next to a consideration of symbolic capital, that social capital is so totally governed by the logic of knowledge and acknowledgement (hence belief), that it always functions as symbolic capital.

But what, exactly, is symbolic capital?

Symbolic capital, rather than constituting a form of capital in its own right, is better understood as being a constituent of all forms of capital, and refers to the belief that confers legitimacy on relations of power. Bourdieu situates symbolic capital as an essential component at the core of all power relations, as a condition of their efficacy since it includes the accumulated praise, prestige and recognition associated with a person or position.

Significantly, symbolic capital only exists in the eyes of others, while the other forms of capital have an independent objectification, be it as money, titles or behavioural attitudes and dispositions. As Bourdieu puts it, symbolic capital is capital in whatever form, 'insofar as it is represented, i.e. apprehended symbolically, in a relationship of knowledge or, more precisely, of misrecognition and recognition, and which presupposes the intervention of the habitus, as a socially constituted cognitive capacity.'[46] Misrecognition refers to the process whereby power relations are perceived not for what they objectively are but in a form which renders them legitimate in the eyes of the beholder, and also involves what Bourdieu calls symbolic violence.

The efficacy of symbolic capital involves symbolic violence in the sense that the intervention of 'knowledge' or categories of perception disguises the real grounds of power, which is the asymmetry of capital ownership, and this overlay of ideology is a violence which is exercised upon a social agent with his own her complicity. Referring to how relations of dominance are maintained, Bourdieu notes that social agents are knowing agents who, even when they are subjected to determinisms, contribute to producing the efficacy of that which determines them insofar as they structure what determines them, via the `fit' between determinants and the categories of perception that constitute them as such. This is how, he says, the effect of domination arises. He further clarifies that he calls *misrecognition* the fact of recognising (or ratifying) a violence which is wielded precisely in as much as one does not perceive it as such.

Importantly, Bourdieu distinguishes between knowledge, as referred to here in the context of symbolic capital and symbolic violence, and scholastic knowledge, especially as readers of Bourdieu have tended to view the two as synonymous. According to Bourdieu, the former kind of knowledge is the product of an act of *practical* knowledge which in no way implies that the object known and recognised even be posited as an object.[47] Moreover, even the question of legitimacy which it apparently answers is not posed explicitly as such; there is, instead, a practical recognition of legitimacy. This is not an act of free consent accomplished as the outcome of an explicit cognitive operation. It is inscribed, rather, in the immediate relationship between a habitus and a situation and is expressed indisputably in the silence of shyness, abstention, or resignation,' by which the dominated manifest practically, without even considering the possibility of doing otherwise, their practical acceptance (in the mode of *illusio*) of the possibilities and the impossibilities inscribed in the field.'[48, 49]

The transmutation of whatever kind of capital into symbolic capital involves labour, as is seen clearly in the case of an economy such as that of Kabylia, where the only form of the circulation of goods is via the gift economy, and where, given the relatively low levels of material wealth, perhaps the most valuable form of accumulation is of symbolic capital, in the form of the prestige and renown attached to a family and a name. Interested relations imposed by kinship, neighbourhood, or work, are transmuted into elective relations of reciprocity, in particular by the sincere fiction of disinterested exchange. Yet, even here, symbolic capital is a transformed and thereby disguised form of physical 'economic capital', an origin it must conceal even as it is what makes it effective, and, moreover, it also always guaranteed 'economic' profits in the long run. Thus, for example, `the owners of the best land and the best oxen are those who can assemble the labour force required for a quick harvest, since they are also richest in symbolic capital, gained by the transmutation of economic assets into aid which builds up obligations.'[50]

To explain the workings of symbolic capital, Bourdieu draws a parallel with the analysis of magic by Marcel Mauss. Thus, as noted in the last chapter, he writes that the problem with magic is not so much to know what the specific properties of the magician, or even of the magical operations and representation are, but rather to discover the basis of the collective belief or more precisely, the *collective misrecognition*, collectively produced and maintained, which is the source of the power the magician appropriates. As regards a work of art, then, he writes that it is

> both true and untrue to say that the commercial value of a work of art is incommensurate with its cost of production. It is true if one only takes account of the manufacture of the material object: it is not true if one is referring to the production of the work of art as a sacred, consecrated object, the product of a vast operation of *social alchemy* jointly conducted with equal conviction and very unequal profits by all the agents involved in the field of production —i.e. obscure artists and writers as well as 'consecrated' masters, critics and publishers as well as convinced vendors.[51]

These contributions, he observes, are what the partial materialism of economism ignores, and which only have to be taken into account in order to see that the production of the work of art, that is of the artist, is no exception to the law of the conservation of social energy. Thus, as Bourdieu notes elsewhere, 'in accordance with a principle which is the equivalent of the principle of the conservation of energy, profits in one area are necessarily paid for by costs in another (so that a concept like wastage has no meaning in a general science of the economy of practices).'[52] As an illustration of the fact that there is no exception to the law of the conservation of social energy, we may consider the persistence of dowry and arranged marriages as well as conspicuous consumption in the modernizing, transnational middle class Indian diaspora. In other words, those who *have* shall have *more* in social life in accordance with the principle of the conservation of social energy.

Significantly, according to Bourdieu, in the symbolic struggle for the production of common sense or, more precisely, for the monopoly over legitimate naming, agents put into action the symbolic capital which they have acquired in previous struggles. This capital may, moreover, be judicially guaranteed, as in the case of titles of nobility or educational credentials, which give one a right to share in the profits of recognition. In this sense, the power of symbolic capital is a power of 'world-making', which is no ordinary phenomena, for it can become a power of constitution. This is because as Bourdieu puts it to change the world, one has to change the ways of world-making, that is 'the vision of the world and the practical operations by which groups are produced and reproduced.'[53] This power of constitution rests on two conditions: firstly, as any form of performative discourse, it has to be based on the possession of symbolic capital; secondly, symbolic efficacy depends on the degree to which the vision proposed is founded in reality. Thus, '*symbolic power is a power of consecration or revelation*, the power to consecrate or reveal things that are already there.'[54] This does not mean, however, that it does nothing, for, a group, a class, a gender, a region, or a nation for example, begins to exist as such, for those who belong to it, as well as for others, only when it is distinguished according to one principle or another, from other groups, that is, through knowledge and recognition. But in the determination of the objective classification and of the hierarchy of values granted to individuals and groups, not all judgments have the same weight, and holders of large amounts of symbolic capital, the *nobiles* (etymologically, those who are well known and recognized), are in a position to impose the scale of values most favourable to their products—notably because, in our modern societies, they hold a practical *de facto* monopoly over institutions which, like the school system, officially determine and guarantee rank.[55] It may be added here, that this is true not only in modern societies, but also in what may be called 'warm' societies and cultures, as in the case of India where the process of sanskritization, for instance, bears this out.[56]

Incidentally, the concept of symbolic capital brings home very forcefully, the fact that though it might be fruitful to regard capital as the energy of social physics, social science is not a social physics. For it is often essential, for capital to function effectively, that it be perceived as being other than what it really is, that is be misrecognized; and since perception or recognition are acts which are products of socially constituted subjectivity, they cannot be analysed within the framework of a physics.[57] An example that clearly shows up the problem with a social physics is that of cyber-endogamy, where technological and physical displacements do not correspond to symbolic and social displacements. In fact, traditional patterns are even reinforced rather than changed.

To conclude our discussion of forms of capital, we will consider its relationship with modes of domination. It has been observed that Bourdieu uses the concept of capital, with the specific meaning he gives to the term, for the analysis of social practice in both precapitalist and capitalist forms of society. Nevertheless, the crucial distinction between the two forms of society is the differentiation of social space, in the case of the latter into autonomous social, economic, and cultural fields, with associated markets and forms of capital. In the former, in the absence of an independent economic field whereby exchanges of goods and services are mediated by the market, symbolic capital has a more central place, and this includes the fact that symbolic power has a direct economic function, as in labour mobilization, for example. Also, while the universe of ideas in traditional societies is characterized by the one single undisputed 'doxa', which means that the symbolic system is both common to all and taken-for-granted, in modern societies, principles of 'heterodoxy' and 'orthodoxy' engage in struggle—a struggle which presumes a universe of discourse. Following from this, in traditional societies, practice is mainly about strategies aimed at the accumulation of (usually symbolic) capital, while in modern societies, collective struggles aimed at power and the imposition of a set of heterodox and orthodox norms and symbols also become significant. Also, given the low level of material resources in them, symbolic violence, rather than the overt expression of differences in wealth is the preferred mode of domination in pre-capitalist societies. The overt and direct exercise of material force would, in fact, be too expensive in material resources to allow for simple reproduction. And lacking, as they do, the objectification of power in institutions such as a market or the church, as well as associated instruments of objectification such as writing, power relations have to be reasserted constantly in direct human interaction, involving the day-to-day work of symbolic violence through obligations and debts, including the complex and continuous weaving of affective bonds. This symbolic capital, a transformed and thereby disguised form of physical 'economic' capital, produces its proper effect only in as such as it conceals the fact that it originates in 'material' forms of capital which are also, in the last analysis, the source of its effects.[58]

In modern societies, in contrast, domination no longer needs to be exerted in a direct, personal way, since it is entailed in possession of the means—that is economic or cultural capital—of appropriating the mechanisms of the field of production and the field of cultural production, which tend to assure their own reproduction by their very functioning, independently of continuous recreation by agents or of any direct intervention by them. Furthermore, while the legitimate culture of class societies is a product of domination predisposed to express or legitimate domination, in little differentiated or undifferentiated societies, in which access to the means of appropriation of the cultural heritage is fairly equally distributed, culture is fairly equally mastered by all members of the group and cannot function as cultural capital, that is, as an instrument of domination, or only so within very narrow limits and with a very high degree of euphemisation. In the former case, because the appropriation of cultural products presupposes dispositions and competencies which are not distributed universally (although they have the appearance of innateness), cultural products are subject to exclusive appropriation, material or symbolic, and function as cultural capital (objectified or internalized). They thus yield a profit in distinction proportionate to the rarity of the means required to appropriate them, as well as a profit in legitimacy, the profit par excellence, which consists in the fact of feeling justified in being (what one is), being what it is right to be.

As regards the creation of capital, the contrast between pre-capitalist and capitalist society is also meaningful, since according to Bourdieu, in the latter, 'Economic power lies not in wealth, but in the relationship between wealth and a field of economic relations, the constitution of which is inseparable from the development of a *body of specialised agents*, with specific interests (and)... it is in this relationship that wealth is constituted, in the form of capital, that is, as the instrument for appropriating the institutional equipment and the mechanisms indispensable to the functioning of the field, and thereby also appropriating the profits from it.'[59] As regards the constitution of cultural capital, according to Bourdieu, 'just as economic wealth cannot function as capital until it is linked to an economic apparatus, so cultural competence in its various forms cannot be constituted as cultural capital until it is inserted into the objective relations between the system of economic production and the system producing the producers (which is itself constituted by the relation between the school system and the family).'[60] In such societies, academic qualifications are to cultural capital what money is to economic capital. Thus, the educational system plays such an important role within Bourdieu's theory, because historically the development of such a system, as a system of certification, created a market in cultural capital within which certificates acted as money in terms of a common, abstract, socially guaranteed medium of exchange between cultural capitals and crucially, between cultural capital and the labour market and thus access to economic capital. In this regard, Bourdieu notes how there is a shift from early capitalism to late capitalism, in modes of reproduction, from *direct* reproduction, where power is transmitted essentially within the family via economic property, to *school-mediated* reproduction, where the bequeathal of privilege is simultaneously effectuated and transfigured by the intercession of educational institutions.

> But again, all ruling classes resort to both modes conjointly (Bourdieu takes pain to stress that the growing *relative* weight of cultural capital in no way effaces the ability of economic capital to propagate itself autonomically) and their partial preference for one or the other will depend on the full system of instruments of reproduction at their disposal and on the current balance of power between the various fractions tied to this or that mode of transmission.[61]

To conclude our discussion of the concept of capital with reference to Bourdieu's theory of the symbolic, we may note that it provides a way of linking material and symbolic resources as bases of power conceptually, given his understanding that different types of capital can be derived from economic capital, together with his analysis of how a misrecognition of this fact is usually essential for their efficacy. The notion of cultural capital, differentiated into its embodied, objectified, and institutionalized forms, gives his theory a means of looking at the fields of cultural production, circulation, and consumption in relation to the concept of habitus as well as to processes of the institutionalization and objectification of cultural phenomena, and also a way of relating subjective and objectified symbolic systems to processes of domination and subordination. The concept of social capital highlights the significance of material and symbolic exchanges between individuals and between groups and the social alchemy of institutionalization, involving physical and symbolic labour. Indeed, all the forms of capital according to Bourdieu involve symbolic labour and are constituted by it, as also in most cases by physical labour as well. In particular, the centrality of symbolic capital in his conceptualization of capital as a form of power involving a process of symbolic violence brings to the fore the multiple roles of the symbolic in his theory of practice.

We will turn to a discussion of his concept of fields next.

ENDNOTES

1. Jan Bremen and E.Valentine Daniel, 'Conclusion: The Making of a Coolie' in *The Journal of Peasant Studies*, Vol. 19, Nos. 3 & 4, April/July 1992, p. 281.
2. Brian Keith Axel, *The Nation's Tortured Body: Violence, Representation, and the Formation of a Sikh 'Diaspora'*, Durham and London, Duke University Press, 2001, p. 228.
3. Anthony Giddens, *The Constitution of Society*, Cambridge, Polity Press, 1984.
4. See Pierre Bourdieu, 'Social Space and Symbolic Space' in *Practical Reason: On the Theory of Action*, Cambridge, Polity Press, 1998, pp. 2–3.
5. Pierre Bourdieu, 'Social Space and Symbolic Power', in *Sociological Theory*, Spring, Vol. 7, No. 1, 1989, pp. 33–4.
6. Pierre Bourdieu, *Pascalian Meditations*, Cambridge, Polity Press, 2000, p. 53.
7. Pierre Bourdieu, *Outline of a Theory of Practice*, Cambridge, Cambridge University Press, 1977, pp. 4–9.
8. Ibid., p. 171.
9. Ibid.
10. Pierre Bourdieu, *Distinction: A Social Critiue of the Judgement of Taste*, London, Routledge and Kegan Paul, 1979, p. 101.
11. The term symbolic is being used as an approximation to denote what is actually only contained in the concept of habitus itself
12. Pierre Bourdieu, *Outline of a Theory of Practice*, p. 72.
13. Pierre Bourdieu, *The Logic of Practice*, Cambridge, Polity Press, 1990, p. 54.
14. Pierre Bourdieu, 'The Philosophical Establishment', in Alan Montefiore (ed) *Philosophy in France Today*, Cambridge, Cambridge University Press, 1983, p. 2.
15. Pierre Bourdieu, *Pascalian Meditations*, Cambridge, Polity Press, 2000, p. 166.
16. Pierre Bourdieu, *Outline of a Theory of Practice*, p. 97.
17. Pierre Bourdieu, *Pascalian Meditations*, p. 160.

18. Pierre Bourdieu, *Outline of a Theory of Practice*, p. 78.
19. Pierre Bourdieu, *Pascalian Meditations*, p. 157.
20. Pierre Bourdieu, *Sociology in Question*, London, Thousand Oaks, New Delhi, Sage Publications, 1993, p. 86.
21. Ibid.
22. Ibid.
23. Pierre Bourdieu and Loic J. Waquant, *An Invitation to Reflexive Sociology*, Cambridge, Polity Press, 1992, p. 139.
24. Pierre Bourdieu, *Pascalian Meditations*, p. 165.
25. Pierre Bourdieu, *The Logic of Practice*, p. 66.
26. Pierre Bourdieu, *Pascalian Meditations*, p. 57.
27. Pierre Bourdieu, 'Particpant Objectivation', in *Man*, Vol. 9, 1 June 2003, p. 286.
28. Ibid., pp. 287–8.
29. Pierre Bourdieu, *Outline of a Theory of Practice*, p. 178.
30. Pierre Bourdieu, 'Forms of Capital', in John G. Richardson (ed) *Handbook of Theory and Research for the Sociology of Education*, New York, Westport, London, Greenwood Press, 1986, p. 241.
31. Pierre Bourdieu, 'Forms of Capital', in John J. Richardson (ed) *Handbook of Theory and Research for the Sociology of Education*, London, Greenwood Press, 1986, pp. 242–3.
32. Pierre Bourdieu, 'Forms of Capital', p. 253.
33. See Pierre Bourdieu, 'Forms of Capital', p. 241–2, and Pierre Bourdieu, *The Logic of Practice*, p. 64
34. Pierre Bourdieu and Loic J. Waquant, *An Invitation to Reflexive Sociology*, p. 99.
35. John Thompson (ed) *Language and Symbolic Power*, Cambridge, Polity Press, 1991, p. 148.
36. Pierre Bourdieu, 'Forms of Capital', p. 252.
37. Pierre Bourdieu and Jean-Claude Passeron, *Reroduction in Education, Society and Culture*, London and Beverly Hills, Sage Publications, 1977, p. 30.
38. Pierre Bourdieu, 'Forms of Capital', p. 244.
39. Ibid., p. 247.
40. Ibid.
41. Ibid., pp. 248–9.
42. Ibid., p. 256, n. 11.
43. Ibid., pp. 249–50.
44. Ibid., p. 251.
45. Pierre Bourdieu and Loic J. Wacquant, *Invitation to Reflexive Sociology*, Cambridge, Polity Press, 1992, pp. 118–9.
46. Pierre Bourdieu, 'Forms of Capital', p. 255, n. 3.

47. Pierre Bourdieu, *In Other Words*, p. 112.
48. Ibid. As noted in the last chapter, the fact that misrecognition occurs through what goes without saying and requires no inculcation, makes Bourdieu's theory of symbolic violence different from Gramsci's theory of hegemony. The former requires none of the active 'manufacturing', of the work of 'conviction' entailed by the latter. See Pierre Bourdieu and Loic J. Waquant, *An Invitation to Reflexive Sociology*, p. 168, n. 123.
50. Pierre Bourdieu, *Outline of a Theory of Practice*, p. 222, n. 32
51. Pierre Bourdieu, 'The Production of Belief: Contribution to an economy of symbolic goods' in in Richard Collins, James Curran et.al. (ed) *Media, Culture and Society: A Critical Reader*, London, Sage Publications, 1986, pp. 131–63.
52. Pierre Bourdieu, 'Forms of Capital', p. 253
53. Pierre Bourdieu, 'Social Space and Symbolic Power', in *Sociological Theory*, Vol. 7, No. 1, Spring, 1989, p. 23
54. Ibid., p. 23.
55. Pierre Bourdieu, 'Social Space and Symbolic Power' in *In Other Words*, Cambridge, Polity Press, 1990, p. 135.
56. The phrase 'warm' societies and cultures is taken from Ravindra K. Jain,' Social Anthropology of India: Theory and Method' in *Survey of Research in Sociology and Social Anthropology 1969-1979*, Vol. 1, Indian Council of Social Science Research, New Delhi, Satvahan Publications, 1985, p. 27.
57. Pierre Bourdieu, *The Logic of Practice*, p. 25.
58. Pierre Bourdieu, *Outline of a Theory of Practice*, p. 183.
59. Ibid., pp. 184–5.
60. Ibid., p. 186.
61. Loic J.D. Wacquant, 'Foreward', in Pierre Bourdieu, *The State Nobility*, Cambridge, Polity Press, 1996, p. xiii.

4

The Symbolic in Relation to Fields and the Notion of an Economy of Practice

Fields

The appearance of the concept of fields in Bourdieu's work can be traced back to *Les Heritiers* the study of French students and their relation to culture, published in 1964, whose English translation, *The Inheritors* was published in 1979. However, in it Bourdieu uses, but does not elaborate upon the concept of fields. The first discussion is to be found in an article entitled 'Intellectual Field and Creative Project', published in 1966. In an interview, Bourdieu himself notes that the concept developed out of the convergence between research into the sociology of art, which he started in 1970 in a seminar at the Ecole Normale, and his commentary on the section on the sociology of religion in Weber's 'Wirtschaft and Gesellschaft'.[1] Aside from this discussion, the concept of fields is more prevalent and thus becomes significant in Bourdieu's writings from the mid '70s on. It may be argued, however, that by the early '70s', the concept had become an integral part of Bourdieu's social theory, which itself first appears in crystallized form in his *Outline of A Theory of Practice*, published in 1972.

However, not unlike the concept of habitus, the concept of field in Bourdieu's sociology can be said to have taken root in the context of Bourdieu's study of the transformations affecting Algerian society during the colonial period. In particular, it was prompted by the observation of an earlier, relatively undifferentiated society giving way to one marked by social differentiation—a differentiation most conspicuously linked to the constitution of an autonomous economic domain within the social formation. The discovery of labour as an economic category and the related formation of a field of economic practice 'per se', made possible activity directed towards exclusively economic goals, subjectively recognized as such. This replaced the play of individual and collective misrecognition of the economy as an economy in precapitalist Algeria—the repression of the objective reality of the processes of the production and circulation of material goods, which were embedded within a logic of symbolic power and its accumulation and distribution in the form of symbolic capital—that is material capital denied as such and recognised as legitimate, in other words, misrecognized as capital.

With this observation, Bourdieu's argument moved towards a critique of what he terms an ethnocentric approach to the analysis of traditional societies, by which he means the application to them of a restricted definition of economic interest, which is in fact the historical product of capitalism. It is possible to see in this historical specificity accorded to the emergence of a restricted 'economic' domain, an anchor point for conceptualizing the emergence of a multiplicity of relatively autonomous domains, designated by the terms 'fields', and it is well to note that Bourdieu also identifies the functioning of these fields in terms of laws obeying a logic deemed to be economic, but not in a narrow 'economic' sense. Thus referring to capitalist social formations, Bourdieu draws attention to the process of the establishment of areas of practice in which symbolic interests, often termed 'spiritual' or 'cultural', are set up in opposition to the field of economic interest, these former being the 'paradoxical product of the ideological labour in which writers and artists, those most directly interested have played an important part, and in the course of which, symbolic interests become autonomous by being opposed to material interest, that is by being symbolically nullified as interests.'[2]

While the changes observed in Algerian society provided a

foundation for the concept of fields it is not applied or even formulated as such in the actual analysis of Algerian reality. As noted earlier, the concept first appears in a clearly discursive form in the article entitled 'Intellectual Field and Creative Project', an article later described by Bourdieu as an attempt to analyse the 'intellectual field' as a relatively autonomous universe of specific relationships.

The intellectual field refers, according to Bourdieu, to the system of social relations within which creation as an act of communication takes place, such that the conceptual construction of the system facilitates assigning the sociology of intellectual and artistic creation its proper object and limits. And what justifies, in Bourdieu's view, the construction of this object, and its treatment as an object of structural analysis and thus its methodological autonomization—including its analysis as a system governed by its own laws—is the fact that it possesses a relative autonomy—an autonomy which is itself the product of a historical process.[3] From this, it also follows that the system cannot be dissociated from the historical and social conditions under which it is established. These conditions influence, for instance, the particular substance of the logic of competition for cultural legitimacy governing the field—a competition conducted in what is termed a 'literary and artistic market', whereby relations are built up among various agents themselves, and between them and their products—all of which go into making the system. In the competition between these agents, the public is the prize, and apparently, also the arbitrator.

The general points about fields that this example illustrates are the following: that fields are relatively autonomous structures of relations between agents that emerge in specific socio-historical contexts; that they are the site of struggles between agents, such as struggles for cultural legitimacy, with their own particular stakes and rewards and that these struggles have a certain logic of their own, influenced, nevertheless, by the general socio-historical situation.

Certain aspects of the way the concept of fields has been used in this early article have, however, been criticized by Bourdieu subsequently, and the move towards a more adequate application is marked, according to him, by the writings concerned with reworking the basic matrix of Weber's sociological analysis of religion. What Bourdieu considers a shortcoming of his own early analysis of the intellectual field is the fact that it does not sufficiently take into account the effect of the relationship between objective positions occupied by individual agents in the field, and that it concentrates instead on the actual interactions between, for example, authors and publishers. In his writings on the sociology of religion, Bourdieu attempts to demonstrate how Weber provides a way of escape from the seeming alternative between the illusion of the absolute autonomy of religious beliefs 'which tends to have us conceive the religious message as a spontaneously generated product of inspiration, and the reductive theory, which sees that message as the direct reflection of economic and social conditions.' This is by taking into consideration the religious work carried out by specialist agents—that is by agents who 'are relatively autonomous in respect of external constraints (economic constraints in particular) and invested with the institutional—or other—power to respond to a particular category of needs proper to determinate social groups by a determinate type of practice or discourse.'[4] Bourdieu's re-reading of Weber shows how 'any analysis of the *logic* of the interactions that may develop between agents in direct confrontation with one another must be subordinated to the construction of the structure of the objective relations between the *positions* these agents occupy in the *religious field*, a structure that determines both the form their interactions may assume and the representation they may have of these interactions.'[5]

In other words, according the Bourdieu, viewed synchronically, fields present themselves as structured spaces of positions, whose properties depend on their positions in these spaces, which can be analysed independently of the characteristics of their occupants—characteristics which in fact, are in part determined by them. Elsewhere, he specifies that the notion of space delineated by him is borrowed from the philosopher P.F. Strawson, according to whom the fundamental property of a space is the reciprocal externality of the objects it encloses. Thus for Bourdieu, social space is a space of social positions external to one another, defined by their relative distance to one another.[6]

Sociology, according to him, has to proceed by looking at the social world as a space with several dimensions, constructed on the basis of principles of differentiation or distribution constituted by the set of properties active within the social universe, or field in question—that is capable of conferring strength, or power within that universe, on their holder. Agents and groups of agents are thus defined by their relative positions within that space—each of them being assigned to a position or a precise class of neighbouring positions (that is a particular region in this space), such that one cannot really—even if one can in thought—occupy two opposite regions of the space. In as much as the properties selected to construct this space are active properties, one can according to Bourdieu also describe it as a field of forces, that is as a set of objective power relations that impose themselves on all who enter the field and that are irreducible to the intentions of the individual agents or even to the direct interactions among the agents.[7]

Bourdieu also maintains that there are general laws of the functioning of fields, which are invariant across different fields —that is across the fields of politics, of philosophy, of religion etc. Each field is defined for example, by specific stakes and interests, irreducible to those of other fields, which are not even perceived by those not themselves equipped to enter the particular field. Moreover, in *The Logic of Practice,* as also in other writings, Bourdieu notes that the fact of shared properties between fields brings into being structural and functional homologies between them which is very significant, as we shall see below, to understand the links between different fields, and the way individuals are part of several fields.

For a field to function, it is necessary, states Bourdieu, that there be stakes i.e. something to gain or lose, and people who undertake to play the game—people endowed with a habitus that implies a knowledge and recognition of the inherent of laws of the game, that is, the way it is organized, the probable outcome, its stakes et cetera. And the structure of a field is the state of relations of force between agents or institutions engaged in a struggle, or if one prefers, the state of the distribution of specific capital accumulated in the course of earlier struggles, which orients later strategies. Social fields are distinguished according to Bourdieu, by the forms of capital deployed in them, and are animated by agents employing optimising strategies – that is strategies to increase their share of the relevant form of capital. The struggle for which a field is the site, has for stakes the monopoly of legitimate violence, or of the specific authority characteristic of the field under consideration, which is also a struggle for the conservation or subversion of the structure of the distribution of capital specific to the field.

Bourdieu notes that those who, in a determinate state of the relations of force, monopolize (more or less completely), the specific capital, the foundation of the power or of the specific authority characteristic of the field, are inclined to strategies of conservation, and in the field of the production of cultural goods, they tend to defend orthodoxy, while those least provided with capital (who are also often new entrants, and hence often young) are inclined to strategies of subversion—those of heresy. Heresy, leading to heterodoxy, is a critical rupture with doxa, often connected to a crisis, which drives the dominant out of their silence, forcing them to produce the defensive discourse of orthodoxy, aimed at establishing an equivalent of the silent adherence to doxa.

An important property of a field, nevertheless, is that all the persons engaged in it have in common certain fundamental interests—those which are linked to the very existence of the field—such that their objective complicity keeps antagonisms under abeyance. Thus, struggle presupposes an accord between all the antagonists on that which merits struggle, and which is relegated to the taken-for-granted, to the state of doxa. This refers to all that which makes the field itself, the game, the stakes, the presuppositions which are accepted tacitly, without conscious knowledge of them, by the fact of playing, of entering into the game.

Significantly, then, those who participate in the struggle, contribute to the reproduction of the game, by contributing, more or less completely, according to the field, to the production of belief in the value of the stakes. New entrants must pay an entrance fee which consists in the recognition of the value of the game, and great attention is always paid to indices of adherance to the game, of investment, and to the practical knowledge of the principles of functioning of the game, in processes of selection and cooption. Even strategies of subversion are contained within limits, under pain of exclusion from the field of the agents pursuing them.

In fact, fields are continually the sites of partial revolutions, that do not call into question the foundations of the game, its fundamental axiomatic, the basis of ultimate beliefs on which all play rests. On the contrary, in the field of the production of cultural goods, such as religion, literature, and art, heretical subversion makes use of a return to the sources, to the origins, to the spirit, to the truth of the game, against its banalization and degradation. The importance of investments in time, in effort, et cetera that are prerequisites for entering the game, protects different games from total revolutions of the type that would destroy not only the dominants and domination, but the game itself. It is a rite of passage that renders practically unthinkable the pure and simple destruction of the game. And through the practical knowledge of the principles of the game which is tacitly demanded from the new entrants, all the history of the game and all the past of the game, are present in each act of the game.

While Bourdieu uses the metaphor of games to explain the concept of fields, he takes pains to specify what makes fields of social practice different from real games. He clarifies, for instance, that unlike the latter, in which the field (whether the pitch or the board on which it is played, the rules, the outcome at stake et cetera) are clearly seen for being the arbitrary social constructs which they are, and where entry into the game takes he form of a quasi-contract, in the case of social fields, embarking on the game is not a conscious act. One is either born into the field or coopted by a slow process of initiation, and the relation of investment or involvement in it is made more total and unconditional by the fact that one is unaware of what it is. This lack of awareness, coupled with investment, makes a certain kind of belief an inherent part of belonging to a field and playing the game—that is belief as enacted belief, or as doxa, 'a pre-verbal taking for granted of the world, flowing from practical sense'.[8]

Bourdieu also emphasizes that while in conjunction with the notion of social space, the concept of fields may be used to represent social reality synchronically, in fact, because fields are products of history, any attempt to consider propositions arising from a synchronic study of a state of the field as essential, transhistoric and transcultural truths, is condemned from the outset. Instead, the sociologist working with the concept of fields must reckon with the fact that the genesis of any field is the result of a historical process of autonomization and internal differentiation. He or she also has to take account of the specific historicity of an already constituted field.

Indeed, the dynamic of struggles which is intrinsic to the concept of fields, gives it a temporal dimension, and it may be said that the history of struggle creates the history of the field. The dialectic of conservation and subversion referred to earlier, as a characteristic of fields, whereby there are on the one side, the dominant figures, who want continuity, identity and reproduction, and on the other, the newcomers who seek discontinuity, difference, revolution, also produces signs of distinction, which mark time. Thus for example, writing in 1977, and referring to the artistic field in France, Bourdieu notes that the names of schools or groups which have proliferated in recent painting (pop art, minimal art, process art, land art, body art etc) are produced in the struggle for recognition by the artists themselves or their accredited critics, and 'as the newcomers come into existence, that is accede to legitimate difference, or even for a certain time, exclusive legitimacy, they necessarily push back into the past the consecrated producers with whom they compared', 'dating' their products and the taste of those who remain attached to them.[9]

Another general point about fields that the above example illustrates is that contrary to the apparent neatness of boundaries suggested by the use of a concept to denote reality, what is often at stake in the struggles characterizing a field, is the very definition of what constitutes the legitimate domain of the field. Thus as in the field of art, so also in other fields, in the field of sport for instance, the social definition of sport is an object of struggle, a struggle along the lines of amateurism vs professionalism, (elite) sport vs popular (mass) sport. However, what is also significant is that these struggles over definitions are themselves part of the larger field of struggles over the definition of the *legitimate body and the legitimate use of the body*—'struggles which, in addition to the agents engaged in the struggle over the definition of sporting uses of body, also involve moralists and especially the clergy, doctors (esp health specialist), pacemakers in matters of fashion and taste (couturiers etc.).'[10] This draws our attention to questions of the relationship between fields, and of the autonomy of fields.

It has been suggested that while sharing certain invariant features, the central axis of the variation of fields is their degree of autonomy. At the same time, it is pointed out that Bourdieu is not entirely consistent in his assessment of just what this autonomy is from. 'At points it is from the dominant class in the field of power (for example in *Homo Academicus*). At points it is from the entirety of the social field.'[11] What does seem clear, however, is that the autonomy of a field is always a relative autonomy, in so far as a field is always embedded within a wider socio-historical context to which it is responsive, and to which one often needs to turn when attempting to explain any instance of social practice. But instead of positing a direct determinism between the wider social context and an instance of social action, the concept of fields acknowledges the possibility of structures which mediate the influence of the wider context. Thus, for example, while discussing intellectual creation, Bourdieu maintains that the influence and constraints exercised by an authority outside the intellectual field is always *refracted* by the structure of the intellectual field. Thus, for instance,

> the relationship which an intellectual has with the social class he comes from or belongs to is mediated by the position he occupies in the intellectual field in terms of which he feels authorized to claim that he belongs to that class (with the choices that implies)

> or on the other hand inclined to repudiate it and to conceal it with shame. Forces of determinism can only become a specifically intellectual determination by being reinterpreted, according to the specific logic of the intellectual field, in a creative project. Economic and social events can only affect any particular part of that field, whether an individual or an institution, according to a specific logic, because at the same time as it is re-structured under their influence, the intellectual field obliges them to undergo a conversion of meaning and value by transforming them into objects of reflexion or imagination.[12]

However, in general, Bourdieu's analyses of fields are particularly concerned with the mediated links between the wider social field as a field of class struggle, and particular social practices. Importantly, the correspondence between class structures and the structure of different fields takes the form of homologies between fields. What this refers to is the fact of a structural correspondence between different fields based on there being certain invariant features of fields, such as the existence of interests, stakes, and struggles between the dominant and the dominated. These, Bourdieu points out, provide hypotheses of enormous heuristic value. Discussing the field of art criticism, for example, and more specifically, the verdicts and opinions of drama critics in contemporary French newspapers, Bourdieu demonstrates how the space of judgements on the theatre is homologous with the space of the newspapers for which they are produced and which make them known, and also with the space of the theatres and plays about which they are formulated – 'these homologies and all the games they allow being made possible by the homology between each of these spaces and the space of the dominant class.'[13] The play of homologies creates conditions for the production and reproduction of class structures via euphemisms or ideological discourse which get their particular symbolic force from the fact that they create a misrecognition of the determination of fields of forces within different fields by class.

In fact, Bourdieu's analysis of each different field can be seen to be similar to his attempt to understand the fields of class in relation to the cultural field, whereby he tries to answer how 'the free, apparently autonomous practices of the agents involved in the two different fields and thus whose actions are governed by a different specific logic of practice, ... so interact as to not just produce but reproduce the class patterns of cultural practice in general and by so doing tend to reproduce the given set of class relations in general.'[14]

In his *Reproduction in Education, Society and Culture* for example, Bourdieu seeks to analyse both the relative autonomy as well as the dependence of the educational system with respect to the social classes. He argues that it is precisely its relative autonomy that enables the traditional educational system to make a specific contribution towards reproducing the structure of class relations. This it does by fulfilling simultaneously its social function of reproducing the class relations by ensuring the hereditary transmission of cultural capital, and its ideological function of concealing that social function by creating the illusion of its absolute autonomy. Thus, the full definition of the relative autonomy of the educational system with respect to the interests of the dominant classes must always take into account the specific services this relative autonomy performs for the perpetuation of class relations.

Despite his unraveling of the complex links between different fields and the field of class struggle, however, Bourdieu's social theory is acutely sensitive to the significance of the autonomy, albeit relative, of various fields. The consequences of this autonomy can be far reaching in other ways as well. For example, even while he posits that the different classes and class fractions are engaged in a specifically symbolic struggle to impose the definition of the social world that is consistent with their interests, and that the field of ideological positions reproduces the field of social positions in a transfigured form, he adds that the interests of the dominant fractions, who seek to impose the legitimacy of their domination through the intermediary of conservative ideologists, are served only incidentally, that is only to the extent that they thereby serve their specific interests as professional producers. Significantly, he observes that 'these ideologists always threaten to divert to their own advantage the power of defining the social world, which they hold by delegation', and indeed, that this dominated fraction of the dominant class 'always tends to set cultural capital—to which it owes its position—at the top of the hierarchy of the principles of hierarchization'.[15]

To do justice to Bourdieu's social theory, however, it is essential to note that whatever the degree of autonomy of a field, the concept of habitus plays a crucial role in linking different fields. Thus finally, it is to the relationship between the concepts of habitus and fields that we must now turn.

Bourdieu's theory of practice rejects distinctions such as that between action and structure, arguing instead for a conception of the present in terms of two histories: the frozen, objectified past manifest in positions and the embodied history manifest in the habitus (the dispositions) of an individual. A discussion of the links between the fields and habitus would refer essentially to the dialectic of objectified history and embodied history in societies characterized by the existence of fields.

According to Bourdieu, 'an institution, even an economy, is complete and fully viable only if it is durably objectified not only in things, that is, in the logic, transcending individual agents, of a particular field, but also in bodies, in durable dispositions to recognise and comply with the demands immanent in the field',[16] He also writes that 'Investment is the inclination to act which is engendered in the relation between a space of play proposing certain stakes (which I call a field) and a system of dispositions adjusted to that game (which I call a habitus), a sense of the game and of the stakes, which implies, to begin with, the inclination and aptitude to play the game, to take interest in the game, to take up the game.'[17] Given the discussion of the concept of habitus in the last chapter, and of the concept of fields here, these statements suggest how the two concepts, used in conjunction, can illuminate some of the complex processes that structure human action.

The habitus, as a system of durable dispositions, exists as a potential for action in every individual, and determines, in the first instance, the inclination to take part in the struggles characterizing particular social fields, the choice, usually unconscious, of these fields, being contingent on the existence of the pertinent capabilities within the habitus. The specific strategies and their results, however, are necessarily dependent on the individual skills of a player, and on the quantity and quality of the capital which an individual agent or group can mobilize in struggles, so that any given practice is the combined outcome of the activation of habitus and deployment of capital, within the parameters of the logic governing a field.

This location of action within the system of fields provides a point of view on practice which inevitably takes into account other actors, since it is a relational construct. Moreover, since both habitus and field are concepts that have a temporal dimension, they make for an understanding of practice which is historically situated, encapsulating both a past and a probable future. Furthermore, the use of the concept of habitus enables us to move from the contingent characteristics of an action within the context of a particular field to a perception of the common principles informing action in more than one field, and thus to an appreciation of the links between different fields. This link by habitus is essentially a link by social class, since the habitus is a product of the incorporation of the symbolic and material environment through early processes of socialization, and social class refers to groups that share a common habitus and possess similar amounts of similar forms of capital.

To sum up the discussion above: the concept of fields facilitates the analysis of the relatively autonomous universe of symbolic interests in a differentiated society, and provides an insight into the ambiguous relationship it has with the field of material interests. It allows us to view the dynamic processes that animate various realms of social life and provides tools for analysing the specific effect of each realm on human practice. The identification of structural homologies between fields, and particularly between the field of social classes and various other fields, makes possible a conceptualization of how social structures are reproduced and transformed, and how individuals and groups form part of these processes, via their systems of dispositions, the possession of different volumes and types of capital, and in accordance with the logic of the fields they participate in.

While the concepts of habitus, capital and of fields, in their interrelationship, provide the basic analytical edifice of Bourdieu's theory of practice, it is significant that he terms his theory a theory of the economy of practice. Thus the notion of an economy of practice provides an explanatory framework which is integral to his theory, and we will conclude our discussion by examining it in some detail.

The notion of an economy of practice

When discussing his theory of practice, Bourdieu often describes it in terms of a project to develop a theory of an economy of practice. A consideration of the points at which in the course of his work, Bourdieu articulates the need to take on such a project, reveals some of the modalities that have shaped the undertaking.

But before we examine these points, two features which appear in his work prior to the proposal of this notion are worth noting, because they introduce certain critical components of the theory, even though it was unarticulated as such, then.

The first is his observation that certain social practices, in some contexts, are governed by a form of calculation that is distinct from explicitly economic calculation characteristic of the capitalist economy. This is as early as in 1963, when in his 'Travail at Travailleurs en Algerie', Bourdieu first analyses a form of calculation opposed to the spirit of calculation imposed by capitalism, that is, calculation in the service of the sense of equity, characteristic of pre-capitalist peasant society in Algeria.[18] The analysis of such practice is then couched, in the conclusion, (with reference both to the traditional Algerian peasant, and the Algerian subproletariat), in terms of a system of dispositions, linked to the economic and social situation 'through the mediation of the objective potentialities defined by and defining that situation.'[19] In other words, objective, collective probabilities—statistically measurable in the form of regularities independent of individual wills—are noted to be concrete data in individual experience, via group or class habitus, even though they may not be available as conscious data to actors. Thus, from the point of view of the analyst, the objective future seems to be the objective principle of the present behaviour of social subjects. He adds however, that the gap between subjective apprehension and the objective truth of the situation varies considerably from one class situation to another. For the present purpose, this is relevant as an early indication of what the economy of practice entails, namely, an objectively discernible system of action with varying degrees of consciousness on the part of subjects of its generative principle, which actualises calculation without the act of calculation.

The second feature is the appearance of certain concepts whose employment may be described as an extended use of economic concepts—beginning with the concept of cultural capital. This, together with the concept of linguistic capital, first appears in a study of inequalities in relation to education and to culture, more generally, and is followed by the use of the concepts of national cultural capital and artistic capital in a study of museum-going.[20] In the latter, he also uses the notion of supply and demand with regard to cultural phenomena, and refers to Weber's notion of a monopoly of the manipulation of cultural goods and the institutional signs of cultural salvation.

The concept of cultural capital is used again, around the same time, both in a study of the school as a conservative force, and in an article on the sense of honour in Kabyle society, where the notions of the capital of honour and of symbolic capital are also advanced.[21] Ideas of cultural wealth and its monopolisation appear again in an article on the perception of art, and they are developed in conjunction with the concept of cultural capital in several successive studies of the educational system. Subsequently, in the 1972 study, *Esquisse d'une Theorie de la Pratique*, published in English as *Outline of a Theory of Practice* in 1977, a proposal for a theory of an economy of practice first makes an appearance.

While grappling with the realities of precapitalist Algeria in *Outline of a Theory of Practice*, Bourdieu asserts that 'the theory of strictly economic practice is simply a particular case of a general theory of the economics of practice.'[22] The development of such a theory, he adds, involves extending 'economic calculation to all the goods, material and symbolic, without distinction, that present themselves as rare and worthy of being sought after in a particular social formation – which may be 'fair words' or smiles, handshakes or shrugs, compliments or attention, challenges or insults, honour or honours, powers or pleasures, gossip or scientific information, distinction or distinctions, etc.'[23]

Furthermore, rejecting as ethnocentric, both the structuralist analysis of matrimonial exchanges in 'primitive' societies, that viewed them as part of an unfounded universal communicative intent, and the 'mechanical' materialism of social analysis that deliberately overlooked or relegated to the superstructure whatever did not conform to economic interests as defined by the capitalist mentality characteristic of the early phase of capitalist development—Bourdieu indicates the possible usefulness of analysing these social realities in terms of an economy of practice. For example, to understand kinship and marriage in Kabylia, Bourdieu found it useful to bring to the fore the interests of agents in appropriating what he terms economic and symbolic capital, for themselves or for the groups of which they were members, each person's relative strength at a particular point of time being based on the possession of these forms of capital. He also highlights the relations of exploitation, in particular those masked by idealized conceptions of kinship, such as the relationship between brothers, that underpinned relationship between various groups and individuals in Kabyle society. By doing so, he claims to demonstrate that the various exchanges in Kabylia, as indeed in all societies, obeyed the logic of costs and benefits, including the costs of transgressing the official norm and the gains in respectability accruing from respect of the rule.[24] He adds that the definition of an economic system as a system governed by laws of interested calculation, competition, or exploitation is one which can rightly be extended to most social arrangements.[25] It is against this backdrop that we ought to view his discussion and inclusion in his sketch for a theory of the economy of practice, of concepts such as those of cultural capital, symbolic capital, capital of trust, investments, and of profits, including that of 'the maximisation of magical profit'.[26]

To glean from the above, why Bourdieu puts forth the notion of a theory of the economy of practice: it would seem to be, in part, at least, a product of his dissatisfaction with current modes of analysing practice, such as those of structuralism and vulgar Marxism, given, especially, his encounter with the realities of traditional Algeria. That this tradition be accommodated within the framework of a dichotomous conception of the traditional versus the modern, was unacceptable to Bourdieu since his study of the impact of the capitalist system on agents who were struggling to survive in the changed situation, showed up the manner in which the encounter of the two systems was a combined product of the precapitalist cosmology and the capitalist reality, in which the reformulation of traditional modes could not be ignored, suggesting that the two systems were marked by discontinuities as well as continuities, which needed to be analysed in terms of a theory capable of accounting for both realities.[27] The understanding that both were characterized by economic systems, defined as systems exhibiting the properties of interested calculation, competition, and exploitation; that there was implicit and/or explicit calculation to obtain what was rare, materially and symbolically; and that the social exchanges between individuals and groups in both were affected by the logic of costs and benefits; opened the knot whereby the two systems occupied two ontological domains, without losing sight of the peculiarities of each.

Turning to the next articulation of the need for a theory of an economy of practice in Bourdieu's work, we find that in the article entitled 'Avenir de classe et causalite du probable' published in 1974, Bourdieu begins by observing that any theory of practice is an attempt to explain the economy of practices—that is to explain 'the logic immanent in actions and in the objective sense of works and institutions...'[28] He then goes on to criticize the theoretical traditions usually invoked to provide such a theory, clarifying, as he does so, that by the economy of practices, he means to refer to

> the specific logic of all the actions which are reasonable without being the product of a reasoned design or, for stronger reason, of a rational calculation; imbued with a sort of objective finality without being consciously organised in relation to an explicitly constituted end; intelligible and coherent without being issued

by an intelligent intention and by a deliberate decision; adjusted to the future without being the product of a project or a plan.'[29]

Though this is by no means a statement by Bourdieu intended to define what he means by the economy of practices, it seems reasonable to draw upon it to arrive at some understanding of the term. What it suggests is that according to him, practices have an aspect which we may term their economy, on the grounds that they are reasonable, that they are imbued by some sort of objective finality, that they are intelligible and coherent, and that they are adjusted to the future. In addition, it is implied that an original theory is required to explain these characteristics, particularly because this economy exists despite the absence of a reasoned design or rational calculation, of conscious organisation in relation to an explicitly constituted end, of an intelligent intention or deliberate decision, or of a project or a plan—that is, in short, without the phenomena usually evoked to explain practices.[30]

The meaning of an economy, in relation to a narrower notion of 'economy' as in economism, is also sharply etched in an article published in 1977, a large extract from which has been translated as 'The Production of Belief'.[31] Here, Bourdieu refers to economies based on disavowal of the 'economic', which present a challenge to all forms of economism, since they 'function, and can function, in practice—and not merely in agents' representations—only by virtue of a constant, collective repression of narrowly 'economic' interest and of the real nature of the practices revealed by 'economic' analysis.'[32] In other words, and as noted earlier with reference to some of the early writings relating the economy of practices and the 'economy' via misrecognition, what is being elaborated upon here is the fact that a theory of an economy of practice must include the play between two kinds of economy, without one being either reduced to the other, or being the exact opposite of the other. What is also being clarified here is that we are not talking of subjective factors alone, but of practice in all its dimensions: that is, it is not merely a question of adding up economy as subjectively experienced, and 'economy' as objectively realised, but the interplay of both in the subjective and objective dimensions.

In addition, Bourdieu points out here, that there is an affinity between the logic of practice in pre-capitalist societies and that which operates within the parameters of a negation of 'economy' in capitalist societies. In fact, Bourdieu says that it is an instance in which the logic of the pre-capitalist economy lives on, with practices functioning as practical negations, in a sense akin to Freud's *Verneinung*. He also adds that in this economic universe, 'the most 'anti-economic' and visibly 'disinterested' behaviours'.... 'contain a form of economic rationality', even in the restricted sense, and 'in no way exclude their authors from even the "economic" profits awaiting those who conform to the law of this universe'.[33] It is in relation to this non-economic economy that the concept of symbolic capital becomes extremely significant, and it has been defined here as `economic or political capital that is disavowed, misrecognised, and thereby recognised, hence legitimate, a "credit" which, under certain conditions, and always in the long run, guarantees "economic" profits.'[34] In other words, 'when the only usable, effective capital is the (mis)recognised, legitimate capital called 'prestige' or 'authority', the economic capital that cultural undertakings generally require cannot secure the specific profits produced by the field—nor the "economic" profits they always imply—unless it is reconverted into symbolic capital.'[35]

In his *Distinction*, (1979), a study in which many of his tools of analysis are deployed to comprehend the realm of 'tastes', Bourdieu begins with the observation that `there is an economy of cultural goods, but it has a specific logic.'[36] Implying that sociology can analyse this logic, he says that this would involve establishing the conditions in which the consumers of cultural goods, and their taste for them, are produced, and at the same time describing the different ways of appropriating such of these objects as are regarded at a particular moment as works of art, and the social conditions of the constitution of the mode of appropriation that is considered legitimate. It needs to be noted here that while dealing with the consumption of art, Bourdieu conceptualises it as a particular case of competition for rare goods and practices.[37] However, the components of an economy of cultural goods enumerated above are not all there is to it: it includes something more, as well. As Bourdieu puts it—'art and cultural consumption are predisposed, consciously and deliberately or not, to fulfill a social function of legitimating social differences.'[38] This heuristic hypothesis is then examined for its validity, with the result that, to quote Bourdieu,

> it is only by increasing the number of empirical analyses of the relations between relatively autonomous fields of production of a particular class of products and the market of consumers which they assemble, and which sometimes function as fields (without ceasing to be determined by their position in the field of social classes), that one can really escape from the abstraction of economic theories, which only recognise a consumer reduced to his purchasing power (itself reduced to his income) and a product characterized, equally abstractly, by a technical function presumed to be equal for all; only in this way is it possible to establish a genuine scientific theory of the economy of practices.[39]

Thus, the 'economism' of marketing research procedures is shown up to be erroneous and unrealistic, while an economy of cultural goods is established as being a complex, but comprehensible reality.

From the point of view of identifying what Bourdieu means by an economy of practice, what is relevant here is firstly, the fact that the reality denoted by the term economy includes the system of the production, distribution, and consumption, not just of material goods and services, but also of symbolic goods and practices, including tastes. It is thus a wider term than that of the economy within the field of the economy. Arguably, it also encompasses the social function of the system—which in this case, is found to be the legitimation of social differences. And finally, and related to the two points noted above, it involves seeing the relationship between various fields, articulated and to an extent determined, as regards their dynamics, by the structures and the habitus of class—that is by the field of social classes. This last is particularly significant, for it links the practices of cultural consumption to other domains, that is those of the economy of social and economic practices, revealing specifically, the homologies between the structures of the space of life-styles and those of cultural consumption—

vindicating Bourdieu's insistence that ' "culture", in the restricted, normative sense of ordinary usage', be brought back 'into "culture" in the anthropological sense' and that 'the elaborated taste for the most refined objects' be 'reconnected with the elementary taste for the flavours of food.'[40] That in describing and analysing tastes thus, Bourdieu deploys the concepts of production, consumption, supply and demand, cultural, educational, economic, social, symbolic, inherited, and acquired capitals, markets, and profits, and that part 11 of the book is entitled *The Economy of Practices,* mean that *Distinction* is a particularly good example of, and compelling argument for the fruitfulness of his notion of a theory of the economy of practice.

In *Le Sens Pratique* published in 1980 (English translation, *The Logic of Practice,* published in 1990), Bourdieu goes a lot further in his delineation of an economy of practice. Reiterating some of the notions noted above, he notes that practices can have principles other than those of mechanical causes or conscious ends, and that they obey an economic logic without obeying narrowly economic interests. 'There is,' he writes, 'an economy of practices, a reason immanent in practices, whose "origin" lies neither in the "decisions" of reason understood as rational calculation nor in the determinations of mechanism external to the superior to the agents.'[41]

The particular context in which Bourdieu expresses these views regarding a theory of the economy of practice is that of a critique of theoretical reason, and more specifically, while discussing the problems of the anthropology of the voluntaristic Sartrian subjectivism, and of rational actor theories. It is implied that Bourdieu's own project avoids the pitfalls of both and also offers an alternative anthropology. In particular, the inability of the former tradition to admit the importance of inculcated dispositions, Bourdieu consistently maintains, prevents it from grasping the sociological moorings of all human practice. In fact, Bourdieu's notion of the dialectic of habitus and structures replaces existentialism's absolute voluntarism and its notion of emotions, passions and actions as games of bad faith. With particular reference to Sartre's thought, Bourdieu's theory of practice unburdens agents of the definition of their practices as oriented towards ends explicitly defined by a free project. He refers, instead, to their dispositions which incline agents to 'cut their coats according to their cloth'—a phrase invoking Marx's views on freedom and necessity. The critique is developed further through the observation that by privileging consciousness, by endowing it with the power to create the world of action, existentialism looks at this world as though it were devoid of objectivity.

As for Rational Actor Theory, what in Bourdieu's opinion unites phenomenological subjectivism and this theory is the fact that the former constitutes one of the two ends of the pendulum between which the latter oscillates, so far as its anthropological content, hardly ever explicitly discussed as such by those who base their analyses on it, is concerned. Indeed, in this context, subjectivism appears in a more extreme form than in existentialism. And this is precisely what makes it imperative for Bourdieu to discuss it in *The Logic of Practice*, specially when the model was fast becoming influential in the social sciences. Referring in particular to its articulation in Jon Elster's *Ulysses and the Sirens*, Bourdieu spells out the problems of the implicit anthropology of this current of thought. Concerned with the ways in which agents exercise choices, this model sees them as dependent on the one hand on the structural constraints (technical, economic, or legal) that delimit the range of possible actions, and on the other hand on preferences deemed universal and conscious or subject to universal principles. Bourdieu describes these two kind of variables as connoting mechanistic economism and finalist economism respectively, the common term economism referring to the fact that the first involves constraints to which the agents are subject by the self-evidence of reasons, and the second their subjection to the logical necessity of a 'rational calculus'. 'Mechanism' refers to the effect of structural constraints which agents are condemned to passively react to while 'finalism' refers to the substitution of the future ends of the project and of intentional action, in this case, the expectation of future profits, for the antecedents of causal explanation. The latter corresponds to the ultra-finalist subjectivism of the Sartrean consciousness 'without inertia' in that it posits continuity and constancy only in faithfulness to oneself (hence the metaphor of Ulysses who bound himself as he sailed by the Sirens).[42] Paradoxically, however, the choosing agent in this theoretical construction is constituted a-priori by the modalities that are considered to determine the exercise of choices, so that what we have here, according to Bourdieu, is an exercise in total fiction masquerading as an account or explanation of rational action. What he finds behind this banality is the absence of an inquiry into the economic and social conditions of economic dispositions which are designated by him as being more or less reasonable (rather than rational) by the sanctions of a particular state of a particular economy.

Elaborating further on the logic of the economy of practice, Bourdieu writes that 'being constitutive of the structure of rational practice, that is, the practice most appropriate to achieve the objectives inscribed in the logic of a particular field at the lowest cost, this economy can be defined in relation to all kinds of functions, one of the which, among others is the maximization of monetary profit, the only one recognised by economism.' He adds that

> if one fails to see that the economy described by economic theory is a particular case of a whole world of economies, i.e. of fields of struggle differing both in the stakes and scarcities that are generated within them and in the forms of capital deployed in them, it is impossible to account for the specific forms, contents and leverage points thus imposed on the pursuit of maximum specific profits and on the very general optimising strategies (of which economic strategies in the narrow sense are one form among others).[43]

Among other things, what needs to be noted here, is that Bourdieu clearly links the notion of an economy of practice to the concept of fields, and as discussed in the previous section, the concept of field is itself defined with reference to forms of capital, markets, interests, and investments—and thus that it is inextricably part of Bourdieu's project of reconstituting economic concepts.

It is also worth noting that the notion of an economy of practice is seen by Bourdieu as having significance for the science of economics itself, and his views on this further clarify what is denoted by the notion. In a particularly valuable paper presented in 1981 at a seminar on the economic model in social sciences, he says that as in the case of all fields, so, too, in the case of the economic field, one has to observe the form taken at a given moment in history by the interest specific to the field, namely, by economic interest.[44] Furthermore, one would have to recognise that there must be, in order for economic interests to exist, the prior existence of a certain belief in the economic game, that makes it possible for people to be interested in the game. Thus the constitution of an economic field is an empirically identifiable, historical process, amenable to being analysed in terms of the concept of fields, rather than being the basis of the concept.

An important implication of this is that the juridically guaranteed structure of the distribution of property, whereby the formation of prices and wages is determined, is seen as a particular, historically specific form of the structuring of power within the economic field. Thus, too, it becomes possible to perceive how and why the political struggle to modify the structure of the economic field is at the heart of the object of economic science. Consequently, he notes, that 'not even the criterion of value, the central bone of contention between economists, can escape being an object of conflict in the very reality of the economic world'.[45] This has the important implication that to be truly rigorous, economic science should include in its very definition of value the fact that the criterion of value is an object of conflict. This, according to Bourdieu, should replace the claim that this struggle can be decided by some objective verdict, as in the attempt to find the truth of exchange in some substantial property of the goods exchanged. Indeed, he adds that it is no small paradox that one comes across the substantialist mode of thought in Marx himself, with the notion of labour-value, considering that Marx denounced in fetishism the product par excellence of the inclination to impute the property of being a commodity to the physical thing and not to the relations it entertains with the producer and the potential buyers.[46]

Having collated these articulations on the theme, we are now in a position to attempt to identify, summarily, what the notion of an economy of practice means by referring to the precise sense of the term economy in it. Given Bourdieu's repeated clarification that his theory of practice is not borrowed from economics, we need to look at the term in its more generic aspect. When we do so, we find that very generally speaking, the term economy refers to 'an orderly interplay between the parts of a system or structure', and there is little doubt that Bourdieu's use of the term implies that, at the very least.[47] In order words, the theory of an economy of practice is a theory that is concerned with the orderly interplay between parts of a system or structure, namely, of a system or structure of practice.

Additionally, economy also refers to 'sparing, restrained, or efficient use, especially to achieve the maximum effect for the minimum of effort.'[48] That this meaning of the term is also implied by Bourdieu becomes evident when we recollect his assertion that the economy of practice constitutes the structure of rational practice, that is, the practice most appropriate to achieve the objectives inscribed in the logic of a particular field at the lowest cost.[49]

The flip-side of this characteristic of a system termed an "economy" is the optimization of the cost-profits balance sheet, which is clearly referred to by Bourdieu, when he says that the most different economies can obey partly or wholly, the principle of economy, bringing into play a form of calculation, of ratio, which aims at ensuring the optimization of the cost profits balance-sheet, and that this can be termed the universality of the principle of economy: that is of the ratio in the sense of calculating the optimum.[50] That this calculation may not be conscious is a point we have already noted.

Thus, an economy may be described as consisting of the orderly interplay of the parts of a system or structure, in which the principle of economy is at play.

It is in this context that we must place Bourdieu's description of an economy of practice as referring to the logic of actions which are reasonable, rational, imbued with objective finality in relation to an explicitly constituted end, intelligible and coherent and adjusted to the future, without reasoned design or rational calculation, conscious organization in relation to an end, an intelligent intention or deliberate decision, a project or a plan, and also without origins in determinations of mechanisms external to the agents. It is also specified that the nature of this logic is distinct from that of conscious calculation, even if it leads to objective results that make it appear to be the product of some such ratiocination; and that it is, nevertheless, this quality that makes it appropriate for us to speak of an economy of practice.

It is also the context in which we must view Bourdieu's definition of an economic system as a system governed by laws of interested calculation, competition, or exploitation—a definition which according to him is one that can be extended to most social arrangements.

A further characteristic of the notion of economy that emerges from our survey of Bourdieu's writings, is that it includes systems of exchange, capable of procuring a certain material or symbolic profit. Thus, since the discipline of economics deals only with material profit, we need to develop, according to Bourdieu, a theory of the economy of symbolic exchanges, which, no doubt, would form part of a theory of the economy of practice.

A fourth meaning of economy can also be identified as part of Bourdieu's usage: and that is, of economy as 'careful management of resources, to avoid unnecessary expenditure or waste'.[51] This becomes clear via his discussion of the economy of logic that is the symbolic accompaniment of practice, which also accomplishes, among other things, a saving of time.

Finally, a fifth meaning of economy, as 'the complex of human activities concerned with the production, distribution, and consumption of goods and services', also finds a place in Bourdieu's conception, with the important qualification that the realm of human practices it refers to includes symbolic practices.[52]

The above, then, is an attempt to answer the question of what Bourdieu means by the economy of practice, by identifying what the notion of an economy means. As this is clarified, it also becomes possible to understand what the notion of an economy of practice entails, namely, that it is a method of object construction that attempts to wrest actions 'from the absurdity of arbitrariness and of motivelessness.'[53] It is a notion that urges us to interpret action as the outcome of an encounter between habitus and field, an encounter whose most significant features can be analysed by the use of interrelated concepts of investments, interests, markets, profits, and forms of capital, whereby human practice is analysed as being amenable to calculation, at least in terms of effort and time, and as being the practice which is also most economical with regard to effort and time. In the preceding sections on habitus, capital, and fields, we have seen how this economy of practice is realized. Our discussion of the notion here throws into relief the distinctiveness of the theory of which it forms a part. While not entirely free from ambiguities, and not worked out in all its details, it is a remarkable effort to grasp the generative principles of human practices in all places and at all times, without losing sight of empirical and historical specificities.

Conclusion

In our discussion of Bourdieu's theory of practice above we have seen that his theory of the symbolic is an intrinsic part of it.

Thus, it was noted that the dispositions of the habitus, as structured structures and structuring structures, consist of embodied symbolic schemes which define a subjectivity that is transindividual and historical. Understood as being among the principles of the generation of practices, the concept of habitus places symbolic phenomena and the processes of their inculcation and effect at the core of Bourdieu's social theory. That the habitus embody social and material structures in terms of their own logic, gives his theory of the symbolic a complexity that allows him to highlight, for instance, the link between symbolic systems and the dimension of power, through the process of misrecognition; and the practical functions of symbolic phenomena, through the notion of practical logic. Moreover, the understanding that the schemes of the habitus are embodied, creates a significant conceptual space for analysing practice, based on a rejection of the dualisms of mind and body, and of the symbolic and the material.

It was also noted that embodied and objectified symbolic systems are conceptualized as potential forms of power, as cultural capital, and also as subject to consecration in the form of institutionalized cultural capital; but also that in all cases cultural capital exists in the form of symbolic capital—that is, a belief in the legitimacy of the power of cultural capital. Social capital, again, has an important symbolic component, insofar as it is based on material and symbolic exchanges and the symbolic constitution produced by social institution. In fact, it was noted that the pursuit of symbolic capital is seen by Bourdieu to be a motor of primary socialization, and that symbolic capital exists as a dimension of the efficacy of all forms of capital including economic capital. Further, the notion of symbolic violence with which the concept of symbolic capital is associated, introduced Bourdieu's analysis of symbolic power, which also places the realm of the symbolic at the centre of Bourdieu's social theory.

As regards the concept of fields: its relevance to Bourdieu's theory of the symbolic was seen to lie, in the first instance, in the fact that it draws our attention to the constitution of relatively autonomous fields of symbolic interests. The introduction of relational structuralism for the analysis of fields by Bourdieu was seen to provide a particularly powerful means to conceptualize their autonomy as well as their links with other fields, specially the field of social classes. Also relevant from the point of view of his theory of the symbolic is the significance of social positions in fields in providing points of view, including points of view on the space of different points of view. The concept was also seen as providing a framework for viewing symbolic struggles within fields as part of power struggles between the dominant and the dominated; between orthodoxy and heterodoxy, while at the same time alerting us to the basic symbolic commitment of all participants to the axiomatics of the field via the notions of doxa and illusio.

Insofar as Bourdieu's theory purports to be a theory of the economy of practice, it subsumes a theory of symbolic phenomena, both in that it is concerned with the economy that characterizes the creation and pursuit of symbolic goods, as well as in that it sees the locus of calculations in the systems of dispositions of agents and their encounter with the structures of fields in particular historical conjunctures. The economy of reasonable action that governs practice, furthermore, finds a particular form of symbolic expression in practical logic and practical sense as conceptualized by Bourdieu.

Having examined how Bourdieu's theory of the symbolic forms part of his theory of practice in these chapters, we will attempt to evaluate some of its strengths and weaknesses through an empirical exemplification in the next chapter.

ENDNOTES

1. Axel Honneth, Hermann Kocyba and Bernd Schwibs, 'The Struggle for Symbolic Order—An interview with Pierre Bourdieu', in *Theory, Culture and Society*, Vol. 3, No. 3, 1986, p. 45.
2. Pierre Bourdieu, *Outline of a Theory of Practice*, p. 177.
3. Pierre Bourdieu, 'Intellectual Field and Creative Project' in *Social Science Information*, 8[2] April 1969, p. 89.
4. Pierre Bourdieu, 'Legitimation and Structured Interests in Weber's Sociology of Religion', in Sam Whimster and Scott Lash (ed.) *Max Weber: Rationality and Modernity*, (London, Allen and Unwin, 1987), p. 11.
5. Ibid., p. 12.
6. Pierre Bourdieu, 'What makes a social class? On the Theoretical and Practical Existence of Groups', *Berkeley Journal of Sociology*, 32, 1987, p. 3.
7. Pierre Bourdieu, 'The Social space and genesis of groups', in *Theory and Society*, Vol. 14, No. 6, Nov. 1985, pp. 723–4.
8. Pierre Bourdieu, *The Logic of Practice*, p. 68.
9. Pierre Bourdieu, 'The production of Belief: Contribution to an Economy of Symbolic Goods', in Richard Collins, James Curran et.al. (ed) *Media Culture and Society: A Critical Reader*, London, Sage Publications, 1986, p. 159.
10. Pierre Bourdieu, 'Sport and Social Class', *Social Science Information*, 17, 6, 1978, pp. 826–7.
11. Scott Lash, *Sociology of Postmodernism*, London, Routledge, 1990, p. 244.
12. Pierre Bourdieu, 'Intellectual Field and Creative Project', pp. 118–9.

13. Pierre Bourdieu, 'The Production of Belief', p. 143.
14. Raymond Williams and Nicholas Garnham, 'Pierre Bourdieu and the Sociology of Culture' in Richard Collins, James Curran et.al. (ed.) *Media, Culture and Society: A Critical Reader*, London, Sage Publications, 1986, p. 127.
15. Pierre Bourdieu, 'Symbolic Power', in *Critique of Anthropology*, 13 and 14, Vol. 4, Summer, 1979, pp. 80–1.
16. Pierre Bourdieu, *The Logic of Practice*, p. 58.
17. Pierre Bourdieu, *Questions de Sociologie*, Paris, Editions de Minuit, 1980, pp. 33–5.
18. Pierre Bourdieu, *Algeria 1960*, Cambridge, Cambridge University Press, 1979, p. 18.
19. Ibid., pp. 92–4.
20. Pierre Bourdieu, 'Heritage Culturel et Inegalites Devant l'ecole et la Culture' in *Colloque D'Arras*, 12–13 June 1965, and Pierre Bourdieu, Alain Darbel with Dominique Schnapper, *The Love of Art*, Cambridge, Polity Press, 1991.
21. Pierre Bourdieu, 'The School as a Conservative Force: Scholastic and Cultural Inequalities', in John Eggleston (ed.) *Contemporary Research in the Sociology of Education*, London, Methuen, 1974, pp. 32–46, and Pierre Bourdieu, *Algeria 1960*, pp. 95–132.
22. Pierre Bourdieu, *Outline of a Theory of Practice*, p. 177.
23. Ibid., p. 178.
24. Ibid., p. 171–83.
25. Ibid., p. 172.
26. Ibid.
27. Pierre Bourdieu, *Algeria 1960*, Cambridge, Cambridge University Press, 1979.
28. Pierre Bourdieu, 'Avenir de classes et causalite du probable', in *Revue Francaise de Sociologie*, xv, 1, January-March, 1974, p. 3.
29. Ibid.
30. It may be noted here, that Bourdieu, while clearly not a rationalist, is not a positivist either, for he subscribes to Bachelard's position, which is also a critique of positivism, that 'the epistemological vector... points from the rational to the real and not, as all philosophers from Aristotle to Bacon professed, from the real to the general'. See Pierre Bourdieu et.al., *The Craft of Sociology*, Berlin, New York, Walter de Gruyter, 1991, p. 36.
31. Pierre Bourdieu, 'The Production of Belief'.
32. Ibid., p. 131.
33. Ibid.
34. Ibid., p. 132.

35. Ibid.
36. Pierre Bourdieu, *Distinction: A Social Critique of the Judgement of Taste*, p. 1.
37. Ibid., pp. 99–100.
38. Ibid., p. 7.
39. Ibid., p. 224.
40. Ibid., p. 1.
41. Pierre Bourdieu, *The Logic of Practice*, p. 50.
42. Jon Elster, *Ulysses and the Sirens*, Cambridge, Cambridge University Press, 1979.
43. Ibid., pp. 50–1.
44. Pierre Bourdieu, *In Other Words*, p. 88
45. Ibid., p. 89.
46. Ibid., pp. 88–90.
47. *The Collins English Dictionary*. 1986, Collins London, Glasgow, p. 484.
48. Ibid.
49. Pierre Bourdieu, *The Logic of Practice*, p. 50.
50. Pierre Bourdieu, *In Other Words*, p. 92.
51. *The Collins English Dictionary*.
52. Ibid.
53. Pierre Bourdieu, 'The Genesis of the Concepts of Habitus and of Fields', in *Sociocriticism*, Vol. 11, No. 2, December, 1985, p. 19.

5

An Empirical Exemplification: The Shah Bano Case

Introduction

Bourdieu's theory of the symbolic, and the theory of practice of which it forms a part, are products of a rigorous dialectic between conceptual traditions and innovations, on the one hand, and empirical observations of particular social realities, on the other. The epistemological status conferred on them by Bourdieu is that of universally valid frameworks of analysis, capable of yielding sociological truths in diverse empirical contexts. This assertion is qualified by the understanding that the theories are not closed, but open ended constructs, and thus subject to change and modification when demanded by subsequent research. They are constituted by conceptual tools that are heuristic devices to be used as such. This quality of Bourdieu's contribution prompts one to undertake in this chapter the exercise of exploring in a preliminary way the strengths and limitations of his theory of the symbolic by viewing it in relation to the symbolic aspects of a selected social reality distinct from the ones analyzed by Bourdieu himself. This reality pertains to an event involving the rights of women in India, namely, the Shah Bano case.

The case has been seen as exemplifying, among other things, a contest between the state and community, over the issue of cultural rights, particularly the right to regulate the spheres of law and memory.[1] In what follows, I will explore how far Bourdieu's theory of the symbolic goes towards illuminating its reality, examining in particular the fruitfulness of the following conceptions:. firstly, the notion of differentiated societies as characterized by doxa, orthodoxy, and heterodoxy; secondly, the definition of the state as an institution having a monopoly over legitimate symbolic violence; and thirdly, the understanding that subordinate social groups, including women, are subject to symbolic violence involving a process of misrecognition.

Before proceeding further, it would be meaningful to briefly outline Bourdieu's concept of history. The significance of this aspect of his work becomes apparent when we attempt to view, through the lens of his conceptual framework, an event located in particular time and space dimensions.

According to Bourdieu, every historical action brings together two states of history: objectified history, that is the history which has accumulated over the passage of time in things, machines, buildings, monuments, books, theories, customs, law, et cetera, and embodied or internalized history, in the form of habitus. The habitus is the product of a historical acquisition, which makes it possible to appropriate the legacy of history. This is so in the sense that 'the institution or objectified, instituted history, becomes historical action, i.e. enacted active history, only if it is taken in charge by agents whose own history predisposes them to do so; who, by virtue of their previous investments, are inclined to take an interest in its functioning, and endowed with the appropriate attributes to make it function'.[2]

The structures of objectified history constitute part of what Bourdieu calls fields, and the relation between habitus and field is conceptualized as two modes of the existence of history. The notion of field implies transcending the conventional opposition between structure and history, conservation and transformation, for fields are sites of struggle, and the relations of power which form their structures provide the underpinnings of both resistance to domination and resistance to subversion. Moreover, to see how struggles account for a transformation of structures, one needs to enter into the details of particular historical conjunctures and analyse the positions in the structure.[3] In fact, Bourdieu argues for a form of structural history, 'which finds in each successive state of the structure under examination both the product of previous struggles to maintain or transform this structure, and the principle, via the contradictions, the tensions, and the relations of force which constitute it, of subsequent transformations'.[4] Indeed history, or time, is at the center of Bourdieu's analysis, in that it is built into his conceptualization of social space. Thus, the model of structure of social space put forth in his study, *Distinction*, for example, is a three dimensional one: in addition to the volume and structure of capital possessed by social agents, it takes into account the evolution over time of these two properties.[5]

By viewing the relation between habitus and field as two modes of existence of history, Bourdieu is able to found a theory of time that breaks with two opposed philosophies of time. On the one hand, 'the metaphysical vision which treats time as a reality in itself, independent of the agent (as in the metaphor of the river) and, on the other hand, a philosophy of consciousness'. This is because 'far from being a condition *apriori* and transcendent to historicity, time is what practical activity produces in the very act whereby it produces itself'. At the same time,

> Practice need not—except by way of exception—explicitly constitute the future as such, as in a project or a plan posited through a conscious and deliberate act of will. Practical activity, in so far as it *makes sense*, as it is *sensee*, reasonable, that is, engendered by a habitus adjusted to the immanent tendencies of the field, is an act of temporalisation through which the agent transcends the immediate present in a practical mobilization of the past and practical anticipation of the future inscribed in the present in a state of objective potentiality.[6]

We may note here that Bourdieu, while excluding the category of subject, which is central to philosophies of consciousness, does not exclude agents. For it is as active participants in historical action that agents either reproduce or transform structures, even as they are products of these structures. Thus social agents are the product of history; of the history of the social field and of the accumulated experience of a path within the specific subfield. But they also make history.

Bearing in mind this conception of history, and the overall aim of this chapter, which is to view the Shah Bano case in the light of Bourdieu's theory of the symbolic, I will proceed next to an account of the case and then move on to its analysis.

The Shah Bano Case

The Shah Bano case refers to the events that followed from a criminal appeal in the Supreme Court of India by appellant Mohammed Ahmed Khan against respondents Shah Bano Begum and others in 1985. The appeal was a response to an application filed by Shah Bano, a divorced Muslim woman, for maintenance under Section 125 of the Criminal Procedure Code, or CrPc for short.

Shah Bano was married to Mohammad Ahmed Khan in 1932, had borne him three sons and two daughters and was driven out of her matrimonial home in 1975. In April 1978, she filed an application against her husband asking for maintenance, and in November 1978, she was divorced by him by an irrevocable *talaq*, or divorce, permitted under the personal law of the Muslims. He defended himself against Shah Bano's petition for maintenance by stating that she had ceased to be his wife after the divorce, that he had paid a maintenance allowance for two years, and had deposited a sum of Rs 3000 by way of dower as per Muslim Personal Law during the period of *iddat* (which normally is three menstrual cycles or the passage of three lunar months for post-menopausal women). The Judicial Magistrate of the concerned High Court, did, however, sanction a small sum to be paid as maintenance in terms of Section 125 of the CrPc, and following a revised petition, the sum was raised nominally. It was then that the husband appealed to the Supreme Court.

The Supreme Court ruled that a Muslim woman unable to maintain herself was entitled to take recourse to Section 125 of the CrPc that requires husbands with sufficient means to pay maintenance to wives or ex-wives who are unable to support themselves. The ruling was based on the understanding that Muslim Personal Law, which limits the husband's liability to provide maintenance to a divorced woman for the period of *iddat* does not deal with a situation of destitution, the prime concern of the provisions of the CrPc.

The judgement provoked widespread consternation in the Muslim community in the country. The *ulema,* or Muslim clerics condemned the judgement as an attempt to undermine the *Shariat,* the source of Islamic law. A large number of Muslims took to the streets to register their protest, accusing the Supreme Court of trespassing on their domain. What added to their outrage was the reference in the judgement to the desirability of evolving a uniform civil code, which questioned the suitability of Muslim personal law, as indeed of all religious personal law, as an agency capable of fostering national integration. This was viewed as a position contrary to the principles of secularism on the basis of which different communities were bound together in India, and as particularly threatening to the Muslims, who as a minority community, had for long, sought through the preservation of personal law, a means of protecting their self identity.

The leadership of the movement came from the ulema and the All India Muslim Personal Law Board (AIMPLB), an organization established in 1974, who were joined by several other Muslim organizations, and by Muslim politicians in centrist parties, such as the Congress and the Janata Dal. They mobilized Muslims in the states of Uttar Pradesh, Bihar, Kashmir, Andhra Pradesh and Kerala, and their campaign spread through religious institutions, mosques, newspapers, and local community leaders. While initially, when it focused on the issue of maintenance rights for women, the movement failed to gain popular support, it gained momentum towards the end of 1985, when it shifted to the much larger issue of the status of the Muslim minority and its right to exist as a religious community in a secular society. Passions were aroused with protests against interference with Muslim Personal Law and by the fuelling of fears of its substitution by a common civil law, which, it was suggested, would spell the death warrant of Muslim identity in a Hindu India.

In April 1985, G.M. Banatwala, a Muslim League member from Kerala, introduced a private bill in Parliament to ensure the continuance of the regime of personal law. In May, six Muslim organizations issued a joint statement expressing fear of the extinction of personal law. The secretary of the AIMPLB explicitly demanded that the government should nullify the judgement by reiterating its commitment to uphold the Muslim personal law. The organization warned the government that 'it would be unwise and against the interests of national unity to arouse fears and apprehensions and to create a sense of religious insecurity'.[7] Numerous public meetings were held in the course of the Shariah week launched in October 1985, culminating in the observation of the All India Shariah Day, marked by street-corner meetings and demonstrations. Doctrinal differences between organizations were underplayed to safeguard personal law, as were regional and class divisions among Muslims. Towards the end of 1985, the fundamentalists persuaded Shah Bano to hold a press conference, where she put her thumb impression on a statement demanding that the Supreme Court withdraw its verdict as it amounted to interference in the Muslim personal law.[8]

However, even as this fundamentalist tide grew, a large number of Muslims saw no conflict between the Supreme Court verdict and Islamic principles. Significantly, it has been noted that many Muslim women were unaffected by the tide and supported the demand for maintenance rights provided under the Criminal Procedures Code. Women who were initially unaware of the maintenance issue became conscious of it as the campaign against the judgement gained momentum. Muslim women groups in Kerala, West Bengal, Bombay and Delhi reaffirmed the right of maintenance and criticized the mullahs or Muslim priests for making religion an instrument of injustice. The formation of the Committee for the Protection of the Rights of Muslim Women in Calcutta, Trivandrum, and Delhi, gave organized expression to such sentiments. It organised public meetings and conventions in different parts of the country to highlight the issue of women's rights, and submitted memoranda to the prime minister emphasizing the need to protect all sections of the minorities, particularly women.[9] These stirrings of protest were strengthened by voices from within the Muslim intelligentsia. Important sections of enlightened and liberal Muslim opinion, drawn from the educated and professional classes, signed a memorandum demanding the preservation of the right of a divorced Muslim woman to claim maintenance from her former husband.[10] In short, the claims of some Muslim leaders that the community was unanimously opposed to the Supreme Court verdict in favour of maintenance, were false.

As regards the government, the ruling Congress Party initially welcomed the Supreme Court verdict, and the prime minister was openly supportive of the Union Home Minister, Arif Mohammed Khan, who denounced the Banatwala Bill in Parliament. However, the defeat of the Congress Party in the by-elections in December 1985 'led the government to execute a *volte face*'.[11] Fearful of further electoral reverses, the government initiated several moves to assuage Muslim feelings. Thus members of the AIMPLB were summoned to Delhi for consultation; Ali Mian, the *alim*, or head, of the Lucknow Seminary, Nadvatal-ulma, was assiduously cultivated; and the prime minister found time to attend the All Momin Conference where he assured his audience that the Muslim personal law will not be modified or altered. In May 1986, the Muslim Women (Protection of Rights on Divorce) Bill, 1985, was introduced in Parliament.[12]

The Bill denied Muslim women the option to avail of Section 125 of the CrPc. It legitimized the arguments of the AIMPLB and the Muslim League that a woman's natal family should maintain her after her divorce and not the husband as she has ceased to be his wife. It provided that the inheritors of her property would be responsible for her maintenance in accordance with the property to be inherited, without fixing the amount of property to be inherited by the divorced woman. Where a divorced woman had no relatives or any one of them did not have enough means to pay the maintenance, it was decreed that the State Wakf Board (the government's endowment board for Muslims) would pay.

In passing the Bill, the government had clearly surrendered to fundamentalist pressures. The Bill was widely criticized, and women's organizations mobilized public opinion, highlighting gender identity and the need to safeguard the rights of women. They pointed out how women's identity often gets subsumed in the larger issue of community identity. Their intervention restored the focus on women, and exposed the subordinate and unequal position of women within the family, that is, with reference to personal laws, and in the public realm, where, for example, women could not avail of Section 125 of the CrPc because that would supposedly threaten community identity.[13] Street corner meetings, protest marches and signature campaigns were organised, but the government refused to recognize the strength of Muslim opposition to the Bill.

It has been pointed out that the most important factor which made the government take such a stance was the need to stem the anger over the Shah Bano verdict, which was losing the Congress its Muslim votes. Moreover, the Bill was a sequel to the communal pressures mounted by Hindu organizations agitating for the reopening of the Babri Mazjid Ram Janam Bhoomi temple in Ayodhya. The temple was opened in February 1986 to appease and conciliate the Vishwa Hindu Parishad and Ram Janam Bhoomi Mukti Samiti, and at this point, Muslim communal leaders threatened to boycott the Congress if the Babri mosque was not restored to Muslims. The Muslim Women Bill was an effort to pacify ruffled Muslim sentiments over the reopening of the disputed Babri mosque and the conservative objections to the Supreme Court verdict. As Zoya Hasan comments 'In this way the Indian State performed a balancing act of accommodating and according protection to all religions and religious sentiments under the umbrella of multi-theocratic pluralism and an ideology of secularism that encourages and protects all religions'.[14] Furthermore, she notes that 'the most pernicious aspect of the controversy was the attempt by the government to defend the AIMPLB sponsored Bill (which would clearly debilitate and deprive the Muslim community) and lament the absence of reformist tendencies among Muslims at the same time'.[15] But while the responsibility of the Muslim

Women's Bill was transferred to the Muslim fundamentalists, in effect, it was an attempt to mollify them.

Analysis

To see what light Bourdieu's theory of the symbolic sheds on this case, we need to remind ourselves that the realm of the symbolic refers, in his work, to mental structures, including schemes and categories of perception, thought, evaluation, and action, both conscious and unconscious, as well as to activities, institutions, and objects pertaining to the same. We can begin the exercise by asking whether the concepts of doxa, orthodoxy, and heterodoxy provide useful tools for analysing how the events related to the case unfolded. This means considering the available empirical evidence regarding the mental make-up of the litigants involved; of the judges in the context of the judgement proclaimed; and of the dramatis personae who participated in the response to the judgement. It may be noted here that 'doxa' refers to the ensemble of common opinions, established beliefs, and received idas, which remain undiscussed. 'Orthodoxy' may be defined as a system of euphemisms, of acceptable ways of thinking and speaking the natural and social world, which rejects heretical remarks as blasphemies. 'Heterodoxy' refers to the existence of competing possibles in the field of opinion.

To look at Shah Bano's actions first: they have to be viewed against the backdrop of her biographical trajectory in a milieu characterized by a subordinate position for women. Illiterate and aging, abandoned by her husband, and living with one of her three grown-up sons, it is unlikely that her legal application for maintenance was based on a conscious decision to fight for her rights. It was more likely the product of an acceptance in the doxic mode of what the significant males in her immediate milieu dictated she do. Regarding their motives in prompting her to do so, it may realistically be doubted if she would have had much control even over the meager sum which she would have been given as maintenance, had she not retracted her claim. This is likely even as her sons were well off enough to be able to support her. Indeed, as journalist Saeed Naqvi has noted, the maintenance claim by Shah Bano followed a series of disputes on the ownership of certain properties, largely inspired by the sons.[16] Thus, what was important in Shah Bano's case of adopting her earlier stance, and of later retracting from it, was not a consciousness of the legal or perhaps even religious correctness or incorrectness of the particular positions taken, but the fact that they were authorized by significant persons—all males—whom she was subordinate to. The 'doxa' that governed her actions made her consistent even when apparently inconsistent. We can also discern the element of misrecognition involved, when we consider her statement to the effect that she was following the dictates of a religious consciousness in changing her stance. For this was in conformity with the orthodox discourse of Muslim clerics which was put up in response to the heterodoxy of the legal verdict and of certain currents of public opinion. While Shah Bano's interests as a woman were thus thwarted, it was precisely her gendered subjectivity that made her complicit in what happened.

Incidentally, the fact that the concept of habitus, which takes into account individual variations in skills and experience, has greater explanatory power than the Durkheimian concept of a collective consciousness, becomes apparent if we compare Shah Bano's actions to those of another divorced Muslim woman, Shehnaz Sheikh, subject to the pressures of a similar milieu. Unlike Shah Bano, the young and educated Shehnaz Sheikh, did not succumb to these pressures, but instead took up the cause of Muslim women, and formed an organization for the same. This was after she petitioned the Supreme Court, challenging the discrimination against women inherent in Muslim personal law on issues of polygamy, divorce, maintenance, custody of children and inheritance.[17]

As for the actions of Shah Bano's husband, Mohd. Ahmad Khan, it must be borne in mind that he was a lawyer with substantial earnings, for whom the payment of maintenance would not have caused great financial hardship. What seems more pertinent is the reference to the limitations of Muslim personal law in the Supreme Court judgement, which ignited the whole issue of the infallibility or otherwise of the Shariat and of certain interpretations of it, and its implications for the status of the Muslim community in India. As a Muslim lawyer, Mohd. Ahmad Khan was perhaps only too conscious, in appealing under Muslim personal law, of these implications, including the role they had played in legal discourse in India so far, and even more, of the sociopolitical support from sections of the Muslim community that such an appeal carried. His actions stemmed from a calculated bet on the strength of the orthodoxy characterizing certain sections of the Muslim community which had figured in legal debates in modern India, and which was very likely a part of his habitus anyway. The calculation involved in his actions was not strictly speaking rational calculation, but the activation of a 'practical sense'. Thus it is significant that, as has been noted, since he had appealed under Muslim personal law and lost, he became an instant hero among the more conservative *maulvi* elements.[18]

As regards the Supreme Court judgement on the case, a notable feature is the fact that in the course of upholding the High Court decision on the provision of maintenance to Shah Bano, it also commented upon several other issues, and we will consider its various components here. With reference to strictly legal aspects, the judgement drew upon colonial legislation, citing the speech of Sir James Fitzjames Stephen, who had piloted the Code of Criminal Procedure, 1872 as Legal Member of the Viceroy's Council. It clarified the purport of the relevant sections of the code within which Section 125 occurred, which, significantly, is not concerned with individual rights, but with 'prevention of vagrancy' as a threat to public order. As Veena Das comments, 'The creation of a legal category of vagrants, as well as the criminalization of 'close relatives' who could be held responsible for supporting indigent relatives, reflected the basic opposition of colonial rulers to the maintenance of unproductive populations'.[19] Within the framework of modern law, which is a product of heterodox discourse, the judgement thus conformed to colonial orthodoxy on strictly legal issues.

In supporting itself against an appeal based on Muslim personal law, however, the judgement went on to the terrain of heterodox beliefs and opinions. It questioned the role of religion as protector of the interests of women; it contested the interpretation of the sacred legal texts offered; and it spoke of the desirability of a common civil code 'to help the cause of national integration by removing disparate loyalties to law which have conflicting ideologies'.[20] This heterogeneity, Veena Das observes, allowed the judgement to become a signifier of issues which touch upon several dimensions, including the nature of secularism, the rights of minorities, and the use of law as an instrument of securing justice for the oppressed.[21] It is reasonable to suppose that the judges concerned had certain convictions with regard to all these issues, and that these convictions formed part of the existing heterodox discourse associated with certain individuals and groups in modern India. Its constituent elements can be analysed briefly as follows.

The unjust treatment of women in religion was illustrated in the opening paragraph of the judgement by quoting from Manu, the author of the ancient Hindu text, the Manusmriti, followed by a statement by Sir William Lane made in 1840, to the effect that the fatal point in Islam is its degradation of women.[22] Veena Das very perceptively identifies the semiotic function of this manner of framing things, which was 'to establish the secular and learned credentials of the judges, for, by a time honoured tradition in our political culture, secular credentials are signaled by handing out in an even manner criticisms of the majority community and minority community'.[23]

As regards the exercise undertaken in the judgement, of examining Islam's position on the issue of maintenance, it is significant that this was not strictly relevant to the legal judgement pronounced. For stating that Section 125 was part of the Code of Criminal Procedures, and not of Civil Law, the judges asserted that they were not concerned with the broad and general question of whether a Muslim husband was liable to maintain his wife, including a divorced wife, under all conditions. The correct subject matter of Section 125 related to a wife who was unable to maintain herself, and their ruling was limited to such a case. Clearly, given the fact that there is a uniform criminal code to which all Indian citizens are subject, the court could not take into account the religion of the persons involved.[24]

Yet, the judgement did examine the question of whether there was any conflict between the provisions of Section 125 and those of the Muslim personal law on the liability of the Muslim husband to provide for the maintenance of his divorced wife. For this, it drew upon legal texts and the *Quran*, and came to the conclusion that there was no conflict. The process by which the judges arrived at this conclusion involved opening up to scrutiny the legal orthodoxy that existed in textbooks on Muslim law. That this exercise provoked such strong reactions from sections of the Muslim community, not all of whom, it may be realistically supposed, were acquainted with these texts, testifies to the extent to which this orthodoxy had become the doxa—unquestioned and taken for granted—for part of the community. Even more powerful was the typical stance of all orthodoxy that characterized the response, which was to not countenance any questioning whatsoever of its contents—and to term any exercise of scrutiny an interference or even blasphemy.[25]

Moreover, it would be naïve to restrict our analysis of this phenomenon to the realm of discourse alone. For as Bourdieu points out, where there is a correspondence between mental structures and social structures, systems of classification are political instruments which contribute to the reproduction of the social world.[26] Thus, the disadvantageous position of women in legal orthodoxy, only served to reinforce and to contribute to the reproduction of their subordinate position in the community. Nevertheless, as the differentiated reaction to the judgement, even within the Muslim community shows, the orthodox response was not an attempt to legitimize doxa in a vacuum, but was a response to the constitution of a field of opinion, which included heterodoxy. The judgement partook of this heterodox discourse, whose voice could be heard in several other responses to the judgement as well.

As regards its perspective on the need to evolve a common civil code, the judgement articulated a stance conforming to one of the major strands in heterodox discourse on the issue of secularism in modern India. Insofar as it posited a contradiction between the existence of a plurality of personal laws based on religion and the interests of the oppressed and of national integration, it represented what may be termed a position of militant secularism. However, it is significant that while positing this, 'there is no attempt in the judgement to explain why different ideologies in the sphere of personal life are seen as intrinsically threatening to national integration'.[27] Also, the question of the rights of women is 'raised but then totally eclipsed by the allegiance to abstractions like public order and national integration'.[28] Questioning the version of secularism associated with the proposal for a uniform civil code further, Zoya Hasan points out that the notion of national integration on which it is based, and whose development can be traced back to the debates in the Constituent Assembly on the same, is not that of the principle of citizenship or the equitable distribution of resources.[29] As this suggests, there is, in contrast both to the position of the militant secularists and the orthodoxy of those in favour of unreformed personal laws, an alternative position in the field of opinion. This is that of secularism in favour of a legal pluralism based on a reform of personal laws in the light of the principles of justice and equality, including gender justice.

That the demand for a uniform civil code was appropriated by Hindu communalists, so that 'women's right is subordinated to imperatives of unity defined by majoritarianism and pluralism defined in terms of minority rights' reflects the extreme vulnerability of the position of women in processes of the Constitution and exercise of law, a vulnerability whose specifity the overall text of the judgement does not take into account, despite its ruling apparently in favour of Muslim women.[30]

The above draws attention to an absence in Bourdieu's theory of conceptual tools for analysing the phenomenon of conflicting and competing orthodoxies in society as are found in the case of communal ideologies in India. It would not do to subsume them under the category of heterodox discourse, for they are characterized by a defensiveness, rigidity and resistance to dialogue, which are typical of orthodoxy. Neither would it do to see them as ultimately the same, or as subspecies of a general orthodoxy, since they are manifestly hostile to each other, with this hostility affecting social processes significantly, even as they play a similarly regressive role in society. It may be argued, however, that while in his schematic presentation of the concept in his *Outline of a Theory of Practice*, Bourdieu presents orthodoxy as a singular phenomenon opposed to heterodoxy, its rendering is far more complex in his various subsequent analyses of the cultural field.[31] In them, there appear struggles between producers with their products to attain to the position of orthodoxy, that is in Max Weber's terms, claims to the legitimate and monopolized use of a certain class of symbolic goods.[32] This suggests a preliminary framework within which communal discourses and practices could possibly be analysed. However, the specificities of the phenomenon of communalism in India would shape the concept, as much as its analysis would be aided by its use.

To return to the Shah Bano case, to understand the orthodox response to the judgement better, it is necessary to see how it was shaped by the existence of a relatively autonomous political field. For the construction of a discourse and doxa that regards Muslim identity as being based on adherence to infallible Islamic personal laws is a historical construction produced in the context of actors and organizations participating in political processes characterizing modern Indian history. This becomes clear when we observe that the 'common sense' among certain sections of the Muslim community that Muslim identity is equal to Muslim personal law, papers over the heterogeneity, which is the true condition of the Muslims in India—a heterogeneity of region, class, caste and culture. In this sense, orthodoxy is a creation which does not preserve an initial doxa but which creates a new doxa. In the process, misrecognition occurs: the diversion of people from their real interests, to the defence of a symbolic entity which furthers the interests of clerics and politicians, being thereby an instance of the exercise of symbolic violence by them. Thus, apart from the hold of orientalist clichés that projected Islam as providing a complete identity, explanation and moral code for Muslims, and colonial stereotypes of an Islamic community organized on a pan Indian or transnational basis, as well as mythical portrayals of Muslim unity in nationalist discourse, what is of particular relevance to us is the existence of practitioners of modern day politics 'who purported to represent the *'millat'*, or the 'community' as a whole, but were actually exploiting Islam and communitarian solidarity as a shield to cover their political designs'.[33] That the Indian state was responsive to pressures from such politicians is, of course, a significant fact, which we will discuss when we examine the notion of the state as an agency with a monopoly over legitimate symbolic violence. What is important from the point of view of understanding the orthodox response to the case, is the presence of organizations with a leadership that had sought to carve out a place for itself in Indian politics through mobilizations on the issue of Islamic law.

Among the organizations which condemned the judgement as interference in Muslim personal law, were the All India Muslim Personal Law Board, the Jamait-ul-Ulema-Hind, the Jamait-e-Islami, the Muslim League; and the Muslim Majlis Mushawarat. While the first is an apex body of several Muslim organizations committed to upholding the sanctity of Muslim personal law, the other organizations are marked by the existence of doctrinal differences between them. Thus, to compare the Jamait-ul-Ulema-Hind and the Jamait-e-Islami, for instance. the Jamait-ul-Ulema-Hind, which took the lead in demanding restoration of the Islamic laws, was founded in 1919 by a group of influential ulama from Deoband. It had worked closely with the Congress in the anticolonial struggle and in the post independence period, it held that both in theory and in practice, democracy and secularism adequately safeguarded and guaranteed the religio-political interests of Muslims. Its leadership, at least up to the 1970s was secure in the belief that an enduring Congress-Muslim alliance was the way out of post-Partition conflicts. In the 1970s, the breakdown of the secular consensus and the spurt in Hindu-Muslim violence across large tracts of the country 'led the jamiyat to invoke specifically Muslim themes of "solidarity", "unity" and "identity", and to organize Muslims in pursuit of religio-political goals'.[34]

As for the Jamait-e-Islami, it was established in 1941 and has as its goal in India and elsewhere in South Asia, the one of seizing the commanding heights of the state and Islamizing state and society. Mushirul Hasan describes it as a retrograde force, 'steeped in religious conservatism and opposed to the "modernizing" processes in education, social reforms and the emancipation of women'. Further, he notes that

> its world view militates against liberal, progressive and enlightened ideas because of an inflexible interpretation of Islamic doctrines and stout resistance to the eclectic Sufi and syncretic trends in Indian Islam. The few cosmetic changes have not changed the Jamaat into a reformist or modernist movement.

Also,

> as a militant expression of orthodox Sunni Islam, its ideology promotes sectarian consciousness, widens the Shia-Sunni rift and creates barriers between communities'. Indeed, 'at the heart of the Jamaat's campaign is the long cherished ideal of creating a pan-Indian Islamic/Muslim identity. [35]

Cutting across differences, the issue of upholding Muslim personal law formed the basis for mobilizing Muslims on a fairly large scale, even as an organization like Majlis-i-Mushawwarat had failed to form a united Muslim front in the country. Yet, in the normal course of things,

> for most Muslims, far removed from and indifferent to the quibblings in the Jamiyat-al-Ulama, Jamaat-I-Islami or the Majlis-I-Mushawwarat, the critical issue was not the fate of the Shariat, which was in any case accepted by the state as sacrosanct, or the validity of the Islamic state idea; it was to establish, for their own survival, and progress, enduring relationships with fellow citizens and with established political parties.[36]

This prompts us to consider also the role of the state in the whole affair, for it has been pointed out that 'what started as an expression of Muslim feelings and misgivings acquired the shape of significant sentiments only as a result of the intervention of specific political processes and developments in the political arena'.[37]

Bourdieu defines the state as the ensemble of fields that are the site of struggles in which what is at stake is the monopoly of legitimate symbolic violence, that is, the power to constitute and to impose as universal and universally applicable within a given 'nation', that is, within the boundaries of a given territory, a common set of coercive norms.[38] Since the state is an ensemble of fields in which different species of capital circulate (for example, economic, military, cultural, juridical, and, more generally, symbolic), the emergence of a specific capital, a properly statist capital, is the result of the process of the rise and consolidation of these fields and the concentration of their different species of capital. This statist capital allows the state to wield a power over the different fields and defines the specific power of the state. It follows, according to Bourdieu, that the construction of the state goes hand in hand with the constitution of the field of power understood as the space of play in which holders of various forms of capital struggle in particular for power over the state, that is, over the statist capital that grants power over the different species of capital and over their reproduction.[39]

In the case of the government's response to the Supreme Court judgement in the Shah Bano case, statist capital was used to modify the balance of forces within the juridical field in a way that confirmed the supremacy of statist capital over other species of capital. That this in turn was the result of the play of forces and struggles within the field of power, for control over statist capital, is borne out by the fact that those who opposed the judgement appealed to the state to modify it, and the government that reversed it, was prompted to do so by considerations of retaining its power. Even when faced with resistance, as it was by the heterodox response to the judgement, and active demonstrations of protest, the balance of forces in the field of power was tilted in favour of an outcome that was in keeping with a process that had been shaping Indian politics for sometime now; a process described as the communalization of the state.

To consider this process briefly: it has been noted that since the 1980s, a significant factor abetting communalism in India has been the role of the ruling party in supporting religious fundamentalist forces, especially Hindu fundamentalists. Thus, writing in 1989, Amrita Chhachhi observes that

> In sharp contrast to the positions in the late 1960s and 70s, the ruling Congress Party has now shifted from its earlier public condemnation of communalisms and of Hindu organizations and support to the victims of minority communities (in particular the Muslims) to a more generalized condemnation of communalism and the foreign hand in public pronouncements along with a series of concessions to communal demands, a refusal to indict individuals identified as being responsible for the violence, and a stifling of secular opinion, both, within and outside the ruling party.[40]

She goes on to say that

> This shift in the stand of the ruling party on communalism was partly due to an electoral strategy to cash in on the 'Hindu vote', especially in north India. When this strategy did not result in large scale support in the 1986 by-elections, there was a shift back to and a succumbing to Muslim fundamentalist demands by pushing through the Muslim Women's Bill. The ruling party played one communalism off another in the electoral numbers game.[41]

However, Chhachhi points out that it would be a mistake to see the consolidation of communalism today only as the backlash of a short-sighted electoral strategy. Among the deeper factors at work is the increasing crisis of the ideological legitimacy of the Indian state and its need for a new hegemonising ideology. For while post-independent India did have in the early period an anti-colonial nationalism to bind together and give legitimacy to the newly created 'nation-state', now 40 years later, given the results of development policies, the state can no longer claim legitimacy from past struggles. The centralizing tendency of the state, moreover, requires some ideology of unity, and the emergence of fundamentalism amongst sections of civil society could provide a basis for such state ideology.

In the attempt to explain this phenomenon further, Bourdieu's conceptualization of the state as an ensemble of fields, rather than as an autonomous apparatus is useful, as it allows us to see the continuity between the state and civil society.[42] But drawing as he does, mainly upon the experience of West European societies, Bourdieu emphasizes the homogenizing thrust of the state. To understand the playing up of differences by the state, as indeed, the creation of new differences by it, as in the case of a communalized state, requires a development of his concept in a different direction. For this purpose, the work by Katherine Verdery on ethnicity, nationalism, and state making is particularly suggestive.[43] Drawing on the anthropologist Brackette Williams' work, Verdery points out that a homogenizing policy creates the 'nation', as consisting of all those the state should administer, because they all ostensibly ' have something in common'. 'State subjects', she writes, 'are most frequently encouraged to have 'in common' (besides their government) shared culture and/or 'ethnic' origin'.[44] Significantly, though, she adds that 'to institutionalize a notion of 'commonality' however, is to render visible all those who fail to hold that something in common'. This means that 'the relentless press toward homogeneity that underlies the totalizing process of making modern nation-states is 'simultaneously a press toward exclusion'. The state is 'the frame for producing visibility through differences whose significance it creates'.[45] Thus

> By instituting homogeneity or commonality as normative, state building gives sociopolitical significance to the fact of difference – that is, it *creates* as significant pre-existing 'differences' that hitherto had not been organised as such. It groups them as differences of ethnicity, gender, locality, class, sexuality and race, each of these defined as particular *kinds* of difference with respect to the state's homogenizing project.

Adapting Bourdieu's language, she suggests that we may see state-making

> As a process that raises 'difference' from the realm of notice, where disputes can occur between the orthodox and the heterodox, the normal and the strange – that is, between the values associated with what are now recognized as significantly different options but were not previously seen to be so.[46]

Attention to this dimension of the role of the state marks a significant development of Bourdieu's notion of the state as an institution with a monopoly over symbolic violence.

Verdery goes on to note that states vary in the intensity of their homogenizing efforts for numerous reasons, such as the degree and nature of the power exercised by political elites and the resistance they encounter. From this it may be argued that the homogenizing policy of the state in India has been subverted by sociopolitical processes into a policy that includes the homogenizing of religious communities into different groups, and playing them off against each other, as a manoeuvre to manage the state's crisis of legitimacy. The contest is now between the emerging orthodox bases of making differences, and other heterodox forces that may prove stronger. That in the process of such state making, identities are created, is a fact which needs to be taken into account to see the link between subjective day to day experiences and macro processes. For conceptualizing this, Bourdieu's analytical framework of a dialectic between habitus and fields is powerful. With reference to the Shah Bano case, this means that the symbolic violence wielded by politicians subscribing to orthodox notions of Muslim identity, was compounded by that wielded by the state.

However, as regards the crisis of legitimation of the state, Bourdieu does not have much to offer. He refers to it just in passing, noting that 'what is problematic is the fact that the established order is not problematic; and that the question of the legitimacy of the state, and of the order it institutes, does not arise except in crisis situations'.[47] This incidentally, is in striking contrast to the work of Jurgen Habermas, who has been concerned with the legitimation crisis of the state in his work, although with reference to advanced capitalist societies.[48] This is so even as Bourdieu's involvement with the phenomenon neoliberalism, which we will consider in the next chapter, did lead him to engage with the changing role of the state in European societies.

Conclusion

The analysis presented above is a tentative one, to explore the potential of Bourdieu's theory of the symbolic in relation to the Shah Bano case in a preliminary way. What emerges from it is the heuristic value of several concepts, beginning with the concepts of doxa, orthodoxy, and heterodoxy. They are found to be useful in mapping the terrain of the symbolic field in which the case is located, as well as in delineating the habitus of the actors involved. In terms of Bourdieu's concept of history, the 'ontological complicity' between habitus and field, that characterizes historical action, leading to social reproduction, is to be found in the case of the events composing the case.[49]

However, as fields are also sites of struggle, we find, not surprisingly, elements of both conservation and subversion, as well as relations of domination and subordination, involving processes of symbolic violence and misrecognition. Thus we have referred to the symbolic violence to which Muslim women are subject, ranging from that perpetrated by men in Shah Bano's family, to that wielded by religious clerics, affecting both men and women, but women particularly. We have also referred to the violence of law, which brings into dispute the rights of women as equal citizens, and the violence of political groups and leaders that create the myth of the homogeneity of the Muslim community regardless of existential heterogeneity. Above all is the symbolic violence monopolized by the state, which in the case of the communalization of the state as in India, creates differences between religious groups, reinforcing the violence of clerics and politicians. In short, the exercise of looking at a new empirical context within the framework of Bourdieu's theory is rewarding, and encourages one to undertake further such analyses in the future. However, we did find certain limitations of Bourdieu's theory of the symbolic in relation to analysing the case, which suggest the need for a creative use of his concepts.

For one, the positing of a single orthodoxy as Bourdieu seems to do in his early work, makes an understanding of competing orthodoxies problematic. However, since in his later studies of the cultural field, Bourdieu does talk of competition for the status of orthodoxy, we seem to have a preliminary basis in his theory for analysing communal ideologies and practices. This, though, would constitute only a starting point.

Secondly, in so far as his analysis of the state focuses on the homogenizing role of the state, the phenomenon of a communalized state would seem to be beyond its purview. However, we have suggested that it is possible to develop his concept of the state in a different direction, drawing on the work of Verdery, so that the role of the state in creating differences gets highlighted.

Finally, there is an absence of a concern with the crisis of legitimation of the state in Bourdieu's work, which it seems is needed to fully appreciate the political dimension of a case such as the Shah Bano case in India. It may be argued, however, that this is something Bourdieu would have taken into account, in his future work, given his concern with the global state of affairs in his later years, which he often described in terms of a crisis. It is to this that we will turn in the next chapter.

ENDNOTES

1. Veena Das, *Critical Events: An Anthropological Perspective on Contemporary India*, Delhi, Oxford University Press, 1995, Chapter 4, p. 84.
2. Pierre Bourdieu, 'Men and Machines' in K. Knorr Cetina and A.V. Cicourel (eds), *Advances in Social Theory and Methodology*, London, Routledge and Kegan Paul, 1981, pp. 305–6.
3. Pierre Bourdieu and Loic J. Wacquant, *An Invitation to Reflexive Sociology*, Cambridge Polity Press, 1992, pp. 89–90.
4. Ibid., p. 91.
5. Ibid., p. 137 fn. 91.
6. Pierre Bourdieu and Loic J. Wacquant, *An Invitation to Reflexive Sociology*, p. 138.
7. *Statesman*, 27 October 1985 quoted in Zoya Hasan, 'Minority Identity, Muslim Women Bill Campaign and the Political Process', *Economic & Political Weekly*, 7 January 1989.
8. Asghar Ali Engineer, *The Shah Bano Controversy*, Hyderabad, Sangam Books Ltd, 1987, p. 63.
9. Zoya Hasan, 'Minority Identity, Muslim Women Bill Campaign and the Political Process', *Economic & Political Weekly*, p. 47.
10. Ibid.
11. Ibid., p. 47.

12. Ibid.
13. Ibid., p. 48.
14. Ibid.
15. Ibid.
16. Asghar Ali Engineer (ed), *The Shah Bano Controversy*, p. 68.
17. Ritu Menon, 'The Personal and the Political; an interview—discussion' in Kamla Bhasin, Ritu Menon and Nighat Said Khan (eds), *Against all Odds*, New Delhi, Isis International and Kali for Women, 1994.
18. Asghar Ali Engineer (ed), *The Shah Bano Controversy*, p. 68.
19. Veena Das, *Critical Events*, p. 97.
20. Asghar Ali Engineer (ed), *The Shah Bano Controversy*, p. 33.
21. Veena Das, *Critical Events*, p. 95
22. Asghar Ali Engineer (ed), *The Shah Bano Controversy*, p. 23.
23. Veena Das, *Critical Events*, p. 98
24. Ibid., p. 97.
25. Pierre Bourdieu, *Outline of a Theory of Practice*, Cambridge, Cambridge University Press, 1986, pp. 167–8.
26. Ibid., p. 164.
27. Veena Das, *Critical Events*, p. 99.
28. Ibid., p. 100.
29. Zoya Hasan, 'Uniformity vs. Equality: Gender Minority Identity and Debates on a Uniform Civil Code' in Reicha Tanwar (ed), *Women: Human Rights, Religion and Violence*, (Nirmal Book Agency, Kurukshetra, 1998, p. 116.
30. Ibid., p. 117.
31. Pierre Bourdieu, *Outline of a Theory of Practice*, p. 268, and subsequently, Pierre Bourdieu, *The Field of Cultural Production: Essays on Art and Literature*, Cambridge, Polity Press, 1993.
32. Pierre Bourdieu, *The Field of Cultural Production*, p. 116
33. Mushirul Hasan, *Legacy of a Divided Nation: India's Muslims Since Independence*, New Delhi, Oxford University Press, 1997, p. 51.
34. Ibid., pp. 213–4.
35. Ibid., pp. 209–10.
36. Ibid., p. 215.
37. Zoya Hasan, 'Minority Identity, Muslim Women Bill Campaign and the Political Process', *Economic & Political Weekly*, p. 47.
38. Pierre Bourdieu and Loic J Wacquant, *An Invitation to a Reflexive Sociology*, pp. 111–2.
39. Ibid.
40. Amrita Chhachhi, 'The State, Religious Fundamentalism and Women: Trends in South Asia' in *Economic & Political Weekly*, 18 March 1989, p. 569.

41. Ibid.
42. Pierre Bourdieu and Loic J Wacquant, *An Invitation to Reflexive Sociology*, pp. 111–5.
43. Katherine Verdery, 'Ethnicity, Nationalism, and Statemaking—Ethnic Groups and Boundaries: Past and Future' in Hans Vermuelen and Cora Govers (eds), *The Anthropology of Ethnicity: Beyond 'Ethnic Groups and Boundaries'*, Amsterdam, Het Spinhuis, 1994.
44. Ibid., p. 45.
45. Ibid.
46. Ibid., p. 46.
47. Pierre Bourdieu, *Practical Reason: On the Theory of Action*, Cambridge, Polity Press, 1998, p. 56.
48. See Jurgen Habermas, *Legitimation Crisis*, trans. T. McCarthy, Boston, Beacon Press, 1975.
49. Pierre Bourdieu, 'Men and Machines' in Cetina K. Knorr and A.V. Cicourel (eds), *Advances in Social Theory and Methodology*, p. 306.

6

Critique of Neoliberalism: Bourdieu in Practice

Introduction

In this chapter I discuss Bourdieu's critique of contemporary society—particularly of neoliberalism and globalization—and his views on how to resist it. While these ideas have been put forward by Bourdieu as a participant in a movement of resistance, rather than as theoretically worked out analyses, their consistency with and relationship to earlier work needs to be brought to the fore.

To do so, I will first trace Bourdieu's biographical trajectory as a critic of society and then note briefly how the basic concepts of his theory of practice and of the symbolic are undergirded by a critical intent. While doing so I will discuss how his approach is committed to the possibility of emancipation with a role for intellectuals in the process. I will then sketch his critique of the current phase of neoliberalism and discuss his alternatives to the current scenario, seeing how his vision is linked to his overall concerns as a sociologist of the symbolic.

Bourdieu's Trajectory as a Critic of Society

Pierre Bourdieu was born on 01 August 1930 to Mme. Noemie Bourdieu and M. Albert Bourdieu—a *fonctionnaire* or civil servant—in Denguin in the Bearn area of the Department des

Basses – Pyrenees – a place he describes as 'a remote village in a remote region of South Western France'.[1]

After studying at the Lycee de Pau, the Lycee Louise-Le-Grand, and the Faculte des Lettres de Paris, Bourdieu joined the Ecole Normale Superieure.[2] He graduated in 1955 as an *Agrege* in philosophy, though he refused to write a thesis in reaction to the pedestrian and authoritarian nature of the education which was on offer.[3] For the following year, he was professeur at the Lycee de Moulins, intending to study biology in order to combine philosophical investigations with his 'inclination towards thoroughness and rigour.'[4] In 1956, however, he was conscripted for two years by the French government and sent to Algeria to help with a pacification programme against the revolutionaries.[5]

While the Algerian experience marked a turning point in Bourdieu's career which we will discuss shortly, it is important to realise that Bourdieu's early philosophical training oriented him in a particular way towards the major debates in French intellectual life in the years to come. This training was less by strict adherance to the prescribed curriculum and more through individual and peer group initiative (the latter is suggested by Bourdieu's use of the pronoun 'we' in talking of it).[6] Phenomenology in its existential form was at the height of its influence when he was a student. Bourdieu had read *Being and Nothingness* in 1949 followed by Husserl (who at that time was hardly known in France), Heidegger, Schutz and Merleau-Ponty.[7] To this extent, he was an early initiate into the phenomenology of his day. Infact, one could also say that he was prepared for the then incipient existential Marxism (Sartre's *Critique of Dialectical Reason* appeared only in 1960) in so far as he was interested in the early Marx and was specially impressed by the *Theses on Feuerbach*. This was a time when, according to Bourdieu, Marxism did not really exist as an intellectual position, though Stalinism was in ascendency. The latter was unacceptable to Bourdieu who, together with some other students of the Ecole, including Derrida, Bianco, Comte, Marin and Pariente, founded a Committee for the Defence of Freedom around 1951.[8] This led to their denunciation as social traitors at a meeting of the Communist Party at the Ecole.[9]

Significantly, though, Bourdieu was inspired to go beyond existentialism and the reading of classic authors. This was through the work of Gaston Bachelard and Georges Canguilhem at the Sorbonne (relatively unknown in the phenomenological era) and Eric Weil, Alexandre Koyre, Martial Gueroult and Etienne Gilson in other institutes. These philosophers stood for a rigorous history of science, philosophy and epistemology—which have indeed been prominent concerns in Bourdieu's work.[10] He had also studied Saussure extensively and thus was able subsequently to engage critically with structuralism.[11] In short, we can conclude that in Bourdieu's social science the epistemological questions which are intrinsic and explicit are grounded in fairly extensive and intensive philosophical study.

A conspicuous feature of the institutional context of Bourdieu's education was its elitist status, including the lycees attended, enrolment at the Ecole Normale Superior, the study of philosophy which for long had occupied in France the highest rung of the ladder of academic prestige (conferring on the teachers and taught the corresponding social reward of distinction), and the taking of an Agrege, considered to be the best guarantee of material security for the French academic.[12] Equally striking, however, was the ambivalence which marked Bourdieu's attitude toward it and which no doubt gave impetus to his to his subsequent deeply probing studies of education. Injustice and the abuse of power, writ large in the Algerian situation he was to encounter, were phenomena he had already been alerted to in the educational context.[13]

However, when from the Lycee de Moulins Bourdieu went to Algeria, it is unlikely that he had anticipated the enormity of the emotional and intellectual shocks he was to experience there. With his cultivated disposition and the choice of philosophy as a vocation, Bourdieu, though a keen observer of foreign affairs, schooled in the Parisian milieu of political debates, was faced with a situation that was a challenge to moral and intellectual integrity. It was here that his idea of a 'métier militant' took shape. His earlier discontent with 'just reading left wing newspapers' (the weekly L-Express used to be the very conscience of the intellectual left, with long articles by Sartre on such matters as torture in Algeria) 'and signing petitions' took on an urgency that made reading books and visiting libraries seem totally inadequate.[14]

After two arduous years in the army in Algeria, while still intending eventually to return to philosophy, Bourdieu began to write a book about Algeria: 'To highlight the plight of the Algerian people and also that of the French settlers, the pieds-noirs, whose situation was no less dramatic, whatever had to be said about their racism etc.'[15] While he agreed with the actions of the French intellectuals against torture and for peace, he was also: 'Appalled by the gap between the views of the French intellectuals about this war [i.e the Algerian war] , and how it should brought to an end, and my experiences, the embittered pieds-noirs as well the military coups, de Gaulle etc.'[16] The research and his book were to be his way of contributing to the struggle including the one with his own conscience for having been merely a participant observer in the war.[17] His first book *Sociologie de l' Algerie* was published in 1958.

For two further years, Bourdieu remained in Algeria, lecturing at the Faculte Des Lettres D'Alger including teaching a course on 'Algerian Culture' at the University of Algiers in 1960 (which was viewed as a provocation by authorities and settler groups for whom the mere acknowledgement of the existence of something like an Algerian culture was tantamount to open support for the National Liberation Front)[18] and conducting field research with the scholars Alan Darbel, Jean Paul Rivet, Claude Seibel, and a group of Algerian students of the Institute de Statistiques d'Alger. This was the basis of two studies *Travail et Travailleurs en Algerie* (consisting of 2 volumes: Volume 1, *Statistical Data* by A. Darbel, Jean Paul Rivet and Claude Seibel and Volume 2, *Sociological Study* by Pierre Bourdieu, a shortened version of which was published in English as 'The Disenchantment of the World' in *Algeria 1960), Le Deracinement,* and several articles analysing the social structure of colonial Algeria and its transformation. Most of this work was published after his return to France in 1960, so that by 1977, 5 books (including some pieces that appeared in more than one collection, at times modified) and three major articles on Algeria were published. In 1958-9 he gave a lecture on Durkheim and Saussure in which he tried to show the limitations of attempts at generating pure theory. Between 1959-60 he revisited Bearn where he had spent many years of his childhood and his research amongst the peasantry there followed by further investigations in 1970-71 were the basis of his study 'Marriage Strategies as Strategies of Social Reproduction', an article published in the *Annales* in 1972. Significantly, Bourdieu regards this research as 'the crossover point, the interface, between ethnology and sociology'.[19]

Bourdieu recollects reading all of Marx's work in the course of his research in Algeria. He was also working on the Marxist notion of relative autonomy in relation to research in art.[20] As regards studies of Algeria itself: he found inspiration from the work of the historians Jaques Berque and Andre Nouschi as well as Emile Dermingham and Charles-Andre Julien.[21] He also came across work that used ethnographic data (mainly detailed records of rituals) stretched to fit a vague Frazerian evolutionary framework, which threw sharply into relief the ethnocentrism of most French scholarship on Algeria including its suitability for justifying the colonial order.[22] In the context of his coming upon innumerable meticulously detailed records of ritual that shed little light on Algerian society and which were not unlike the records of American Indian mythologies used by Levi-Strauss purportedly to illuminate the essential reality of social structures, he was provoked to take a critical stance towards Levi-Straussian structuralism, though it did find a place in Bourdieu's own theoretical framework, subsequently. Indeed, when Bourdieu returned to France in 1960, structuralism had replaced existentialism as the dominant intellectual paradigm.

From 1960 to 61, Bourdieu was a lecturer at the Faculte des Letters de Paris and worked as an assistant to Raymond Aron. It was also sometime during this period that he attended Levi-Strauss' seminars at the College de France. From 1961 to 1964, he lectured at the Faculte des Lettres de Lille. He then returned to Paris as Director of studies at the Ecole des Haute Etudes. By 1966, the Ecole had set up an intensive training programme in sociology—a period which coincided with what Bourdieu describes as 'the high water mark of the 'Lazarsfeldian' invasion in France'. According to Bourdieu: 'through some interesting techniques which needed to be learnt and I had learnt, he (i.e Lazarsfeld) was imposing something else, an implicit positivistic epistemology that I didn't want to accept.'[23] The result was the book entitled *Le Metier de Sociologue* published in 1968 (English translation: *The Craft of Sociology* published in 1991). This work was directed against,

> two contrasting errors against which sociology had to define itself. The first one, which could be called theoreticist, was symbolized by the Frankfurt school, in other words people who, without doing any empirical research denounced the positivist danger everywhere (Lucien Goldmann was the French representative of that current) the second that could be called positivist was symbolized by Lazarsfeld.[24]

Interestingly, the year of publication of *Le Metier de Sociologue* marks more than one important 'event' in French intellectual and political history: the May '68, movement, on the one hand, and the rise of the Althusserian theoreticist wave on the other. Bourdieu was active before and during the '68 uprising, speaking at various universities at the invitation of student groups. Closer to Boudieu's own trajectory, this was the year when the Centre de Sociologie European was founded, of which Bourdieu became director.

In 1970, Bourdieu's *La Reproduction* was published. Its translation into English, *Reproduction: In Education, Society and Culture* in 1977 is what established Bourdieu's identity for a long time in the English speaking world as primarily a contributor to the sociology of education. 1972 saw the appearance of *Esquisse d' une theorie de la pratique* (English translation—*Outline of a theory of Practice* published in 1977), Bourdieu's first major theoretical work, and in 1975, he launched his journal, *Actes de la Recherche en Sciences Sociales* 'devoted to deconsecrating the mechanisms by which cultural production helps sustain the dominant structure of society'.[25] In 1979, the widely read and influential work, *La Distinction* (English translation—*Distinction* published in 1979] was published, and in 1980, *Le Sens Pratique* (English translation—*The Logic of Practice* published in 1990), displacing *Esquisse* as the major statement of Bourdieu's theory of practice. In 1981: 'following various episodes of internal politics in the wake of Raymond Aron's retirement, and in competition with Boudon and Touraine, Bourdieu was appointed to the chair at the College de France.'[26].

In 1984, the appearance of Bourdieu's *Home Academicus* (English translation-*Homo Academicus* published in 1988) was a landmark – being an analysis of academia itself. Bourdieu continued to write and publish profusely in the following years, and also to intervene publicly on a number of topics of his competency: education, television, publicity. Over the years, he was also intermittently involved in anti-racism struggles with the group SOS-Racisme without formally joining it. He joined Michel Foucault in organizing action in favour of Poland to protest the meek reaction of France's Socialist government to Jaruzelski's military coup in December 1981. 1989 saw the publication of *La Noblesse d'Etat,* (English translation *The State Nobility* published in 1996), a study of elite schools and the field of power, *Les Regles de l' art,* a study of the literary field, appeared in 1992 (English translation *The Rules of Art* published in 1996), *La Misere du monde,* a work on human suffering,as a consequence of the policies of economic liberalization, in 1993 (English translation *The Weight of the World* published in 1999). *Libre-echange,* a dialogue with the artist Hans Haacke was published in 1994 (English translation *Free Exchange* published in 1995), and *Meditations pascaliennes,* a critique of scholastic reason, in 1997 (English translation *Pascalian Meditations* published in 2000). Following the coming down of the Berlin Wall, Bourdieu launched *Liber,* a European review of books, to facilitate the formation of a European 'collective intellectual', an intellectual being defined as autonomous yet committed, engaged, yet subject to no criteria of political 'orthodoxy'.[27]

Through the 1990s and till his death in January 2002, Bourdieu was a vocal spokesperson against neoliberalism and globalization, addressing trade union federations and rallies of striking railway workers, other public sector employees, the unemployed, and others. In 1995, he founded the group Raisons d' agir to undertake a programme of militant research and publication. A collection of Bourdieu's texts written or spoken was published by it as *Contre-Feux* in 1998 (in English translation as *Acts of Resistance: Against the New Myths of our Time*). In 1996, he presided over the 'Etats Generaux du Movement Social', an organization of European social movements, which he was involved with since its inception.

However, while a look at the points in his biographical trajectory at which he was provoked to take a critical social stance does introduce Bourdieu as a social critic, of particular relevance to us is the critical intent that informs his social theory.

Theory with a Critical Intent

A close look at Bourdieu's theory of practice and the related theory of the symbolic reveals the critical intent of his intellectual project. Born of a dialogue with contemporary intellectual trends and an encounter with empirical realities in Algeria and in France, the theory unsettles many commonsense assumptions and their counterparts in theoretical traditions.

To begin with, the critique of subjectivism and of objectivism that it entails, questions, on the one hand, the absolute voluntarism of the pure subject, a notion with widespread popular appeal, as well as Rational Actor Theory, its contemporary intellectual incarnation, and, on the other, the notion of a deterministic course of history that agents are passively subject to, a view for which the more fatalistically inclined among individuals and groups, including certain social movements, have an affinity, and which also constitutes the other end of the pendulum towards which the Rational Actor Theory swings. By conceptualising practice as the outcome of a dialectic between habitus and field, Bourdieu makes room for an understanding of historical action as openended within limits, and, in differentiated societies, as shot through with myriad possibilities via the play of doxa, orthodoxy, and heterodoxy. In particular, the relative autonomy of the symbolic order conceptualized by Bourdieu, can, according to him, leave a margin of freedom for political action aimed at reopening the space of possibles, especially in periods in which expectations and chances fall out of line. As he puts it, 'the belief that this or that future, either desired or feared, is possible, probable or inevitable can, in some historical conditions, mobilize a group around it and so help to favour or prevent the coming of that future.'[28] Generally, what is implied by favourable historical conditions is a situation such that the structures contested by an utterance or action be in a state of uncertainly and crisis, favouring uncertainly about them and an awakening of critical consciousness of their arbitrariness and fragility. This gives an action or utterance aimed at challenging the objective structures some chance of being recognized as legitimate.

Secondly, a concern with relations of domination and subordination is a marked feature of Bourdieu's analytical framework. Starting with the conceptualization of the structuring of the primary habitus, with the notion of the embodiment of structures of power as well as of the participation in the power play implied by symbolic dependence, the theory breaks away from the apolitical stance of the structural functionalist, the phenomenological, and the structuralist traditions. The structuring of social space by the differential distribution of various forms of capital similarly brings to the fore the dimension of power. Significantly the identification of other forms of capital besides economic capital, provides a more nuanced and comprehensive understanding of relations of domination and subordination. The identification of symbolic capital in particular provides an insight into the role of symbolic power in social life, and marks a distinctive advance over the Marxist theory of class. In relation to the same, the rejection of the mind-body duality also leads to the notion of practical comprehension or belief, which sees systems of the legitimation of power at a level below that of consciousness, unlike what is implied by the notion of ideology. The concepts of misrecognition and symbolic violence, moreover, provide important tools for analysing the dynamics of the structuring, reproduction, and transformation of relations of power. In particular, they facilitate an understanding of how those subjected to domination accept their subordination even without the use of overt force by the dominant. The entire conceptual apparatus of Bourdieu's theory of practice, including the dialectic between habitus and field, the distribution of forms of capital, and the process of the structuring and restructuring of habitus, comes into play in the analysis of how misrecognition and symbolic violence contribute to the maintenance of systems of dominance in society. For as Bourdieu writes, 'One of the most powerful mechanisms of the maintenance of the symbolic order is the two-fold naturalization which results from the inscription of the social in things and in bodies with the resulting effects of symbolic violence.'[29]

It is important to note, however, that as a critical intellectual, Bourdieu does not view asymmetries of power as immutable and irreversible. While wary of the constructivist view that sees power as a purely symbolic phenomena, Bourdieu nevertheless posits the possibility of agents grasping the reality of social processes and seeking to overcome misrecognition. What Bourdieu terms 'socioanalysis' is a possibility which follows from a more general feature of his work as identified by Loic J. Wacquant, which is that 'from the standpoint of the individual, it gives tools for distinguishing zones of necessity and of freedom, and thereby for identifying spaces open to moral action.' This collective counterpart to psychoanalysis may help `unearth the *social* unconscious embedded into institutions as well as lodged deep inside of us,' much as the latter frees us from the individual unconscious that drives or constricts our practices.[30] The application of socioanalysis is evident in Bourdieu's own work. Beginning with his study of Bearnais peasants, familiar from his childhood, where he applied methods of investigation previously used to uncover the logic of kinship relations in the foreign universe of Algerian peasants and workers, it is particularly clear in *Homo Academicus*. In the latter, since it is a study of academia, a universe to which Bourdieu himself belonged, the subject of the work is himself an object of analysis. More generally, Bourdieu regards socioanalysis in this sense to be an essential part of social science, a part of reflexivity as he conceives it. However, we must remind ourselves of Bourdieu's criticism of the scholastic illusion inherent in the description of resistance to domination in the language of consciousness, as among Marxists and feminists who expect political liberation to come from the 'raising of consciousness', ignoring the inertia resulting from the inscription of social structures in bodies, for lack of a dispositional theory of practices.[31] In other words, socioanalysis by itself may not be sufficient to modify actions and relationships.

It is not just in the context of socioanalysis, however, that Bourdieu envisages an important role for intellectuals in movements for emancipation. His conception, rooted in a historical and analytical understanding of the intellectual field, formed the basis for his own interventions in the public sphere, and needs to be briefly considered here.

To begin with, Bourdieu suggests using the title intellectual for cultural producers who fulfill two conditions: firstly, who are members of an intellectually autonomous field, independent of religious, political, economic, or other powers, and who respect that field's particular laws; and secondly, who deploy their specific expertise and authority in their particular intellectual domain in a political activity outside it.

The emergence of relatively autonomous intellectual fields is traced to a historical process that began in the Middle Ages, with philosophy as the first scholastic domain, and later, in Renaissance Italy, with the gradual constitution of the scientific, literary, and artistic fields. What makes these intellectual fields relevant from the point of view of human emancipation is the fact that it was the new agents who made up these fields who initiated the process of the invention of the universal, according to Bourdieu. Characterized by a social break with the economy and the world of practice, that is, freed from the urgencies of the world, these fields were the site for the creation of specific rules and regulations favouring systematization and rationalization, and so for an advance of various forms (scientific, legal, artistic, et cetera) of rationality and universalization. However, noting that this does not by itself ensure the participation of intellectuals in politics, Bourdieu traces historically the constant shift in attitudes of intellectuals regarding politics—'a balancing act between engagement in current events and retreat to the ivory tower'.[32]

In France, a turning point came at the end of the nineteenth century, with literary, artistic, and scientific field attaining a high degree of autonomy, and the most autonomous agents of these autonomous fields realizing that their autonomy was not identical with a rejection of politics, and that they could intervene in politics as artists, writers, and scholars. Particularly significant was Emile Zola taking a stand in the Dreyfus Affair. What Zola exemplifies is an intellectual constituted as such by intervening in the political field in the name of autonomy and of the specific values of a field of cultural production which has attained a high degree of independence with respect to various powers. The intellectual then asserts himself against the specific laws of politics (which Bourdieu terms those of Real Politik and reasons of state) as defender of universal principles that are in fact the result of the universalization of the specific principles of his own universe. Thus, Bourdieu states, the first objective for a movement of intellectuals is to work collectively towards the defence of their own interests and towards the means necessary for the protection of their autonomy. Incidentally, it may be noted that the seeds of Bourdieu's notion of an intellectual as outlined here, had already been sown during his experience in Algeria. The upholding of universal values in the face of a narrow nationalism that Zola's stance in the Dreyfus case represented, has affinities with Bourdieu's being in Algeria as a member of the French army, and critiquing colonialism.

Bourdieu enumerates the historical factors which authorize intellectuals in their universalist ambitions. The first is the very appearance of a field where the defence of universal causes is rewarded. This makes it possible to rely on the symbolic profits associated with these actions to mobilize intellectuals in favour of the universal. The second is the existence of means of objectification, such as sociology, which offer a way of discovering the particular social and economic conditions underlying the claims of intellectuals to the universal, and thereby the means to associate the pursuit of the universal 'with a constant struggle for the universalization of the privileged conditions of existence which render the pursuit of the universal possible.'[33] No doubt, Bourdieu's own interventions in the fields of educational policy and television were clearly inspired by such an aim.

In contemporary times, Bourdieu gave a call for a corporatism of the universal, a conscious and organised mobilization of intellectuals in the face of new threats to the autonomy of cultural fields. These include threats posed by the state for whom culture has become an instrument and concern of politics, as well as by the increasing penetration of the world of art and science by the world of finance. In the cultural field itself, he points to the logic of commercial production increasingly marginalizing avant garde production. Finally, he refers to the control of power-brokers over the means of circulation—particularly via the media—tending to strip intellectuals of their prerogatives to evaluate themselves and their production according to their own criteria. However, Bourdieu does not see this defence of autonomy as its own end, but as a means to extend the intervention of intellectuals in politics.

But the dialectic between the specific logic of the intellectual fields and the logic of political intervention is a complex phenomenon. Thus there is, for instance, as Bourdieu enumerates in his discussion of forms of scholastic fallacy, a tendency for intellectuals to universalize the particular case, that is, of the privilege constituting the scholastic condition. Noting the case of Habermas, for example, he observes that the epistemocentric illusion which leads him to make the universality of reason and the existence of universalizable interests the basis of rational consensus is based on unawareness (or repression) of the conditions of access to the political sphere and of the factors of discrimination (such as sex, education, or income) which limit the chances of access not only to positions in the political field but, more profoundly, to articulated political opinion and consequently to the political field. More generally, there are according to Bourdieu, advocates of an abstract universalism which ignores the conditions of access to the universal, and which generally serves to justify the established order.[34] Moreover there is also what he terms

> 'the obscurantism of the Enlightenment' [which] can take the form of a fetishism of reason and a fanaticism of the universal which remain closed to all traditional manifestations of belief and which, as is shown for example by the reflex violence of some denunciations of religious fundamentalism, are no less obscure and self-opaque than what they denounce.[35]

Significantly, he refers to some contemporary forms of Islamic fundamentalism as being perhaps a distorted riposte to the 'ambiguous aggression of the imperialism of the universal', homologous to Herder's reactive nationalism as a riposte to the French revolutionaries' faith in the imperialism of the universal.[36] At the same time, seemingly radical denunciations of any form of belief in the universal, 'in the values of truth, emancipation, in a word, Enlightenment, or of any affirmation of universal truths and values, in the name of an elementary form of relativism which regards all universalistic manifestoes as pharisaical tricks intended to perpetuate a hegemony', are in a sense more dangerous than abstract universalism and also another way of accepting things as they are.[37]

Bourdieu's own position is that of fighting at the same time against the mystificatory hypocrisy of abstract universalism and for universal access to the conditions of access to the universal, 'the primordial objective of all genuine humanism.'[38]

The situation is also complicated because, if one recalls the social conditions of the emergence of universes in which the universal is generated, one finds that the advent of reason is inseparable from the progressive autonomization of social microcosms based on privilege, 'sites for the progressive invention of modes of thought and action that are theoretically universal but monopolized in practice by a few'.[39] This results in an ambiguity expressed in simultaneous or alternate aristocratic contempt for the 'vulgar' and an unconditional generosity towards an unconditioned 'humanity' on the other. In fact, in so far as it is made possible by a privilege that is not aware of itself, reason contains the potentiality for an abuse of power. Produced in legal, scientific, and other fields as a result of skhole, or leisure, and engaged in the division of labour of domination, 'it has a rarity which causes it always to function as (cultural or informational) capital and also, in so far as the economic and social conditions of its production remain misrecognized, as symbolic capital and therefore both as a source of material and symbolic profits and as an instrument of domination and legitimation'. Further, 'it even offers the supreme form of legitimation, with *rationalization* (in both Freud's and Weber's senses) or, more precisely, universalization, which is the sociodicy par excellence'.[40] One therefore has to acknowledge the unequal distribution of the social conditions of access to the universal, and appeal to what Bourdieu terms a Realpolitik of the universal, so as to favour:

> access everywhere and by all means to all the instruments of production and consumption of the historical achievements that the logic of the internal struggles of the scholastic field, institutes as universal at a given moment in time (while taking care not to turn them into fetishes and to strip them, by remorseless critique, of all they owe merely to their social function of legitimation).[41]

The Realpolitik of the universal would aim to defend the social conditions of the exercise of reason and to endow reason with instruments which are the conditions for its fulfillment in history. He adds that it should also aim to rehabilitate practical reason, thus subverting the social division between theory and practice in representations and in practices, and which would enable a recognition of the plurality of forms of 'intelligence', so far monopolized by the verdicts of the educational system.

Furthermore, intellectual fields are no exceptions to the characterisation of fields as sites of struggle, monopolies, and relations of domination and subordination. Yet, referring in particular to the scientific field, Bourdieu argues that it is at the same time an exceptional universe, in that in it, the necessity of reason is instituted to varying degrees in the reality of structures and dispositions, and the logic of competition in it imposes cross controls which give their full efficacy to mechanisms of universalization. He describes the field as possessing an intrinsic duality which lends itself to two simultaneous readings. 'The pursuit of the accumulation of knowledge is inseparably the quest for recognition and the desire to make a name for oneself; technical competence and scientific knowledge function simultaneously as instruments of accumulation of symbolic capital; intellectual conflicts are always also power struggles, the polemics of reason are the contests of scientific rivalry, and so on'.[42] Of course, it is only to the extent that the field is autonomous, that its participants are constrained to use only instruments of discussion or proof corresponding to the scientific demands in the matter, and are therefore obliged to sublimate what Bourdieu calls their *libido dominandi* into *libido sciendi* that can only triumph by answering a demonstration with a refutation, one scientific fact with another scientific fact, that the field can be a site of the progress of reason. That the constraints favouring such actions are inscribed in the institutionalized procedures regulating entry into the game, in the conditions of exchanges, in the mechanisms of the field and in the dispositions of the agents which are the product of this set of effects, makes for a field whose rules are respected for a strength which is both logical and social. This is what leads Bourdieu to propose that the realistic description of the scientific field be treated as a kind of reasonable utopia of what a political field conforming to democratic reason might be like; 'or more precisely, as a model which, by comparison with the observed reality, would indicate the principles of action aimed at promoting the equivalent, within the political field, of what is observed in the scientific field in its most autonomous forms'.[43] He refers in particular to the phenomenon of regulated competition controlled by its own immanent logic, through social mechanisms capable of forcing agents to behave 'rationally' and to sublimate their drives.[44]

Bourdieu's suggestion for implementing practically the Realpolitik of reason is to use the ordinary means of political action—creation of associations and movements, demonstrations, manifestoes, et cetera.

> Aimed at setting up or reinforcing, within the political field, the mechanisms capable of imposing the sanctions, as far as possible automatic ones, that would tend to discourage deviations from the democratic norm (such as the corruption of elected representatives) and to encourage or impose the appropriate behaviours, aimed also at favouring the setting up of non-distorted

> social structures of communication between the holders of power and citizens, in particular through a constant struggle for the independence of the media.[45]

Bourdieu's critical theory and his views on the participation of intellectuals in politics were to find a major testing ground in the phenomenon of neoliberalism and its impact on society. It is to his engagement with these that we will turn next.

Critique of Neoliberalism

As noted above, from the 90s onwards, Bourdieu was intensely concerned about the phenomenon of neoliberalism and its impact on society, and was an active participant in movements resisting it. His analysis of it, while not the subject of any one work, is contained in numerous writings, in published speeches, interviews, petitions, and manifestoes.

Bourdieu analyses neoliberalism as the implementation of a utopia of unlimited exploitation via a political programme, with the aid of neoclassical economic theory. It is understood as deriving its social force from the political and economic strength of those whose interests it defends – shareholders, financial operators, industrialists, conservative politicians or social democrats converted to laissez-faire, and senior officials of the financial ministries. It is seen as favouring the separation between the economy and social realities, constructing in reality an economic system corresponding to theoretical description. The policy making it possible, that of financial deregulation, is, through the transforming and destructive action of political measures, aimed at putting into question all the collective structures capable of obstructing the logic of the pure market. These include the nation state, 'whose room for manoeuvre is steadily shrinking; work groups, with for example the individualization of salaries and careers on the basis of individual performance and the consequent atomisation of worker; collectives defending workers' rights – unions, societies, and cooperatives; even the family, which, through the segmentation of the market into age groups, loses some of its control over consumption.'[46]

Bourdieu describes how, with the globalization of financial

markets, (which, however, does not mean the emergence of a homogeneous market, but one dominated by certain economies, with the policy of a particular state largely determined by its position in the structure of the distribution of finance capital), together with the progress of information technology, there is an unprecedented mobility of capital, leading to the following consequences: investors (or share holders) concerned with their immediate interests, that is the short-term profitability of their investments continuously compare the profitability of the largest companies and, according to Bourdieu, appropriately sanction relative failure. It would be more correct, however, to say, (as Bourdieu does not), that rather than a conscious sanctioning of relative failure, what actually happens is that there is an attempt by failing companies to inflate profits and get higher shares for profit gains, and ultimately, it is as a consequence of the logic of the market that the attempt to create an image of success results in failure.[47] Bourdieu goes on to suggest that companies exposed to this permanent threat have to adjust ever more rapidly to the demands of the markets, and they get the support of shareholders to impose their will on managers, laying down guidelines for them, through the finance department, to shape their policies on recruitment, employment, and wages. Here, once more, a correction may be in order, in that it is not really an imposition of an explicit or conscious will that sets this process into motion, but the unconscious will of the market, which pushes managers to show they are reducing costs.[48] This undoubtedly leads, as Bourdieu analyses, to the absolute reign of flexibility, with recruitment on short-term contracts or on a temporary basis and repeated 'downsizing'. There is also the creation within the company itself of competition between autonomous 'profit centres' such as between teams forced into providing their own services and finally, between individuals, through the individualization of the wage relation. This is through setting of individual objectives, individual appraisal interviews, personal increments or bonuses based on individual competence or merit, individualized career paths, strategies of 'responsibilization' tending to secure the self exploitation of some managers, who while remaining wage-earners subject to strong hierarchical authority are at the same time held responsible for their sales, their products, their brands, their shop etc., like 'independent' proprietors, and the demand for 'self appraisal' which extends the 'involvement' of employees, in accordance with the techniques of 'participatory management'. All these are methods of rational control which impose overinvestment in work, weakening or destroying collective references and solidarity.[49]

However, 'the ultimate basis of this economic order placed under the banner of individual freedom is indeed the *structural violence* of unemployment, of insecure employment and of the *fear* provoked by the threat of losing employment'.[50] Taking the example of France, Bourdieu notes that this job insecurity is in the private sector as well as the public sector; in industry, but also in the institutions of cultural production and diffusion—education, journalism, the media, et cetera. Bourdieu also quotes British studies which show that Thatcherite policies have resulted in enormous insecurity and distress not only among manual workers but also in the middle classes. The same can be seen in the US, where there is a great rise in the number of insecure, underpaid jobs. In the petition called 'The Cause of the Unemployed', issued in 1998, Bourdieu observes that 'when the stock exchange rejoices, the unemployed suffer,' referring thereby to the effectiveness of peoples' belief that there is a negative relationship between the size of the workforce in a company and the profit margin of that company. Indeed, 'mass unemployment remains in fact the most effective tool in the hands of employers with which to impose the stagnation or lowering of wages, to push up working rhythms, to deteriorate working conditions, to increase job insecurity, to impose flexibility, to create new forms of domination in the work place and to dismantle the legal protection of workers.'[51] Significantly, Bourdieu concludes thus that the cause of the unemployed is also the cause of the excluded, casual workers, and wage earners who work under the same threat.

Bourdieu also highlights the fact that even if one does not mechanically equate unemployment and crime, it remains true that urban violence has its roots in unemployment, generalized social insecurity, and mass poverty. Consequently, the hidden face of neoliberal employment policies are threats to reopen correctional institutions or suppression of family allowances to parents of trouble makers, and other such measures, which are a movement towards what has virtually been realized in the US, namely, the reduction of the state to its policing function. Invoking the law of the conservation of violence, Bourdieu points out the cost of neoliberal policies, for, 'all violence is paid for, and, for example, the structural violence exerted by the financial markets, in the form of lay offs, loss of security, etc. is matched sooner or later in the form of suicides, crime and delinquency, drug addictions, alcoholism, a whole cost of minor and major acts of violence.'[52]

The regression of the Welfare State is a major consequence of neoliberal policies, and is fuelled by what Bourdieu terms the myth of globalization, a polysemous term which really refers to an ideeforce, or key idea, and which is a reality only with regard to the unification of financial markets. Thus European workers are asked to compete with the least favoured workers of the rest of the world: workers in countries with no minimum wage, long working hours, low wages, without trade unions, where there is child labour, and so on. With these as models, flexible working is imposed, meaning night work, weekend work, irregular working hours, 'things which have always been part of the employers' dreams'.[53] This is so even though in fact the competition experienced by workers is largely intra-European. While what is emphasized is the extra-European threat, the main danger is that European countries with less social welfare and lower wages can derive a competitive advantage from this. However, as regards the intra-European threats, too, it has been shown that it is more rhetoric than actual fact. Here, Bourdieu seems to accept as valid an analysis which is incorrect, though not uncommon among northern leftists.[54] Nevertheless, it is true that the more advanced countries are forced to abandon their welfare systems in order to resist. As Bourdieu points out, this implies that in order to break out of this spiral, the workers of the advanced countries have an interest in combining with the workers in less developed countries to protect their social gains and to favour their generalization to all European workers.

Significantly, references to developments in the symbolic order are salient in Bourdieu's analysis of neoliberalism, for, according to him, the maintenance of the symbolic order is the condition of the functioning of the economic order. Thus globalization, he clarifies, is not a new phase of capitalism, but a 'rhetoric' invoked by governments in order to justify their voluntary surrender to the financial markets and their conversion to a fiduciary conception of the firm—that is of the firm as a trustee with regard to its shareholders and employees. 'Far from being the inevitable result of the growth of foreign trade—as we are constantly told—deindustrialization, growing inequality and the retrenchment of social policies are the result of domestic political decisions that reflect the tipping of the balance of class forces in favour of the owners of capital '[55] This significantly, is a fact that even a lot of political economists do not recognize, reifying as they do, finance capital as the cause of economic processes.[56] The emergence of a doxa, a whole set of presuppositions imposed as self evident, such as, for example, that maximum growth and therefore productivity and competitiveness are the ultimate and sole goal of human actions; or that economic forces cannot be resisted; is the result of a labour of symbolic inculcation involving intellectuals, journalists and businessmen, which began a long time ago and continues now. Through the media, and in everyday use, too, a language made up of euphemisms, tends to imply that the neoliberal message is a universalist message of liberation. The commonplaces of neoliberal ideology owe most of their power to convince to the prestige of the place whence they emanate, and to the fact that they are everywhere powerfully relayed by supposedly neutral agencies ranging from major international organisations such as the World Bank, the IMF, European Commission, and the OECD, conservative think tanks, and philanthropic foundations, to the schools of power. The process constitutes a form of symbolic violence that relies on a relationship of constrained communication to extract submission.

Transformed by perpetual media repetition into a universal common sense, these commonplaces succeed in making one forget that they express in a distorted form the complex and contested reality of a particular historical society 'tacitly constituted into the model and measure of all things: the American society of the post-fordist and post-Keynesian era, the world's only superpower and symbolic Mecca'.[57] This is a society characterized by the deliberate dismantling of the social state and the correlative hypertrophy of the penal state, the crushing of trade unions and the dictatorship of the 'shareholder-value' conception of the firm, and their sociological effects—that is, the generalization of precarious wage labour and social insecurity, turned into the privileged engine of economic activity.

The educational system and academia work in more ways than one in maintaining this symbolic order. For one, the strength of neoliberal ideology is that it is based on a kind of social neo-Darwinism in that it is a philosophy of competence according to which it is the most competent who govern and who have jobs, which implies that those who do not have jobs are not competent. Among the workers exposed to casualization, for example, the principle of the division between those who are thrown back into the reserve army and those who are kept in work lies in academically guaranteed competence, which is also the basis of the division, within the technologically advanced company, between the executives or technicians and the production line workers, 'the new pariahs of industrial society.'[58]

> The generalization of electronics, IT and quality standards, which requires all wage earners to retrain and perpetuates the equivalent of school tests within the enterprise, tends to reinforce the sense of insecurity with a sense of *unworthiness*, deliberately fostered by the hierarchy. The occupational world, and by extension the whole social world, seems based on a ranking by 'competence', or, worse, of 'intelligence'.[59]

Thus, the poor are now not just immoral, alcoholic and degenerate, they are stupid, they lack intelligence. Manual workers, particularly, are thrown into demoralization, devaluation and political disillusionment, expressed in crisis of activism, or worse, in a desperate rallying to the themes of quasi-fascist extremism.

At the other end, high ranking economists make a decisive contribution to producing and reproducing the neoliberal utopia, and for this they have sufficient specific interests in the field of economic science itself. 'Cut off by their whole existence and above all by their generally purely abstract and theoretical intellectual training from the real social and economic world, they are, like others in other times in the field of philosophy, particularly inclined to take the things of logic for the logic of things.'[60] Their theory is founded on a total abstraction, for in the name of a narrow and strict conception of rationality as individual rationality, it brackets the economic and social conditions of rational orientations and the economic and social structures that are the condition of their application. Even if some of the consequences of neoliberalism horrify some of these economists, this does not really take away from the satisfaction of seemingly seeing in reality the ultra-consistent utopia to which they devote their lives, that of rational actors calculating profits and losses in an unfettered market place.

Overall, the destruction of a civilization that Bourdieu feared neoliberalism may lead to, is a phenomenon he was no doubt sensitized to perceive by the experience of the destruction of traditional culture by colonialism in Algeria. The destruction of civilizations by colonialism is a fact of history—whether we consider Asia, Africa, or Latin America—and the signs of a phenomenon capable of doing the same for the developed world, were surely not going to be missed by as experienced a social observor as Bourdieu.

However, recognizing neoliberalism as a political project, and actively participating in movements opposing it, Bourdieu was optimistic about the fortunes of resistances to it. The anti-austerity strikes in December 1995 in France, which brought over 2 million disaffected workers and students onto the streets of Paris and other cities, and forced the Chirac-Juppe government to withdraw most of the series of budget cuts which would have drastically lowered the standard of living of public employees, was followed by a number of other actions of resistance in France, as well as in other countries of Europe, and even in Korea. In this context, Bourdieu put forward his ideas regarding how neoliberalism could most effectively be resisted, what forms of organisation need to be created; and what alternatives there could be to the current scenario. It is significant that for this he urged a coming together at an international level, and first, at the level of Europe, of intellectuals, writers, artists and others with those whom he termed the minor state nobility—that is those belonging to the spending ministries concerned with public services, as well as trade unions, work councils, progressive social movements such as the Greens and others, and all adversely affected by neoliberal policies. The ultimate aim was the creation of transnational authorities charged with controlling the dominant economic forces and subordinating them to truly universal ends.

In his address to the Greek Trade Union Confederation in 1996 Bourdieu expressed his concern over what he termed the involution of the state—its regression from a social state to a penal state—which had to be resisted. Historically, the development of the state from one that was characterized by a concentration of physical and economic force, to one marked by a concentration of cultural capital; and then of authority; was simulteneously, according to Bourdieu, a process of the gradual autonomisation of the state. This autonomy made it partially independent of dominant social and economic forces and allowed the bureaucracy to inflect the will of the dominant groups, to interpret them, and sometimes to inspire policies. In any country, the stronger this state was, (which morever, exists in two forms; in objective reality, in the form of a set of institutions, such as rules, offices, agencies, et cetera, and also in peoples' minds), the greater was the resistance to neo-liberal doctrine and policy. That the state exists in peoples' minds is particularly important, according to Bourdieu, for, as he puts it elsewhere, the norm of disinterested loyalty to the public good that it upholds in principle, has encouraged a certain disposition among sections of the bureaucracy, of an interest in disinterestedness. Thus, it exists in the dispositions of those in the state responsible for social policies, 'who are incharge of organizing aid to the long term unemployed, and worried about the breakdown of social cohesion, unemployment etc., and opposed to the finance people who only want to hear about the constraints of globalization and the place of France in the world'.[61] Then again, there is also part of what he calls the minor state nobility, the left hand of the state, all those called 'social workers', as well as secondary and primary teachers, who perform their jobs to compensate for the most flagrant inadequacies of the logic of the market, who are no longer being given the means to really do their job. They represent a force in the old order whose survival needs to be protected, and which is being progressively dismantled. In workers' minds, too, the state exists in the form of subjective law, as attachment to 'established rights' whose dissolution must be prevented. Thus, Bourdieu notes that dominated groups in society have an interest in defending the state, specially the 'universal' functions it fulfills, and he adds that this can in fact be fulfilled as well or better, by a supranational state. At the European level, this would allow the work of combining the greatest social advances of the various national states and a subordination of the creation of the single market to the implementation of the social measures designed to counter the likely social consequences that unbridled competition will have for wage earners.

Among the measures which Bourdieu proposed must be negotiated immediately at the European level were: the definition of minimum wages; measures against the corruption and tax fraud which reduce the contribution of financial activities to public spending, indirectly resulting in excessive taxation of labour; and against social dumping between directly competing activities, drawing up a code of common social rights; a common investment policy corresponding to the general interest, with priority to strategies aimed at safequarding non-renewable resources and the environment, developing trans-European transport and energy networks, developing public housing and urban regeneration, investment in research and development in health and protection of the environment, the financing of new and apparently more risky activities, in forms unknown to the financial world (small businesses, self employment). While it should be clarified that in this list of proposals, the notion of social dumping is based on a misconstrual of the facts of intra-European competition, more generally, Bourdieu suggested that these measures would replace the naturalized economy of neoliberalism with an economy of happiness, based on human initiatives and will.[62] In place of the present economic theory which, when it assesses the costs of a policy, does not take social costs into account, there should be, he urged, an economics which takes note of all the profits, material and symbolic, individual and collective, associated with activity, and also all the material and symbolic costs associated with inactivity or precarious employment.

In view of Bourdieu's earlier analyses and proposals regarding the role of intellectuals in the project of human emancipation, it may be meaningful to consider what he has to say specifically about intellectuals in the movement against neoliberalism. The most important point in this regard is Bourdieu's view that intellectuals bear a great deal of responsibility for the creation of such a movement because the nature of political domination is not only economic but also intellectual, 'it lies also on the side of belief.'[63] They have to participate, alongside associations and unions in particular, who are in a position to exert a real influence on the future of society, by inventing new forms of collective political work, in breaking with the new faith in the historical inevitability professed by theorists of liberalism. They can help to draw up rigorous analyses and inventive proposals about the major questions which the orthodoxy of the media and politics makes it impossible to raise. Thus, for example, they can examine the question of the unification of the world economy and the economic and social effects of the new international division of labour, or of the supposed iron laws of the financial markets; or the question of the function of education and culture in economics where information has become one of the most decisive productive forces, and so on. Though in this list of areas of research, the notion of information as a productive force has been shown to be erroneous by political economists, the general point being made is that relevant research is essential in order to challenge autocratic technocracy without falling into populism which has so often betrayed social movements.[64] Then again, researchers can, as a first contribution, analyze the production and distribution of neoliberal discourse, mapping out the networks of the circulation of ideas, subtended by a circulation of power, and make these analyses generally available, in a form accessible to all. Moreover, he points out that in general, the authority effect of neoliberal thought has to be fought with an authority effect—for this ideology dresses up simply conservative thought in the guise of pure reason, and has to be fought with reasons, arguments, refutations, demonstrations: all implying scientific work. Intellectuals can also contribute to the fight against saturation by the media, which produces demoralization and demobilizes peoples' resistance.

Conclusion

Bourdieu's evolution as a social critic and as a critical theorist led to his engagement as an intellectual with the phenomenon of neoliberalism in his later years. As regards the links between Bourdieu's theory of the symbolic and his analysis of neoliberalism: to begin with, insofar as Bourdieu conceptualized challenges to the established order, such as the ones he himself was associated with, as being effective in situations of crisis, it can be inferred that he viewed the current historical conjuncture as a critical one. One clear index of this is the widespread suffering caused by neoliberal policies, and documented in Bourdieu's own study, *The Weight of the World*, and elsewhere. However, it is to be noted that he has not analysed the elements and nature of this crisis in any great detail.

Then again, the fact that the economic order of neoliberalism is strongly supported by a symbolic order, vindicates Bourdieu's insistence on the importance of symbolic power in maintaining systems of dominance, and of symbolic capital as being an essential aspect of economic capital for its social effectiveness. In particular, the analysis of how economic capital, in the form of finance capital, is misrecognized as symbolic capital, in the form of a belief in the doxa of neoliberalism, provides an instance of the fruitfulness of his concept of symbolic violence, and its relevance for understanding the current situation. Furthermore, the fact of the existence of resistances to neoliberalism points to their being heterodoxy in the situation, and Bourdieu was concerned about adopting novel means of organization to deal with the variety of responses and approaches characterizing the scene. One can speculate that he found in this variety, forms of symbolic revolution, which made him optimistic about the future.

Some inconsistencies may, however, also be noted.

Callinicos points out that Bourdieu's political interventions against neoliberalism fell more into the pattern of the Zola-Sartre model than the 'corporatism of the universal proposed in *The Rules of Art*. 'It is the conservation of an entire civilization rather than merely the autonomy of the fields of cultural production that preoccupies Bourdieu in *Contre-feux*' (Eng. Trns. *Acts of Resistance*).[65] He also identifies certain problems with Bourdieu's model of the intellectual. He points out that in so far as in Bourdieu's conception, the intellectual's *political* authority derives from the extra-political, the rigour of critique belongs to the domain of the autonomous field of cultural production, so that in the public sphere her political audience is not entitled to follow her unless they themselves are suitably qualified. This is unsatisfactory, as political arguments and interventions should surely be amenable to criticism by all those capable of engaging in the public sphere—a group in principle coextensive with the entire adult population. 'Bourdieu does not seem to envisage a domain where intellectual and public life meet to thematise issues specific to the political, a domain where political discourse possesses its own rationality'.[66] However, it can be argued that by urging intellectuals to use their authority in an autonomous field to participate in the political field, Bourdieu envisages the possibility of intellectuals being able to transcend the seeming esotericism of their disciplines, to communicate with a wider public, and participate in the political domain in pursuance of a Realpolitik of reason.

Then again, Bourdieu's characterisation of the dispositions

of teachers and social workers as disinterested and virtuous in relation to the goal of human emancipation appears discordant in relation to other analyses. Referring to teachers paid by the state or the university, Bourdieu in his *Reproduction: In Education, Society and Culture*, for instance, writes that they find themselves in the conditions most conducive to misrecognition of the objective truth of their task, via the ideology of 'disinterestedness'.[67] Symbolic violence is thus a corollary of this ideology. So also, with reference to social workers, there is the observation of an ambivalence of effect, as in *The Weight of the World*, where we have testimonies of people finding the intervention of social workers in their lives to be an affront to their qualifications and abilities.[68]

These inconsistencies point towards a more general problem with Bourdieu's concept of symbolic capital. For by positing that the quest for symbolic capital is a basic attribute of human nature: as that which creates an interest in performing an action, so that even disinterestedness, universality, generosity, and virtue and their realization are linked to it: and simultaneously asserting that symbolic capital is intrinsically exploitative; Bourdieu's conceptual framework does not allow for the possibility of genuine emancipation. Thus Bourdieu suggests in his *Pascalian Meditations* that symbolic capital is a basic desiradatum of social existence, for 'symbolic capital rescues agents from insignificance, the absence of importance and meaning'.[69] At the same time, he writes that symbolic capital 'is not a particular kind of capital but what every kind of capital becomes when it is misrecognized as capital, that is, as force, a power or capacity for (actual or potential) exploitation, and therefore recognized as legitimate.'[70] Even the fact of the ambiguity of the gift in precapitalist societies which he so insightfully analyses, does not lead him to ask the question of the possibility of real generosity being realized. So also while he suggests substituting for the question of knowing if virtue is possible, the question of knowing if one can create universes in which people have an interest in the universal, he does not adequately confront the problem created by his notion of interest as being impelled by the search for symbolic capital, and thus involving misrecognition and symbolic violence.[71] Indeed, as noted in Chapter 2 previously, the lack of a notion of power as other than domination, of power as a positive resource that does not involve exploitation; seems to lead to some problems in Bourdieu's theory of the symbolic.

However, these conceptual problems do not negate the fact that his engagement with the current historical conjuncture provided a major illustration of the vital role intellectuals can play in the project of human emancipation. It also demonstrated practically the potentially positive role of symbolic power, and this might well have become the basis for Bourdieu inflecting his concept of power in a different direction.

ENDNOTES

1. Craig Calhoun et.al. (ed), *Bourdieu: Critical Perspectives*, 1993, Cambridge, Polity Press, p. 269.
2. *Who's Who in France 1983–1984*, p. 135.
3. Richard Jenkins, *Pierre Bourdieu*, 1992, London and New York, Routledge, pp. 13–4.
4. Axel Honneth, Hermann Kocyba and Bernd Schwibs, 'The Struggle for Symbolic Order', *Theory, Culture and Society*, Vol. 3, No. 3, 1986, p. 39.
5. Richard Harker, Cheleen Mahar and Chris Wilkes (ed), *An Introduction to the Work of Pierre Bourdieu*, 1990, London, Macmillan, p. 40.
6. Axel Honneth, Hermann Kocyba and Bernd Schwibs, 1986, p. 36.
7. Ibid., p. 37.
8. Pierre Bourdieu, *In Other Words*, 1990, Cambridge, Polity Press, p. 3.
9. Axel Honneth et.al., 1986, p. 35.
10. Ibid., p. 36.
11. Ibid., p. 38.
12. Theodore Zeldin, *France 1848-1945*, Vol. II, *Intellect, Taste and Anxiety*, pp. 207–20.
13. Axel Honneth et.al., 1986, pp. 36–7.
14. Ibid., p. 39.
15. Ibid., p. 38.
16. Ibid.
17. Ibid.
18. Pierre Bourdieu and Loic J. Wacquant, *An Invitation to Reflexive Sociology*, 1992, Cambridge, Polity Press, p. 45, Fn. 81.

19. Pierre Bourdieu, *In Other Words*, p. 59.
20. Ibid., p. 7.
21. Pierre Bourdieu, *The Logic of Practice*, 1990, Cambridge, Polity Press, p. 3.
22. Ibid., pp. 2–3.
23. Pierre Bourdieu, Jean-Claude Chamboredon and Jean-Claude Passeron, *The Craft of Sociology*, 1991, Berlin, New York, Walter de Gruyter, p. 247.
24. Ibid., pp. 247–8.
25. Alan Bullock and R.B. Woodings (ed) *The Fontana Dictionary of Modern Thinkers*, p. 91.
26. Richard Jenkins, 1992, p. 15.
27. Pierre Bourdieu and Loic J.Wacquant, *An Invitation to Reflexive Sociology*, p. 57.
28. Pierre Bourdieu, *Pascalian Meditations*, 2000, Cambridge, Polity Press, p. 235.
29. Ibid., p. 181.
30. Pierre Bourdieu and Loic J.Wacquant, *An Invitation to Reflexive Sociology*, p. 49.
31. Pierre Bourdieu, *Pascalian Meditations*, p. 172.
32. Pierre Bourdieu, 'The Corporatism of the Universal: The Role of Intellectuals in the Modern World' in *Telos*, No. 81, Fall 1989, p. 100
33. Ibid., p. 110.
34. For another version of an argument against 'abstract universalism' and for the questioning by post colonial thought of Enlightenment categories in the very spirit and even name of these categories, so that Enlightenment thought may be renewed by and from the margins, see Dipesh Chakrabarty, *Provincializing Europe*, 2007, Princeton, Princeton University Press.
35. Pierre Bourdieu, *Pascalian Meditations*, 2000, Cambridge, Polity Press, p. 78. It also seems pertinent in this context to refer to the evocation of the "radical" Enlightenment by Akeel Bilgrami as a counterpoint to the orthodox Enlightenment's legacy of "thick" rationality which resembles Bourdieu's 'obscurantism of the Enlightenment' and `imperialism of the universal'. See Akeel Bilgrami, 'Occidentalism, the very idea: An essay on the Enlightenment and enchantment' in *Economic & Political Weekly*, 19–25 August, 2006, Vol. XLI, No. 33.
36. Ibid., p. 78.
37. Ibid., p. 70.
38. Pierre Bourdieu, *Pascalian Meditations*, p. 71.

39. Ibid., p. 77.
40. Ibid., p. 78.
41. Ibid., p. 80.
42. Ibid., p. 110.
43. Ibid., p. 126.
44. Ibid.
45. Ibid.
46. Pierre Bourdieu, *Acts of Resistance*, 1998, Cambridge, Polity Press, p. 96.
47. Conversation with Prof. Jayati Ghosh, Centre for Economic Studies and Planning, Jawaharlal Nehru University, New Delhi.
48. Conversation with Prof. Jayati Ghosh.
49. Pierre Bourdieu, *Acts of Resistance*, pp. 97-8.
50. Ibid., p. 98.
51. Petition, Le Monde, 17 January, 1998.
52. Pierre Bourdieu, *Acts of Resistance*, p. 40.
53. Ibid., p. 34.
54. Conversation with Prof. Jayati Ghosh, Centre for Economic Studies and Planning, Jawaharlal Nehru University, New Delhi.
55. Pierre Bourdieu and Loic J. Wacquant, 'New Liberal Speak : Notes on the New Planetary Vulgate', in Le Monde Diplomatique 554, May 2000.
56. Conversation with Prof. Jayati Ghosh.
57. Pierre Bourdieu and Loic J. Wacquant, New Liberal Speak: Notes on the New Planetery Vulgate, 2000.
58. Pierre Bourdieu, *Acts of Resistance*, p. 99.
59. Ibid.
60. Ibid., p. 101.
61. Ibid., p. 34.
62. Conversation with Prof. Jayati Ghosh, Centre for Economic Studies and Planning, Jawaharlal Nehru University, New Delhi.
63. Gunter Grass and Pierre Bourdieu, 'A Literature from Below'. 3 July 2000, The Nation [on line] Available at: http//post.thenation.com/issue/000703/0703gross.shtml/ [Accessed 24-10-2001]
64. Conversation with Prof. Jayati Ghosh, Centre for Economic Studies and Planning, Jawaharlal Nehru University, New Delhi.
65. Alex Callinicos, 'Social Theory Put to the Test of Politics: Pierre Bourdieu and Anthony Giddens', in *New Left Review*, No. 236, July/August 1999, p. 98.
66. Ibid., p. 99.
67. Pierre Bourdieu and Jean-Claude Passeron, *Reproduction In*

Education, Society and Culture, 1977, London, Sage Publications, p. 66.

68. Pierre Bourdieu et.al., *The Weight of the World*, 1999, Cambridge, Polity Press, p. 38.
69. Pierre Bourdieu, *Pascalian Meditations*, p. 242.
70. Ibid.
71. Pierre Bourdieu, *Practical Reason: On the Theory of Action*, 1998, Cambridge, Polity Press, p. 89.

7

Conclusion

Pierre Bourdieu's social theory is a formidable combination of theoretical and empirical rigour and innovativeness whose influence has grown steadily, first within France and then internationally, across disciplinary boundaries between sociology, anthropology, and history. Its impact on sociological theory is likely to intensify over the years, for as Loic Wacquant puts it, 'I think it is going to take us 30 to 50 years to draw out fully the implications of his' (that is, Pierre Bourdieu's) 'work'.[1]

The process of the importation of this theory from France into the English-speaking world has not, however, been without its pitfalls, that have left their imprint on the quality of the engagement of the wider sociological community with it. It was in the mid 1970s just as Bourdieu had achieved a major position in French academia and as his influence was growing through teaching and the creation of the Centre for European Sociology at the Ecole des Hautes Etudes en Sciences Sociales in Paris, that his main writings began to be translated into English. It has been pointed out, that about this time, in the aftermath of the late 1960s, a new generation of scholars in Anglo-American universities were searching for new orientations, and their explorations led them to French social theory, beyond Sartre, Levi-Strauss and Althusser, to Bourdieu, Foucault, and Jacques Derrida.[2] However, though the scenario is somewhat brighter today than it was earlier, the observation made at the beginning of the 1990's, that Bourdieu's work, 'so catholic and systematic in both scope and intent has typically been apprehended and incorporated in 'bits and pieces'' and that '*in globo* it is still widely misunderstood', is still valid today. 'The confounding variety of interpretations, the mutually exclusive criticisms, and the contradictory reactions it has elicited' testify to the fact that the systematic nature and main thrust of Bourdieu's endeavour have often remained hidden from view.[3] In this context, this study has been an attempt to overcome fragmentation by traversing across a wide range of Bourdieu's writings, spanning several decades.

It has been observed that generally, the impact of Bourdieu's work has moved along distinct disciplinary and sub-disciplinary lines, largely because unlike France, where the borders between sociology, anthropology, history and philosophy are easy to cross, this is not the case in most Anglo-phone countries. Thus, to identify these lines with reference to the relevant works by Bourdieu: specialists in education have focused on his *Reproduction in Education, Society & Culture*, anthropologists have concentrated on his ethnographies of Algeria and *Outline of a Theory of Practice*, while sociologists of culture, aesthetics and class have engaged primarily with *Distinction*. Interpreters in distinct domains have ignored each other and it is only in recent years that one finds attempts to grapple with his contribution across substantive and theoretical demarcations. Misunderstandings have also been a product of the fact that the very dualisms which Bourdieu's work seeks to transcend: micro/macro; agency/structure; interpretive/positivist; function/conflict; etc. still structure the perceptions of sociologists, who thereby receive it in terms of these alternatives, and distort its meaning. Lack of familiarity with the continental strands of social theory and philosophy which form the backdrop to Bourdieu's intellectual project has further contributed to misreadings.

While this study has focused on Bourdieu's theory of the symbolic from the perspective of Bourdieu's overall approach to social phenomena, its constituent elements have been discussed mainly by scholars working within the framework of the sociology of culture. In that context, the statement that

> The number one growth area in sociology at the beginning of this closing decade of the twentieth century—in the USA, in Britain,

> in Germany, and surely elsewhere too—is the sociology of culture. And the most influential sociologist of culture is, without parallel, Pierre Bourdieu,[4]

is significant. It was in the 1970s and 1980s that Marxist social science, particularly in Great Britain sought 'to restore, via the appropriation of ideology and culture as legitimate objects of analysis, an active model of man to the center of the theoretical stage'.[5] This project, concerned broadly with the cultural reproduction of class society, owed much in addition to English culturalists such as Hoggart, Hobsbawm, E.P. Thompson and Raymond Williams, to the theoretical contributions of Gramsci and Althusser, and increasingly in the 1980's, to Pierre Bourdieu. Noting the potential significance of his contribution to media and cultural studies; Nicholas Garnham and Raymond Williams in 1986, observed how in a movement of critique in the classic Marxist sense, Bourdieu confronts and dialectically supercedes the partial and opposed positions characterizing the field.[6] These were, in a first stage of development, the rise out of literary studies of a culturalist Marxism in opposition to both the subjectivism of Leavisite literary criticism, and to the empirical, ahistorical sociology of mass communication and popular culture with roots in American society, and in a second stage, the development under the influence of Althusser and Lacan of a theoreticist Marxism, soon challenged from within by an older Marxist tradition reasserting the value of empirical work and the social efficacy and explanatory power of economic and class determinants. A materialist theory of culture that transcended both theoreticism and economic reductionism was precisely what was needed and Bourdieu had to offer. Indeed, already in 1978, Stuart Hall had located Bourdieu's significance in his synthesis of the Marxist position with structuralism—a dialectical resolution which offers the possibility of 'an adequate Marxist theory of ideology'.[7]

The characterization of Bourdieu's theory as Marxist has not, however, gone unchallenged, which is in keeping with our earlier observation of the conflicting interpretations of his work. E.P. Thompson, while pausing to draw breath and suggest alternatives during his expose of the pernicious effect of

Althusserian structuralism, proposes that those who have fallen into such errors 'might commence their re-education by attending to Pierre Bourdieu', but then disappoints, insofar as he does not engage any further with Bourdieu's work.[8] The convergences and divergences with the work of Anthony Giddens have also been the subject of some analysis, though Giddens' own comments on it are disappointingly sparse. In his *Central Problems in Social Theory* he credits Bourdieu with adopting 'a standpoint in some respects similar to that which I want to suggest here', but nowhere offers a sustained analysis of that standpoint.[9]

While there is a burgeoning secondary literature on Bourdieu's contribution coming from many countries in recent years, and though Bourdieu was an internationalist who strove to promote dialogue within the world community of intellectuals, the impact of Bourdieu's theory needs to be located and assessed in relation to French social theory in particular. This is so not only because it is only in the French sociological field that his work fully makes sense as an intellectual intervention but also because it is often in conjunction with the contribution of other French scholars that his work has been received elsewhere.

It has been remarked that the field of French sociology which was inhabited by Bourdieu is not readily amenable to any straight forward plotting of positions, capital, and fields, but certain broad features can be outlined. One may refer to the era through which the field was passing as Bourdieu emerged as a major figure, as an era of post structuralism and postmodernism. The earlier era, however, was marked by tendencies which are important referents for the evolution of Bourdieu's theory. That was an era dominated by structuralism, though it is to be borne in mind that structuralism was not a monolith but a complex intellectual phenomenon, embracing Levi-Strauss, Saussure, Chomsky, Althusser and others. There was also what may be termed the phenomenological revolution in social science, 'taking its lead in France from Merleau Ponty and developing into a sociology of everyday life'.[10] The feminist revolution was on the ascendent, as was the Marxist challenge of the 1960s and

1970s. It has been observed, however, that none of these new tendencies offered an orthodoxy, and that for those searching for intellectual idols in the years to come soon after, there was the somewhat dismal prospect of a decaying structuralism, a Marxism under attack from the so-called 'new philosophy' of Bernard-Henri Levi, Andre Glucksmann et. al., Foucault's continuing attacks on the pretension of Marxism as a formalistic and universalistic science, and a polyglot and dispersed feminist movement.[11] Furthermore, there was also a lack of symmetry between social movements and social theory, and 'instead of the political cohesiveness of previous years, the followers of social theory now appeared more closely directed towards their work and less towards their politics'.[12]

As regards sociology in particular, it was difficult to find schools as such, though as Richard Harker et.al. point out, functionalism was cautiously being rediscovered; American sociology was being slowly investigated; 'other alien beings (Norbert Elias, Habermas, Giddens) were being examined often for their possible use-value.'[13] It was in this context that Bourdieu began to be counted as one amongst the key figures in a disaggregated sociological field, together with Crozier, Touraine, Boudon, Foucault, Baudrillard and Morin.

Above all, however, 'the seeming disintegration of fixed positions in the field must be connected to the underlying intellectual current associated with this dis-aggregation, the move to postmodernism'.[14] This trend resonated in the works of Derrida, Kristeva, and Foucault, among others, and was accompanied by a sense of loss, 'a loss of the generalizing principle which had coordinated both theories and researchers across political and empirical terrains in a previous era. In its place, postmodernism offers a plurality of cultures, a plurality of theories, newly reconstructed foundations of legitimate discourses, a loss of faith in totalizing politics, and a rejection of the entire modernist apparatus of culture, science, and reason'.[15]

While Bourdieu's social theory evolved in the midst of these currents, it has quite rightly been remarked by Harker et.al. that it remained at a distance from them. Thus while sharing some of the deconstructionist concerns of Derrida, Bourdieu's work rejects his nihilist relativism. Touraine's voluntarist aspirations have no place in Bourdieu's dialectical conception of agency and structure. And while there are affinities with Foucault's arguments concerning symbolic systems, and both rejected the attempted Marxist takeover of radical thought, retaining radicalism outside Marxism, their work can be distinguished along several dimensions. There is

> Bourdieu's adherence to a theory of social class (however much modified) over and against Foucault's wholesale rejection; Foucault's self conscious rejection (avoidance of) state power contrasted with Bourdieu's fascination with the categorizing and limiting mechanisms by which the state 'acts to legitimate'; finally Foucault's thorough celebration of relativism in contrast to a mediated form of universalism in Bourdieu's method.[16]

Though Bourdieu rejected claims that he was universalistic in the specific sense of theoretical universalism associated with the 'great masters', one can agree with Richard Harker et.al. that he was a methodological universalist in a world inhabited by theoretical relativists. This gave his social theory and the school of sociology that he established in France a very significant place in the field of French social theory. If he was able to provide an alternative to the options of theoreticism and positivist empiricism that prevailed in the previous era, by marrying theoretical and empirical rigour in his work, in the context of postmodernism, he provided the alternative of a new Enlightenment approach, in which, moreover, civic engagement was increasingly to play a part. In the case of the latter, it is notable that Bourdieu's political interventions grew in a climate of a resurgent radicalism in France, opened up by the strike wave of 1995. The intellectual backlash against neo-liberalism and a growing interest in radical ideas

> was accelerated but not created by the events of 1995 and had been apparent in various guises throughout the early 1990s, ranging from the Air France strikes and school student protests of 1993, to the impressive vote for the Trotskyist candidate Arlete Laguiller in the May 1995 presidential elections, the success of events as the International Marx Conference organised by the

> *Actuel Marx* review in September 1995, and in the content and popularity of various books published during the first half of the decade, from Jacques Derrida's *Spectres of Marx* (1993), to Bourdieu's own *The Weight of the World* (1993)—a bestseller—Alain Badiou's *Ethics* (1993) and Daniel Bensaid's *Marx L'Intempestif* (1995).[17]

Impressionistically, one can say that important changes were occurring and are continuing to occur in the field of French social theory, reflecting and refracting changes in the wider social field, and Bourdieu's work has played and will continue to play a significant role in these, though a more precise delineation would require detailed research and analysis.

Against the backdrop of the impact of Bourdieu's theory on sociological theory in general and on French social theory in particular, we may briefly recall the main features of his contribution towards a theory of the symbolic, as identified in this study.

Bourdieu's theory of the symbolic brings together and simultaneously surpasses through critique three distinct modes of analysing symbolic systems. These are: the approach that views them as structuring structures; that which analyzes them as structured structures, and that which regards them as instruments of domination. While the first, or the neo-Kantian approach provides through the work of Durkheim and Mauss, the starting point for a sociology of symbolic forms for Bourdieu as well, he rejects the notions of social consensus, of a collective consciousness, of the dualities of mind and body and of the individual and the social, as well as the objectivist epistemology it entails. The second approach or the structuralist approach is incorporated in the theory insofar as it offers an alternative to the substantialist mode of thought, and draws attention to the *opus operatum* of symbolic systems. But it is critiqued for its idealist objectivism, and linked to a theory of practice that does not view the coherence of symbolic systems as emanating from universal structures of the mind, but from structures of the material and social environment that engenders human practice and is constructed by it. The third approach is found in the works of Marx and Weber, though in distinctive forms in each.

Bourdieu's theory highlights the relationship between power and symbolic systems, as do both of them. However, it does not conceptualize symbolic systems as intellectual constructs necessarily involving conscious thought as does the Marxist tradition, nor as legitimizing systems involving lucid consciousness as does the Weberian. It offers instead the notions of misrecognition and symbolic violence which focus on embodied beliefs and their role in sustaining relations of power. The reduction of ideological products to class interests is also critiqued, and the relative autonomy of the cultural field is highlighted.

Further, these approaches are synthesized by Bourdieu leading to the proposition that symbolic systems exert a structuring power in so far as they are structured, and that it is as structured and structuring instruments that symbolic systems fulfill their political function as instruments of domination.

As regards the intellectual traditions that have gone into its constitution, the theory is also linked to the perspectives of relational structuralism and phenomenology, articulated in a manner that transcends the objectivism of the former and the subjectivism of the latter. As discussed in Chapter 2, the way in which relational structuralism is used to construct the concepts of field and of habitus has important implications for the analysis of symbolic systems. Phenomenology provides a means of incorporating subjective reality into the framework of analysis, but is also subjected to critique before it is included in the theory.

In so far as Bourdieu's theory of the symbolic is embedded within the more inclusive framework of a theory of practice, its characteristics can only be fully understood in relation to it. The conceptual system constituted by habitus, capital, and field leads to Bourdieu's notion of practice, and symbolic phenomena are both components of all three and analyzable in terms of them. To begin with, the habitus is in part a symbolic structure, since it consists of schemes of perception, thought, evaluation and action. The structuring of habitus relates agents to material and social structures through a dialectical process impelled by a search for symbolic capital, in which the inculcation and naturalization of cultural arbitraries takes place, and the habitus in turn structures the context in which practice occurs. The understanding that the schemes of the habitus are embodied creates a conceptual space based on a rejection of the dualisms of mind and body and of the material and the symbolic. The structuring and restructuring of habitus is seen as taking place in the context of different fields, in which agents participate in the first instance by accepting the field's doxa and the consequent activation of a practical sense rather than conscious reflection and calculation.

The structures in which habitus generates practices are crucially shaped by the distribution of, and struggle for, different forms of capital in the fields in which agents act. The concepts of economic, cultural, social and symbolic capital are a very significant part of Bourdieu's theory of the symbolic since they allow him to relate symbolic processes to the dimension of power. They also underline the fact that his theory is undergirded by a non-economistic political economy perspective, because while it is asserted that economic capital is at the root of all forms of capital, at the same time, it is posited that symbolic capital is essential for the efficacy of all forms of capital.

Bourdieu's concept of fields draws attention to the relative autonomy of arenas where symbolic interests and symbolic phenomena come into play, at the same time as it highlights how symbolic systems form part of the constitution of all fields. This is not least because social positions in fields are linked to points of view, including points of view on the space of different points of view. The understanding that participation in fields is via illusio and adherence to doxa and that the schemes of the habitus are refracted through the structures of fields, further makes the concept of fields relevant to a full understanding of his theory of the symbolic.

Finally, the notion of an economy of practice provides his theory of practice in general, and therefore his theory of the symbolic as well, with a metatheoretical system of explanation. Since the pursuit of symbolic goods forms part of his conception of the economy of practice, his theory of the symbolic is a central component of his explanatory framework, and also an intrinsic part of its underlying anthropology.

Some of the strengths of Bourdieu's theory of the symbolic become apparent when it is used to analyse a new empirical context, as has been done by many of his followers, and has been attempted in Chapter 5 of this study. The usefulness of the concepts of doxa, orthodoxy, and heterodoxy, of the notion of the state as an institution with a monopoly over legitimate symbolic violence, and of the concepts of misrecognition and symbolic violence have been illustrated with reference to the Shah Bano case in India. However, the analysis also demonstrates the need to take seriously Bourdieu's view that these concepts are heuristic devices; for it suggests that they need to be extended and modified to some extent to be fully meaningful in a new context.

Certain unresolved dimensions of Bourdieu's theory of the symbolic also emerge when it is viewed in relation to his critique of neoliberalism and participation in the movement opposing it. While social critique is an inherent aspect of his intellectual project, the suggestions for an alternative social order do not seem to be adequately conceptualized. Thus his conception of the role of intellectuals in social movements does not clearly suggest a way of overcoming the gulf between the bases of intellectual authority and public participation in political debates. Nor does his vision of public workers in social sectors as repositories of qualities that can resist the destruction of civic virtues resonate unambiguously with his observations regarding their social role in his theoretical and empirical studies. These problems point towards a general problem with his concept of symbolic capital. That the quest for it is inherent in human nature on the one hand, and that on the other, its possession is the basis of exploitation, leaves little room for a clear conception of the possibility of human emancipation. As was pointed out in Chapter 2, and again in Chapter 6, the fact that power, including symbolic power, is not conceptualized other than in terms of domination and exploitation, is a serious limitation of Bourdieu's theory of the symbolic.

In fact, assessments of Bourdieu's theory of the symbolic, or at least of some major aspects of it, usually subsumed under discussions of the sociology of culture, and often focused on his study *Distinction* have been made by several scholars. We shall consider some of them here.

Writing in 1982, Pekka Sulkunen attempts to review the whole of Bourdieu's cultural sociology, 'aiming to place it in a theoretical context and to draw out its implications in view of studies of contemporary cultural studies'.[18] He observes that though the diversity of Bourdieu's interests and fields of empirical research may divert readers from a search for a common and integrating problematic in his thinking, there is in fact a substantial problematic and a methodological point of view. The problematic consists in revealing and bringing to light the hidden forms of domination that are consciously and unconsciously reproduced in everyday life. The methodological point of view lies firstly, in his perspective on social institutions, such as kinship in Kabylia, as being forms of domination and fields of contestation for positions rather than a function of the total society or a definite set of rules or behavioural norms, and secondly, in his analysis of the cultural system of society as not only a structure of *given* meanings, but also a field of action. 'Culture is a meaning structure, but is produced, reproduced and *used* by acting *subjects*'.[19]

According to Sulkunen, his substantial problematic leads Bourdieu to grapple, as in *Distinction*, with the specific nature of mature capitalist society, where the cultural forms in which class differences appear in everyday life are no longer self evident, as they were even up to the 1950s. As Sulkunen interprets his work, it is relevant, according to him, to note that

> The working class has become less and less distinguishable and is less and less distinguishable itself as a class. On the other hand, the power of the dominant class is no longer only divided between their national fractions, but increasingly also between the national bourgeoisies and such supranational centers of power as the multinational corporations and international organizations. Facing the weakening of traditional correspondence between class position, political organization and cultural practices, it is in the area of 'private' life, style and taste, where the apparition of the class structure in capitalist societies must be found.[20]

It is this that makes comprehensible the focus of *Distinction* on life styles, and the use of the metaphor of capital for cultural practices, 'since the social relationship of everyday life have been turned into markets of esteem'.[21]

The concept of habitus has been identified by Sulkunen as by many others as the basic notion in Bourdieu's methodological position. But he also finds a certain ambiguity in it. He points out that since the habitus is defined as a generating principle of style that endures the changes in objective living conditions while it is also conditioned by them 'we can never be sure to which end the explanation of cultural phenomena should appeal: to the function with respect to living conditions or to the durability of cultural codes'.[22] This ambiguity he traces to the context of anthropological traditions and the French intellectual scene in which Bourdieu's ideas emerged. The context was characterized by two oppositions: the first between functionalism and semiological anthropology, the second between structuralism and existentialism. Noting that the notion of habitus provides Bourdieu with a way of rejecting functionalism because it implies that social agents are constantly producing new meanings, and that far from being determined by the existing institutions, their actions are a way of using them in the struggle for dominance, power and prestige, Sulkunen finds the same argument being used to reject structuralism. For since the habitus is constantly being formed in the daily practices of individual subjects, it does not follow any mechanistic formal or 'algebraic' logic, even as it is a structured system of meanings. 'People do not simply reproduce their meaning systems, they also produce and use them. One must see classes and their members not just as actors in a prefabricated play but also as creative subjects'.[23] Sulkunen, nevertheless, concludes that while Bourdieu's argument aims more fire against the semiotic and structuralist ends of the two dimensions identified above than their respective polar opposites—namely, functionalism and subjectivism, the vagueness of the concept of habitus can be attributed to the fact that Bourdieu does not totally desert the structuralist camp either. In fact, the concept could be seen as a working compromise between the oppositions of the two dimensions. The vagueness of the concept reminds us that while it is necessary to see human practices as structured by meaning systems and as their expressions, they also serve various functions determined by objective conditions of existence, and while they are parts of a structure, they are carried out, produced, reproduced and used by living individuals. Significantly, Sulkunen does not see this vagueness as a weakness. While it may not be conducive to the systematic generation of precise hypotheses which can be rigorously tested by mathematical and statistical methods, he is doubtful whether the appearance of methodological rigour is ever anything more than just an appearance.

> Sociology is a creative science, one of the forms in which society thinks of itself, and the only way of avoiding error is to be aware of the alternatives offering themselves as guiding principles in interpreting concrete phenomena.[24]

According to him, it is precisely this awareness combined with flexibility that Bourdieu has, and which is reflected in his interpretations of cultural forms in modern France.

Further, pointing out that many of the themes on middle class culture found in Bourdieu's work are not new as such, Sulkunen identifies the novelty deserving the greatest merit in his analysis of modern France to be its comprehensiveness. His analysis brings to light the structure of French society. The few lacunae he finds in it include the following: firstly, there is the absence of comparisons with other countries. He points out for example that Bourdieu's denial of the possibility of an autonomous working class culture could gain much from a look at 'pub-culture' in Britain and the extensive working class cultures and their role in the political mobilization of the working class in Scandinavia. Secondly he wonders to what extent the two large working class parties in France could maintain their strength if the cultural practices of the working class were so totally obedient to the codes dictated by the elites, so totally void of autonomous creative power as Bourdieu describes them. 'What is the 'functionalism' of working class style and aesthetic taste if it is not a conscious and subconscious rejection of the coquetry of the bourgeoisie'? he asks.[25] To be fair to Bourdieu, however, it can be argued, contrary to

Sulkunen, that his analysis of working class culture does not infact, suggest that it follows the dictates of the elites. Sulkunen may, however, be correct in perceiving a relative neglect of its more creative dimensions, and of the dialectics of its relationship with ruling class culture.

Focusing on Bourdieu's analysis of language as an arena of power, John Thompson in his assessment is less inclined than Sulkunen to defend the lack of precision in Bourdieu's concepts. He begins by noting that Bourdieu's concept of symbolic violence directs us towards a reflection on the forms in which relations of communication are inter-woven with relations of power. He goes on to argue that the concept of symbolic violence, however fruitful it may be in practice, is unrefined at a theoretical level and is linked to questionable assumptions concerning social reproduction. He also suggests that Bourdieu's preoccupation with *style*, with the way things are said and with the profits obtained thereby, leads him to neglect the *content* of what is said. He thus fails to give sufficient attention to the question of *meaning* (or signification) and he strips away all too abruptly the *rational* features of linguistic communication.

Thompson puts forward his argument regarding the concept of symbolic violence by examining in detail the notions of recognition and misrecognition that form part of it, and finds them vague and ambiguous. In any particular case of symbolic violence, what these notions fail to specify is the degree of misrecognition and recognition and their forms. Thus, the example Thompson gives of a student who, in the course of an interview for admission to a university, strives to eliminate the more prominent aspects of a class and regional accent and to speak a more 'scholarly' English, subsumes numerous different possibilities.

> At one extreme, the student may assume that 'scholarly' English is correct or proper English and is therefore the English to be emulated, acquired and spoken; at the other extreme, the student may recognize 'scholarly' English to be a particular form of English employed by certain groups in certain places, may reckon that they use of this form will improve his or her chances of obtaining a university place, but may despise this form of language and

> have no wish to acquire it. No doubt there could be senses in which recognition and misrecognition entered into both extremes, but the senses are evidently very different.[26]

As this example illustrates, the concept of symbolic violence fails to do justice to the different strategies which may be implicit in, and the different consequences which follow from, the practices which appear to fall within its scope.

Underlying the ambiguities in the concept, Thompson finds a questionable implicit assumption—namely, that social reproduction presupposes a certain kind of *consensus* with regard to the values or norms which are dominant in the society concerned. This is because of the idea that symbolic violence involves a form of complicity of the dominated. While Thompson is quick to add that Bourdieu does not conceive the legitimacy granted to dominant values and norms as being based on a free and fully conscious act on the part of agents but in fact as a *practical* consensus, he nevertheless suggests reasons for rejecting this assumption. He thinks such an assumption presents a misleading view of the conditions underlying the stabilizations of, in particular, contemporary capitalist societies. Arguably, their stabilization rests not so much upon an implicit consensus among social members, but upon a pervasive *fragmentation* of the social order and a proliferation of divisions between its members.

> Social theory can relinquish the need to find a conductor for the concert of social reproduction, not so much because this is a concert performed without a conductor by the harmonizing effects of the habitus, but because social reproduction is less a concert than a cacophony of discordant and divergent notes.[27]

That the hostility and skepticism of particular groups and classes does not necessarily threaten stability of the social order is because oppositional attitudes do not necessarily generate a coherent alternative view which would provide a basis for political action. 'The reproduction of the social order may depend less upon a consensus with regard to dominant values and norms than upon a *lack of consensus* at the very point where oppositional attitudes could be translated into political action'.[28]

This is indeed an incisive comment on the notion of symbolic violence, and directs one to a possible weakness in Bourdieu's theoretical framework.

As regards Bourdieu's emphasis on style in his analysis of language, Thompson relates this to his taking over from Saussure the conception of value, and using it to conceptualize the 'value' of a linguistic product. For Saussure, the value of a term is determined by its *difference* with regard to the other terms which compose the system of which it is part. This idea is translated by Bourdieu into a sociological framework whereby the differences expressed in language are related to a hierarchical system of social differences. Hence the value of a linguistic product is determined by its *social distinction*, that is, by its relation to other products on a market which is structured in specific ways. Agents seek to maximize their material and symbolic profit by adopting a particular style of expression or by realizing their expressions in a particular form. However, as Thompson points out, speaking is not just a matter of style, but also involves saying something about something. It is this which Bourdieu neglects, and thereby also leaves out of his theory an analysis of meaning in language. This is identified as a serious lacuna in an otherwise significant contribution to the analysis of ideological phenomena.[29] However, to conclude that Bourdieu neglects meaning in language would be to take an incomplete look at his work, and to overlook his innovative readings of texts such as those of Heidegger in *The Political Ontology of Martin Heidegger*, where form and content are both in close focus, and are shown to merge.[30] Also significant is his notion of 'understanding' as exemplified by the interviews conducted in *The Weight of the World*.[31] In fact, it would be pertinent to draw attention to the concept of habitus, which provides a locus for bringing together the analytically separable but socially conjoined aspects of style and meaning in language.

As regards the link between language and power, while Thompson concurs with Bourdieu that the utterance of speech acts involves the implementation of institutionally established relations of power, he disagrees with his view that the power of words is exclusively and *in toto*, the power to mobilize the authority conferred on the agent by the group which he or she represents. Thompson gives several examples of every day speech which are not 'authorized' by any 'institution' and which could nevertheless be said to be acts of power, to provide his point, and he is convincing.[32]

Finally, Thompson finds in Bourdieu's analysis of language a serious problem with regard to the relationship between language and the notion of reason or rationality. Bourdieu's contention that the power of language comes from the outside, or from the institution that authorizes it, leaves no room for the possibility that linguistic expressions might have a 'rational force' or a force of conviction of their own. In fact, as Thompson points out, statements claim to say something that is true, and they have a 'rational force' in so far as their claims can be sustained by reason. This is quite different from their being sustained by authority bestowed by an institution. Bourdieu's analysis of language and power thus seems to be far from complete and unflawed. However, Bourdieu would counter this Habermasian critique by not accepting the grounding of reason in transhistoric structures of consciousness or language, which, according to him, is a position which partakes of a transcendentalist illusion of which historical sciences must rid themselves.[33]

Axel Honneth too finds Bourdieu's transposition of the Saussurian notion of value onto a sociological framework problematic, as he explains in his article on Bourdieu's sociology of culture.[34] Referring to *Distinction* as a study which is a bold extension of the idea of symbolic competitive struggles from the Algerian context to the situation of a highly developed society, Honneth identifies the real goal of Bourdieu's inquiry as being 'to decipher the social logic governing the inculcation of the group-specific taste dispositions, lifestyles and habits which exist alongside each other within the social space'.[35] Bourdieu's guiding hypothesis, according to Honneth, is that the various tastes, habits and lifestyles of social groups represent the current strategies, hardened into habit, of a competitive social struggle. Further, Honneth also deduces that Bourdieu's real explanatory aim is to explain the fact that members of a given occupational group by and large make the same or similar judgements of taste, without falling back on the traditional mode of deriving differences in taste cultivation from economically conditioned possibilities of consumption alone.

Following the trajectory of Bourdieu's analysis, Honneth notes that the concept of 'distinction' is the theoretical key to understanding the everyday culture of the ruling classes, and implies having an approximate idea of the taste culture relative to which acts of cultural distinction are oppositionally performed. Bourdieu thus necessarily analyses in his study the tastes of the lower classes, using as he does so, his concept of habitus. According to Honneth, the concept of habitus depends on a reductionist model of representation, focusing on collective perceptual schemas and orientations that ensure that economic constraints and collective life chances are translated into the apparent freedom of an individual way of life, but precluding theoretical sensitivity to other embedded cultural meanings and their expressive or identity confirming elements. The interpretation of the group-specific behavioural model follows a strictly functionalistic viewpoint of cultural adaptation to social class situations so that 'the varied tasks of ensuring collective identity (including oppositional strategies of resistance)—which everyday culture also accomplishes – which is documented in more recent writings on cultural history' remain unacknowledged.[36]

Honneth is also critical of Bourdieu's analysis of the ruling class, the actual site of the symbolic struggles. Bourdieu analyses the struggles among the three occupational groups contending for the claim to the highest rank in the hierarchy of social recognition—the group of tenured intelligentsia, well paid intellectuals and artists, the group of independent professionals, and finally the group of owners and managers of large-scale industry—all three united by their cultural demarcation from the working class and middle class, and by the endeavour of each to acquire the greatest exclusiveness. Insofar as their struggle with each other includes a contest over the standards socially determining the value of a cultural lifestyle, Bourdieu, according to Honneth, alludes to a theory of domination, by terming these contests 'struggles for the basis of legitimate domination' , but, does not actually work it out in his book. In fact, to understand the struggle over 'marks of distinction' and standards of cultural validity, Bourdieu should have distinguished more clearly between a struggle over distribution and a normative-practical struggle.[37] Indeed, Honneth thinks that at the theoretical level, Bourdieu leaves us in the dark as to the role collective taste cultures play in contemporary societies.[38]

Honneth goes on to elaborate upon a further problem which he regards as inherent in Bourdieu's theory as a whole. According to him, in Bourdieu's analysis, the forms of life and taste dispositions which different groups, at any given time, pass on through processes of cultural socialization, have a purely instrumental function.

> They so adapt individual group members to their specific class situation that these individuals unwittingly, as the result of their valuations and judgements of taste, carry out the appropriate strategic actions, aimed at the improvement of their social position. The group specific life-styles are, as it were, only the cultural embodiments of a position-dependent calculus of utilities, which all social groups seem to follows as a matter of habit.[39]

In Honneth's view, a theoretical problem arises, however, from the fact that these groups are also seen as trying to distinguish themselves from one another by learning to inculcate mutually demarcated life styles—in other words, as pursuing the project of 'distinction'. The significance of group-specific forms of taste as captured by the concept of habitus, and this significance as figured in the concept of distinction, exist side by side without a sufficient clarification of their relationship to one another.

Even when Bourdieu, at some points, employs a structuralist conceptual scheme, so that he takes the 'meaning' or 'value' of a social group to be formally determined by its mere 'difference' from neighbouring groups, Honneth thinks his train of thought has more wide-reaching implications. For it implies that different life styles are not just symbolic forms of expression of the strategies for action with which the different occupational groups attempt to assert their social superiority over other social groups, but the cultural forms of life in which the social groups first endeavour to maintain their collective identity.

> Social groups now seek to demarcate themselves from one another by using symbolic distinction, as far as their economic means will allow, in order to give expression to their own life situation and to socially assert the associated value complexes. Bourdieu must therefore assume an internal connection between everyday culture and norms of action, between symbolic forms of expression and particular value conceptions—whereas, earlier, when he spoke of the symbolic striving for distinction merely as a strategic means, he had to assume that the cultural forms of life are themselves the symbolic forms of expression of collective considerations of utility.[40]

According to Honneth, if the utilitarian motive was the only one at work, we cannot understand why social groups should compete among themselves for 'marks of distinction', why they therefore try to enforce their own current standards of cultural self-presentation over those of other groups. 'For only if we assume that the social groups see in their own lifestyle not just a means of improving their own class position, but especially the symbolic expression of their own value complexes, can we sensibly proceed from the assumption of a competition between collective lifestyles'.[41] Otherwise, every social group would always know, after carefully weighing utilities, how to adapt its own everyday culture to the styles which have most recently come to dominate in society.

> The peculiar tenacity with which the social groups hold onto their taste cultures and forms of life in the face of historical change and social transformations cannot be understood via the explanatory model provided by Bourdieu's utilitarian concept of action.[42]

Honneth proposes, in this context, the relevance of the thesis that in the arena of collective lifestyles competing moral and cultural models of a society can stand opposed to one another. The struggles for the social recognition of moral models clearly obeys a different logic from the types of struggles which occur over social distribution. The point, according to him, is, that the social recognition of a lifestyle and of the values it symbolically represents depends on the degree to which the currently held norms of action and value conceptions have found social acceptance. But the central economic concepts upon which Bourdieu's cultural analysis is based compel him to subsume all forms of social conflicts under the type of struggles which occur over social distribution. In short, Bourdieu by passes the problem of how within a society the esteem, the distinctive worth of a life style is socially determined. 'While the economic struggle over distribution is thus a dispute amongst combatants solely mindful of their own utilities, in the moral-practical struggle each of the opposing groups fights for the others normative approval.[43]

> Thus Bourdieu's study repeatedly gives rise to the erroneous idea that the social recognition of a life style and of the values it embodies can be gained in the same way as an economic good. Only by decisively abandoning the utilitarian framework of his empirical analysis could he have avoided making this crucial misunderstanding.[44]

However, it should be pointed out that Honneth's review of Bourdieu's sociology of culture is based on certain misinterpretations. To see Bourdieu's explanatory system as being based on the principle of utility maximization, albeit not necessarily conscious or intentional, and to define the utilitarian 'motive' as analysed in *Distinction* as being the struggle to maintain or improve ones' social standing, is to miss out on the wider theoretical framework, though implicit, within which his study of tastes is embedded. This is of explaining taste cultures in relation to processes of the production, reproduction, and transformation of French social structure.

While it is true that the emphasis in *Distinction* is on reproduction, the point is, that the concept of reproduction itself implies, and the study also bears out, that there be a focus on the structuring of practices that create commonalities and differences, including cultural solidarities and cultural loyalties within groups as well. That Bourdieu does not explicitly pose the question of why social groups hold on as tenaciously as they sometimes do to their lifestyles, does not mean that he does not answer it. His analysis is of how the social order is reproduced by class habitus, not in an objective, mechanical way, but through a subjectively perceived, interpreted, and felt sense of ones' place. 'The cognitive structures which social agents implement in their practices are internalized, 'embodied' social structures.'[45] As Bourdieu puts it

> What individuals and groups invest in the particular meaning they give to common classificatory systems by the use they make of them is infinitely more than their 'interest' in the usual sense of the term; it is their whole social being, everything that defines their own idea of themselves, the primordial, tacit contract whereby they define 'us' as opposed to 'them', 'other people', and which is the basis of the exclusions ('not for the likes of us') and inclusions they perform among the characteristics produced by the common classificatory system.[46]

In other words, there is an understanding of why people adhere to their way of life, and even of why they value it.

Nevertheless, Honneth's proposition that cultural struggles and moral struggles may be at odds in the arena of lifestyles is insightful, and Bourdieu indeed does not engage with this aspect in his study. What is also valid is Honneth's criticism of the functionalistic effect of the use of the concept of habitus in this work, in so far as it leaves little room for descriptions of a culture of resistance, or for that matter, of counter hegemony. This is notwithstanding Bourdieu's view that the alternative of submission and resistance that has traditionally framed the question of dominated cultures needs to be rejected, since it 'prevents us from adequately understanding practices and situations that are often defined by their intrinsically double, skewed nature.'[47] The paradox of the dominated from which there is no way out, is that 'Resistance may be alienating and submission may be liberating.'[48]

Though he is critical of the above mentioned aspects of his theory, Honneth nevertheless lauds Bourdieu's attempt to weld together domains of analysis conventionally separated particularly in Marxist scholarship, namely, those of cultural reality and of socio-economic conditions. In his understanding, Bourdieu is a Marxist, and this is also the view of Raymond Williams and Nicholas Garnham who introduce Bourdieu's sociology of culture as being centrally concerned with the defining problems of historical materialism.

Williams and Garnham argue that the central problem of historical materialism is that of reproduction, both at a material and symbolic level, and that it is what Bourdieu's theory of practice is addressed to. This is clear from the fact that while Bourdieu has concentrated upon the exercise of what he calls symbolic power, that is, on the mode of domination, his theory is cast in resolutely materialist terms, linked to the analysis of the mode of production of material life. Secondly, it is apparent in the fact that Bourdieu's work is cast in the form of a 'critique' in the classical sense practiced by Marx himself. Thus his theoretical and empirical analysis of symbolic power lies at the very heart of his wider general theory, just as theories of fetishisation and ideology do in Marx's work, because it provides the very conditions of its own potential scientificity. Insofar as Bourdieu sees the sociology of symbolic power as also the science of the social conditions determining intellectual practice, the exposure of these conditions is the condition for achieving an always partial because always socially conditioned escape from ideology into scientific practice and for revealing the historically defined limits of available truth. They add that this is always a political act, 'because it is the misrecognition of these conditions and limits that is the condition for the exercise of symbolic power to reinforce the tendency to reproduce the existing structure of class relations.'[49]

Garnham and Williams do, however, raise some questions regarding Bourdieu's work. Firstly, like Sulkunen, they point to the need for comparative work to analyze the similarities and differences inscribed in different histories of the strategies of domination and resistance employed by the dominant and dominated classes and between fractions of the dominant class. Secondly, they point to the need to research into the effect on the operation of symbolic power of the increased intervention of economic capital directly into the field of the production of symbolic goods via the so-called culture industries and the ways this might effect the field of force in the struggle between the fractions of the dominant class in a situation in which the economic interests of the dominant fraction directly threaten the cultural interests of the dominated fraction.

They also discuss the question of Bourdieu's politics. Writing in 1986, they say that 'if to be as objective as possible about the possibilities of a major and immediate transformation of the social formation of advanced capitalism is to be pessimistic, then Bourdieu is, rightly in our view, pessimistic'.[50] This should not, however, obfuscate from view, they think, his commitment to a materialist theory of class struggle and of the position of symbolic struggle within that wider struggle; nor the fact that as in *Distinction*, he exhibits a very rare attribute of the left, namely a positive and unpatronizing valuation of the cultural values and aspirations of the working class which at the same time never lapses into naïve populism or workerism. Finally, it must also be noted that his theory, while focused on the problem of symbolic power, allows fully for the concrete analysis of the specific contradictions between the objective social conditions determined by the mode of production and consciousness and practices of classes and class fractions, contradictions that might offer the concrete possibility of revolutionary mobilization and action. They do, however, discern a functionalist/determinist residue in Bourdieu's concept of reproduction which leads him to place less emphasis on the possibilities of real change and innovation than either his theory or his empirical research makes necessary. In conclusion, they consider the epistemological problem of the social conditions of Bourdieu's own intellectual practice. 'If Bourdieu's is a progressive political intervention, as he clearly believes and with which we agree', they write, 'does the structure of the symbolic field according to his own theory doom the intervention to recuperation and futility or on the other hand are there conditions under which the logic proper to the symbolic field can produce contradictions at the symbolic level such that they no longer tend to reproduce the given set of class relations.'[51]

As regards the identification of Bourdieu as a Marxist, we need to remind ourselves, as noted in Chapter One, that Bourdieu was strongly critical of the tendency to treat Marx, Weber and Durkheim as denominationally discrete intellectual totems. Borrowing from all three, and indeed from diverse other sources as well, Bourdieu's sociology nevertheless has some strong affinities with the work of Marx, which he engages with in a critical and creative way. The fact that he is a materialist, aligned to a project of human freedom from domination; that the Theses on Feuerbach which is the leitmotif of his book *Outline of a Theory of Practice* situates his work as an extension of Marx's own insight on the need to focus on practice to overcome the shortcomings of both idealism and reductive materialism; that a focus on history and class struggle is intrinsic to his theory: all go towards making the view that he is a Marxist seem plausible. However, more appropriately, the question of whether he is a Marxist or not may be regarded as irrelevant; as being little more than a contribution to academic politics. It is more meaningful, perhaps, to note that the questions posed in the 1980s by Garnham and Williams regarding Bourdieu's politics were, in some measure, answered theoretically and practically by his writings and activism in the following decade, as has been discussed in Chapter Six above.

Reflecting the diversity of Bourdieu's intellectual antecedents and the richness of his own contribution, we find that while Honneth, Garnham and Williams emphasize the Marxist lineage of Bourdieu's thought, Dreyfus and Rabinow in their article entitled 'Can there be a science of existential structure and social meaning?' focus on how Bourdieu has continued and enriched the line of modern thought that runs from Durkheim and Weber through Heidegger to Merleau-Ponty and Foucault.[52] What they question however is the idea implicit in Bourdieu's project that there can be a *science* of existential structure and social meaning. They distinguish two components of Bourdieu's work—an ontologically informed research programme which they term an 'empirical existential analytics', and a scientific theory of social meaning (Bourdieu's theory of symbolic capital), which they argue is a specific and contestable interpretation of who we are and what we are always up to. They hold that while objective description is the appropriate way to approach what human being *are* and how their social practices cohere, 'the *meaning* of human action is not accessible to scientific theory; to understand the significance of human action requires an interpretive approach.'[53]

As regards the ontology informing Bourdieu's research programme, Dreyfus and Rabinow show how Bourdieu extends and makes concrete through his concept of habitus, Heidegger's existential ontology which remains at an abstract level, and Merleau-Ponty's account of embodiment which relates action to the perceptual field only in a general way. Bourdieu's use of phenomenological ontology

> allows us to see the way in which the bodily habitus anchors the homologies and analogies of the social field, how the ability to respond appropriately to events in the world arises from skills without recourse to rules and representations, and how what it is to be something in the social world is determined by and reciprocally determines practice.[54]

As regards Bourdieu's science, this, according to Dreyfus and Rabinow, rests on an explanatory principle that accounts for the significance of *all* practices beyond their local sense, and consists of the assertion that 'social life is a race of all against all'. As Bourdieu elaborates, 'The competition for a social life that will be known and recognized, which will free you from insignificance, is a struggle to the death for symbolic life and death'.[55] Difficulties arise from the fact that his explanatory system denies the validity of the manifold significance of the practices to their practitioners . The theory then, since it is a theory of human being, and not a theory of nature, has to account both for why the practitioners are deluded and the scientist is not. As regards the disparity between appearance and reality, Bourdieu is led to claim that the practices only work because their true meaning is repressed, denied, disguised, concealed and so on. His concept of illusio names the self-deception necessary to keep players involved in the game. However, Dreyfus and Rabinow point out that this strategy would work only if there were an invariant, contentful human nature underlying and explaining appearances. If that is not the case, the theory has to answer objections such as Popper's, that its re-description of the phenomenon cannot be falsified and, consequently, that it is not a science. Thus the more common sense denies that *all* action is motivated *solely* by the attempt to use the structure of the social field to increase symbolic capital, the more the scientist sees evidence of the necessity of preserving the *illusio* in order for the system to work. Denying the surface meaning of the phenomena, the scientist uses the objections of the actors that they are being misinterpreted as further evidence for the universal principle being affirmed. This would be scientific only if the theory has independent evidence, such as successful prediction and control. Otherwise, the theory will be able to take care of all anomalies, but only by making it impossible for there to be true anomalies.

A second objection to Bourdieu's version, of a demystifying methodology, according to Dreyfus and Rabinow, is that symbolic capital is circularly defined, so that whatever one acquires by one's social behaviour can be tautologically re-encoded in terms of symbolic capital. 'Everything, from accumulating monetary capital to praise for being burned at the stake, automatically counts as symbolic capital. To say that whatever people do they do for social profit does not tell us anything if profit is defined as whatever people pursue in a given society.'[56]

Dreyfus and Rabinow think that the two problems mentioned above arise because in order to have a science, Bourdieu needs to claim that there is an analog to human nature and use it as a universal, explanatory principle. In their view, Bourdieu needs to abandon the empty claim that the struggle for symbolic capital alone constitutes human beings and the social field, and hence the claim of practicing a science, while retaining the underlying metaphysics of meaning as a heuristic principle. If the principle is understood as totalizing then

(i) It conceals what does not fit, or else
(ii) It requires a repression account of exceptions, and
(iii) The resulting demystifying methodology can never take actors' self understandings at face value (not that they are always right, but the idea that a specific illusion is required to make the system work demands that the actors can never be right about their specific motivations).

In their overall assessment of Bourdieu's work, Dreyfus and Rabinow point to a contradiction in Bourdieu's adoption of a phenomenological ontology, on the one hand, and acceptance of the will to truth of the Platonic Metaphysical tradition on the other. While the phenomenon of the ontological complicity of social space and habitus leads to the thesis that one is inevitably situated within one's culture's understanding of reality, it is the Platonic view that truth can be arrived at by a completely detached unsituated thinker which is the metaphysics that makes modern science possible. Dreyfus and Rabinow conclude that Bourdieu would do well to abandon the claim to be speaking from a uniquely authentic position and to admit 'that his Wissenschaft belongs not among the natural sciences but among the human ones.'[57]

It may be argued, however, that Bourdieu himself suggests that his concepts be used heuristically, and that his method of participant objectivation does not entail taking a distant, detached position, but a form of reflexivity that infact situates the observer vis-à-vis what is observed, but not in an obscure and uncontrolled manner.Dreyfus and Rabinow are correct in perceiving a tension between the hermeneutic and scientific aspects of Bourdieu's work, but it is a tension which he resolves in an innovative and original way.

As the discussion above of some selected assessments of his work shows, Bourdieu's theory of the symbolic has evoked a good deal of creative engagement and also provoked criticisms. It seems meaningful at this point to recognize that, as Brubaker puts it,

> One can most profitably read Bourdieu by treating the concepts, propositions, and theories set forth in his work not, in the first instance, as bearers of logical properties and objects of logical operations, but as designators of particular intellectual habits o sets of habits. The more general and abstract the concept or proposition, the more important it is to read it in this dispositional manner.[58]

This in turn, reminds us that Bourdieu's theory of the symbolic, and the theory of practice within which it is embedded, are products of a scientific habitus, which includes the conviction that 'a true theory is one which accomplishes and abolishes itself in the scientific work it has helped produce.'[59] Thus the practice of theory outside the context of research is somewhat meaningless, and there are severe limitations inherent in a theoretical evaluation of his theory, including his theory of the symbolic.

Not surprisingly, there has appeared a steady stream of studies using his conceptual framework to analyze different facets of cultural life in France, many of which have been published in his journal *Actes de la recherché en sciences sociales*. Bourdieu's influence is, of course, not confined to France, and has expanded over the years to include France's continental neighbours, Eastern Europe, Scandinavia, Asia, Latin America and the United States. Among other things, this has thrown up the challenge of discerning between aspects of his theory which are context specific and those which have a universal import.

For sociologists in India, who are socialized into rejecting the dichotomy between sociology and social anthropology, the appearance of Bourdieu's *Outline of a Theory of Practice* in the late seventies was greeted with enthusiasm as a potential breakthrough in theoretical debates between functionalism, structuralism, and Marxism that had hitherto dominated the scene. The book was my first encounter with Bourdieu, and the beginning of an engagement with his writings, first through discussions with colleagues at the Department of Sociology, Jamia Millia Islamia, New Delhi, and then as a PhD scholar at Cambridge, UK. Bourdieu's analyses in *Algeria 1960* in particular resonated with the kind of problems researchers in the Indian context were grappling with, given that a tribal population as well as a peasantry were major constituents of the social landscape, together with significant inroads being made by a capitalist economic and socio-cultural order. The acceptance of *Distinction* when it appeared in English translation in 1984 as part of a general and unified approach to social phenomena, despite the focus on the culture of an advanced capitalist country, was also easier here, because of the co-existence of pre-modern and modern phenomena in the social context.

The prospect of researching Bourdieu's contribution did, however, lead to the attempt at a more context specific understanding of his enterprise. In the process, Bourdieu's own conceptual framework of fields allowed one to grasp the location of Bourdieu's thought in the French intellectual scene as well as in the wider field of world sociology. An insight into the reasons for Bourdieu's thematic focus on issues of culture and power was also provided by taking into account the significance of colonialism in Algeria and the vicissitudes of French society in the post-war period.

The post-modernist tide that virtually swept across all university departments in the 1980s made one's engagement with Bourdieu's thought sharper in terms of the attempt to grasp his basic assumptions and test the continuing relevance of his endeavour rooted in reason and science. In the process, the sense in which he is an Enlightenment thinker without being anachronistic became clearer.

As one proceeded to examine Bourdieu's theory of the symbolic, it became apparent that it must be viewed in relation to his overall intellectual project. His attempt to transcend the many dualisms in social thought that have hindered the progress of social science informs this theory as well, and it has in turn generated findings that validate his attempt. This in itself is a contribution to sociology of immense significance.

Returning to the Indian context after reviewing and appraising Bourdieu's sociology of the symbolic, one is led to explore its potential relevance to the analysis of symbolism and society here. While the experiences of colonialism and post coloniality and of the diversity of cultures characterizing Indian reality seem to suggest that Bourdieu's conceptual tool kit may have to be inflected in certain ways, even extended, and perhaps modified to yield meaningful results, it most certainly provides useful heuristic devices to open up and explore areas of analysis. The resolution of the problem of agency and structure offered by the concepts of habitus and fields can go a long way towards yielding ethnographies that reveal the richness of phenomenological experience without losing sight of the macro-processes that shape reality. The concepts of habitus, symbolic capital, symbolic power, and symbolic violence could be extremely useful for analysing the material and discursive practices that go to make up the institution of caste in particular, and other forms of domination and subordination as well. The function of education as a mechanism of social reproduction would have to be analysed in the context of a society where there is a scarcity of formal institutions, monopolized by an urban minority, itself stratified, so that its contribution as an agency for the creation of a national culture is not very pronounced. The impact of the electronic media in creating subcultures, and the role of the film industry as a culture industry would need to be highlighted, as would the pervasive power of oral traditions in society. Indeed, there are two significant contributions to the study of schools in India that draw upon Bourdieu's work: Meenakshi Thapan's *Life at School* (1991) and Sanjay Srivastava's *Constructing Post-colonial India: National Character and the Doon School* (1998).

The concepts of doxa, orthodoxy and heterodoxy can potentially clarify some of the links between politics and culture, including the currents of religious fundamentalism and the forces opposed to them. The notion of the relative autonomy of fields can enable a discernment of the complex relationship between political representation and people, avoiding the short-circuit of equating professed ideologies with beliefs.

As regards culture in the restricted sense, the existence of rich literary and artistic traditions calls for a mapping of their fields as fields of production and consumption, and their relationship with culture in the wider sense. Bourdieu's studies of Flaubert and Manet could well provide models for such a mapping, though the coexistence of pre-modern and modern forms and institutions would call for a nonlinear rendering of their histories. In literature, the emergence of movements of the dominated classes, such as the Dalits, would demand careful analysis, in view of Bourdieu's characterization of intellectuals as constituting the dominated fraction of the dominant class,(though it may be argued that this is not a generalization in Bourdieu's oeuvre, but the statement of a specific empirical fact).

Bourdieu's analysis of how relations of dominance and subordination are sustained and exacerbated by processes of neo-liberal globalization makes his theory of the symbolic very relevant to some of the urgent issues that societies are facing worldwide. As the doxa of neo-classical economic theory has governments in thrall, Bourdieu's efforts at its demystification call for sustained work in specific contexts and possibly the wielding and exercise of symbolic power by sociologists to influence processes of social change.

The potential relevance of Bourdieu's theory of the symbolic for the analysis of symbolic processes in the Indian context suggests possibilities for further research and innovation. Bourdieu's contribution has already inspired scholars all over the world, and his legacy of 'métier militant' has made sociology richer for all times to come.

ENDNOTES

1. Loic J. Wacquant, *The Chronicle of Higher Education*, Friday, 25 January 2002.
2. Craig Calhoun et.al. *Bourdieu: Critical Perspectives*, Cambridge, Polity Press, 1993, p. 7.
3. Pierre Bourdieu and Loic J. Wacquant, *An Invitation to Reflexive Sociology*, Cambridge, Polity Press, 1992, p. 4
4. Scott Lash, *Sociology of Postmodernism*, London and New York, Routledge, 1990, p. 237.
5. Richard Jenkins, 'Critical Note—Pierre Bourdieu and the Reproduction of Determinism' in *Sociology*, 1984, 16, p. 270.
6. Nicholas Garnham and Raymond Williams, 'Pierre Bourdieu and the Sociology of Culture: An Introduction' in Richard Collins et.al. (ed) *Media, Culture and Society: A Critrical Reader*, London, Sage Publications Ltd, 1986, pp. 116–7.
7. Stuart Hall, *On Ideology*, London, Hutchinson, 1978, p. 29.
8. Richard Jenkins, 'Critical Note—Pierre Bourdieu and the Reproduction of Determinism' in *Sociology*, 1984, 16, p. 270 quoting E.P. Thompson, *The Poverty of Theory*, London, Merlin Press, 1978, p. 366.
9. Anthony Giddens, *Central Problems in Social Theory*, London, Macmillan, 1979, p. 217
10. Richard Harker et.al., *An Introduction to the Work of Pierre Bourdieu: The Practice of Theory*, Houndmills, Basingstoke, Hampshire, London, Macmillan, 1990, p. 198

11. Ibid., p. 199
12. Ibid.
13. Richard Harker et.al., *An Introduction to the Work of Pierre Bourdieu: The Practice of Theory*, Houndmills, Basingstoke, Hampshire, London, Macmillan, 1990, p. 198.
14. Ibid., p. 198.
15. Ibid., p. 200
16. Ibid.
17. Jim Wolfreys, 'In Perspective: Pierre Bourdieu' in *International Socialism Journal*, No. 87, Summer 2000.
18. Pekka Sulkunen, 'Society Made Visible – On the Cultural Sociology of Pierre Bourdieu' in *Acta Sociologica*, 25(2) 1982, p. 104.
19. Ibid., p. 106.
20. Ibid., p. 107.
21. Ibid.
22. Ibid., p. 108.
23. Ibid., p. 109–10.
24. Ibid., p. 110, See also Pierre Bourdieu and Loic J. Wacquant , *An Invitation to Reflexive Sociology*, Cambridge, Polity Press, 1992, p. 23 and p. 23, fn.41.
25. Ibid., p. 113.
26. John Thompson, *Studies in the Theory of Ideology*, Cambridge, Polity Press, 1984, pp. 60–1.
27. Ibid., p. 62.
28. Ibid., p. 63.
29. Ibid., p. 65.
30. Pierre Bourdieu, *The Political Ontology of Martin Heidegger*, Cambrige, Polity Press, 1991.
31. Pierre Bourdieu et.al., *The Weight of the World*, Cambridge, Polity Press, 1999.
32. John Thompson, *Studies in the Theory of Ideology*, Cambridge, Polity Press, 1984, p. 68.
33. Pierre Bourdieu and Loic J. Wacquant, *An Invitation to Reflexive Sociology*, Cambridge, Polity Press, 1992, p. 47.
34. Axel Honneth, 'The Fragmented World of Symbolic Forms: Reflections on Pierre Bourdieu's Sociology of Culture' in *Theory, Culture and Society*, Vol. 3, No. 3, 1986, pp. 55–6.
35. Ibid., p. 58.
36. Ibid., p. 61.
37. Ibid., p. 63.
38. Ibid.
39. Axel Honneth, 'The Fragmented World of Symbolic Forms:

Reflections on Pierre Bourdieu's Sociology of Culture' in *Theory, Culture and Society*, Vol. 3, No. 3, 1986, p. 63–4.
40. Ibid., p. 64
41. Ibid.
42. Ibid.
43. Ibid., p. 65.
44. Ibid.
45. Pierre Bourdieu, *Distinction: A Social Critique of the Judgement of Taste*, London, Routledge and Kegan Paul, p. 468.
46. Ibid., p. 478.
47. Pierre Bourdieu and Loic J. Wacquant, *An Invitation to Reflexive Sociology*, Cambridge, Polity Press, 1992, p. 23.
48. Pierre Bourdieu, *In Other Words*, Cambridge, Polity Press, 1990, p. 155.
49. Nicholas Garnham and Raymond Williams, 'Pierre Bourdieu and the Sociology of Culture: An Introduction' in Richard Collin, James Curran et.al. (ed) *Media, Culture & Society: A Critical Reader* New Delhi, London, Sage Publications, 1986, p. 118.
50. Ibid., p. 129.
51. Ibid., p. 130.
52. Hubert Dreyfus and Paul Rabinow, 'Can there be a science of existential structure and social meaning? In Craig Calhoun, Edward Li Puma and Moishe Postone (ed): *Bourdieu: Critical Perspectives*, Cambridge, Polity Press, 1993, pp. 35–44.
53. Ibid., pp. 35–6.
54. Ibid., p. 38.
55. Dreyfus and Rabinow in Craig Calhoun, Edward Li Puma and Moishe Postone (ed), *Bourdieu: Critical Perspectives*, p. 39, quoting Pierre Bourdieu, *In Other Words: Essays Toward a Reflexive Sociology*, Cambridge, Polity Press, 1987, p. 196.
56. Dreyfus and Rabinow in Craig Calhoun et.al. (ed) : *Bourdieu: Critical Perspectives*, p. 42.
57. Ibid., p. 44.
58. Rogers Brubaker, 'Social Theory as Habitus' in Calhoun, Li Puma and Postone (ed), *Bourdieu: Critical Perspectives*, Cambridge, Polity Press, 1993, p. 220.
59. Pierre Bourdieu and Loic J. Wacquant, *An Invitation to Reflexive Sociology*, Cambridge, Polity Press, 1992, p. 159.

References

Asad, Talal, 1983, 'Anthropological Conceptions of Religion: Reflections on Geertz' in *Man*, 18 March.

Axel, Brian Keith, 2001, *The Nation's Tortured Body: Violence, Representation and the Formation of a Sikh 'Diaspora'*, Durham and London, Duke University Press.

Bernstein, Richard J, 1985, *The Restructuring of Social and Political Theory*, Oxford, Methuen and Co. Ltd.

Bilgrami, Akeel 2006, 'Occidentalism, the Very Idea: An Essay on Enlightenment and Enchantment' in *Economic & Political Weekly*, 19–25 August, Vol. XLI, No. 33.

Bourdieu, Pierre 1965, 'Heritage Cultural et Inegalites devant I'ecole et la Culture' in *Colleque D' Arras*, 12–13 June.

Bourdieu, Pierre 1968, Structuralism and the Theory of Sociological Knowledge' in *Social Research*, Vol. 35, Part 4, Winter.

Bourdieu, Pierre 1969, 'Intellectual Field and Creative Project' in *Social Science Information*, 8(2) April.

Bourdieu, Pierre 1974, 'Avenir de classe et causalite du probable' in *Revue Francaise de Sociologie*, XV, I, January–March.

Bourdieu, Pierre 1974, 'The School as a Conservative Force: Scholastic and Cultural Inequalities' in John Eggleston (ed) *Contemporary Research in the Sociology of Education*, London, Methuen.

Bourdieu, Pierre 1977, *Outline of a Theory of Practice*, Cambridge, Cambridge University Press.

Bourdieu, Pierre and Jean-Claude Passeron, 1977, *Reproduction: In Education, Society and Culture*, London and Beverly Hills, Sage Publications.

Bourdieu, Pierre, 1978, 'Sport and Social Class' in *Social Science Information*, 17, 6.

Bourdieu, Pierre, 1979, *Algeria 1960*, Cambridge, Cambridge University Press.

Bourdieu, Pierre, 1979, 'Symbolic Power' in *Critique of Anthropology*, 13 and 14, Vol. 4, Summer.

Bourdieu, Pierre, 1979, *Distinction: A Social Critique of the Judgement of Taste*, London, Routledge and Kegan Paul.

Bourdieu, Pierre, 1979, *The Inheritors: French Students and Their Relation to Culture*, Chicago, Chicago University Press.

Bourdieu, Pierre, 1980, *Questions de Sociologie*, Paris, Editions de Minuit.

Bourdieu, Pierre, 1981, 'Men and Machines' in K. Knorr Cetina and A. V. Cicourel (ed) *Advances in Social Theory and Methodology*, London, RKP.

Bourdieu, Pierre, 1983, 'Erving Goffman, Discoverer of the Infinitely Small' in *Theory, Culture and Society*, Vol. 2, No. 1.

Bourdieu, Pierre, 1983, 'The Philosophical Establishment' in Alan Montefiore (ed) *Philosophy in France Today*, Cambridge, Cambridge University Press.

Bourdieu, Pierre, 1985, 'The Genesis of the Concepts of *Habitus* and of *Field*', in *Sociocriticism: Theories and Perspectives*, Vol. II, No. 2, December.

Bourdieu, Pierre, 1985, 'The Social Space and Genesis of Groups' in *Theory and Society*, Vol. 14, No. 6, November.

Bourdieu, Pierre, 1986, 'Forms of Capital' in John G Richardson (ed) *Handbook of Theory and Research for the Sociology of Education*, New York, Westport, London, Greenwood Press.

Bourdieu, Pierre, 1987, 'What Makes a Social Class? On the Theoretical and Practical Existence of Groups' in *Berkeley Journal of Sociology*, 32.

Bourdieu, Pierre, 1987, 'Legitimation and Structured Interests in Weber's Sociology of Religion' in Sam Whimster and Scott Lash (ed) *Max Weber: Rationality & Modernity*, London, Allen and Unwin.

Bourdieu, Pierre, 1988, *Homo Academicus*, Cambridge, Polity Press.

Bourdieu, Pierre, 1989, 'Social Space and Symbolic Power' in *Sociological Theory*, Vol. 7, No. 1, June.

Bourdieu, Pierre, 1989, 'The Corporatism of the Universal: The Role of Intellectuals in the Modern World' in *Telos*, No. 81, Fall.

Bourdieu, Pierre, 1989, 'Social Space and Symbolic Power' in *Sociological Theory*, Spring, Vol. 7, No. 1.

Bourdieu, Pierre, 1990, *The Logic of Practice*, Cambridge, Polity Press.

Bourdieu, Pierre, 1990, *In Other Words*, Cambridge, Polity Press.

Bourdieu, Pierre, Jean-Claude Chamboredon and Jean-Claude

Passeron, 1991, *The Craft of Sociology*, Berlin, New York, Walter de Gruyter.

Bourdieu, Pierre and Alain Darbel, 1991, *The Love of Art*, Cambridge, Polity Press.

Bourdieu, Pierre, 1991, *Language & Symbolic Power*, Cambridge, Polity Press.

Bourdieu, Pierre, 1991, *The Political Ontology of Martin Heidegger*, Cambridge, Polity Press.

Bourdieu, Pierre and Loic J Wacquant, 1992, *An Invitation to Reflexive Sociology*, Cambridge, Polity Press.

Bourdieu, Pierre, 1993, *The Field of Cultural Production: Essays on Art and Literature*, Cambridge, Polity Press.

Bourdieu, Pierre, 1993, *Sociology in Question*, London, Thousand Oaks, New Delhi, Sage Publications.

Bourdieu, Pierre and Hans Haacke, 1995, *Free Exchange*, Cambridge, Polity Press.

Bourdieu, Pierre, 1996, *The State Nobility*, Cambridge, Polity Press.

Bourdieu, Pierre, 1996, *Rules of Art*, Cambridge, Polity Press.

Bourdieu, Pierre, 1998, *Practical Reason: On the Theory of Action*, Cambridge, Polity Press.

Bourdieu, Pierre, 1998, *Acts of Resistance*, Cambridge, Polity Press.

Bourdieu, Pierre et.al., 1999, *The Weight of the World*, Cambridge, Polity Press.

Bourdieu, Pierre and Guntar Grass, 2000, 'A Literature from Below', *The Nation* [on line] Available at http://past.thenation.com/issue/000703/0703 grass.shtml [Accessed 24-10-2000]

Bourdieu, Pierre and Loic J Wacquant, 2000, 'New Liberal Speak: Notes on the New Planetary Vulgate', revised version of a translation by David Macey of an article that originally appeared in Le Monde Diplomatique, 554, May.

Bourdieu, Pierre, 2001, *Masculine Domination*, Cambridge, Polity Press.

Bourdieu, Pierre, 2003, 'Participant Objectivation' in *Man*; Vol. 9, 1 June.

Breman, Jan and E Valentine Daniel, 1992, 'Conclusion: The Making of a Coolie' in *The Journal of Peasant Studies*, Vol. 19, Nos. 3 and 4, April/July.

Brubaker, Rogers, 1985, 'Rethinking Classical Theory: The Sociological Vision of Pierre Bourdieu' in *Theory and Society*, Vol. 14, No. 6, November.

Calhoun, Craig, Edward Li Puma and Moishe Postone (ed), 1993, *Bourdieu: Critical Perspectives*, Cambridge, Polity Press.

Carroll, John B (ed), 1956, *Language, Thought and Society: Selected Writings of Benjamin Lee Whorf*, New York, John Wiley & Sons.

Cassirer, Ernst, 1953, *The Philosophy of Symbolic Forms,* New Haven, Connecticut, Yale University Press.

Chakrabarty, Dipesh, 2007, *Provincialising Europe,* Princeton, Princeton University Press.

Chakravarti, Uma, 2000, 'State, Market and Freedom of Expression: Women and Electronic Media' in *Economic & Political Weekly,* 29 April.

Chhachhi, Amrita, 1989, 'The State, Religious Fundamentalism and Women: Trends in South Asia' in *Economic & Political Weekly,* 18 March.

Das, Veena, 1995, *Critical Events: An Anthropological Perspective on Contemporary India,* Delhi, Oxford University Press.

Dews, Peter, 1987, *Logics of Disintegration,* London, New York, Verso.

Dumont, Louis, 1970, *Homo Hierarchicus: The Caste System and its Implications,* London, Weidenfeld and Nicolson.

Durkheim, Emile and Marcel Mauss, 1963, *Primitive Classification,* Chicago, The University of Chicago Press.

Durkheim, Emile, 1965, *The Elementary Forms of the Religious Life,* New York, The Free Press.

Elster, Jon, 1979, *Ulysses and the Sirens,* Cambridge, Cambridge University Press.

Engineer, Asghar Ali, 1987, *The Shah Bano Controversy,* Hyderabad, Sangam Books Ltd.

Foucault, Michel, 1980, *Power/Knowledge,* Sussex, The Harvester Press.

Giddens, Anthony, 1978, *Durkheim,* Glasgow, Fontana Press.

Giddens, Anthony, 1979, *Central Problems in Social Theory,* London, Macmillan.

Giddens, Anthony, 1984, *The Constitution of Society,* Cambridge, Polity Press.

Goffman, Erving, 1961, *Asylums: Essays on the Social Situation of Mental Patients and Other Inmates,* Harmondsworth, Penguin Books.

Habermas, Jurgen, 1975, *Legitimation Crisis,* Boston, Beacon Press.

Hall, Stuart, 1978, *On Ideology,* London, Hutchinson.

Harker, Richard, Cheleen Mahar, Chris Wilkes (ed), 1990, *An Introduction to the Work of Pierre Bourdieu,* London, Macmillan.

Hasan, Mushirul, 1997, *Legacy of a Divided Nation: India's Muslims Since Independence,* Delhi, Oxford University Press.

Hasan, Zoya, 1989, 'Minority Identity, Muslim Women Bill Campaign and the Political Process' in *Economic & Political Weekly,* 7 January.

Hasan, Zoya, 1998, 'Uniformity vs. Equality: Gender, Minority Identity and Debates on a Uniform Civil Code' in Reicha Tanwar (ed) *Women: Human Rights, Religion and Violence,* Kurukshetra, Nirmal Book Agency.

Honneth, Axel, 1986, 'The Fragmented World of Symbolic Forms: Reflections on Pierre Bourdieu's Sociology of Culture', in *Theory, Culture and Society*, Vol. 3, No. 3.

Honneth, Axel and Hermann Kocyba, 1986, 'The Struggle for Symbolic Order—An Interview with Pierre Bourdieu' in *Theory, Culture and Society*, Vol. 3, No. 3.

Jain, Ravindra K, 1985, 'Social Anthropology of India: Theory and Method' in *Survey of Research in Sociology and Social Anthropology 1969-1979*, Vol. 1, Indian Council of Social Science Research, New Delhi, Satvahan Publications.

Jain, Ravindra K, 2004, 'The Dynamics of Indian Diaspora' (Unpublished Paper).

Jalal, Ayesha, 2003, 'Women and Religion' in *Economic & Political Weekly*, 8 February.

Jenkins, Richard, 1984, 'Critical Note—Pierre Bourdieu and the Reproduction of Determinism' in *Sociology*, 16.

Jenkins, Richard, 1992, *Pierre Bourdieu*, London and New York, Routledge.

Lardinois, Roland, 2002, 'Pierre Bourdieu (1930-2002): A Sociologist in Action' in *Economic & Political Weekly*, March 16.

Lash, Scott, 1990, *Sociology of Postmodernism*, London, Routledge.

Levi-Strauss, Claude, 1967, *Structural Anthropology*, Vol. 1, New York, Anchor Books.

Marx, Karl, 1974, *Economic and Philosophical Manuscript of 1844*, Moscow, Progress Publishers.

Marx, Karl and Frederick Engels, 1976, *The German Ideology*, Moscow, Progress Publishers.

Menon, Ritu, 1994, 'The Personal and the Political—An Interview-Discussion' in Kamla Bhasin, Ritu Menon and Nighat Said Khan (ed) *Against All Odds*, New Delhi, Isis International and Kali for Women.

Nelson, Cary and Lawrence Grossberg (ed), 1988, *Marxism and the Interpretation of Culture*, Urbana, University of Illinois Press.

Oommen, T.K., 2002, *Pluralism, Equality and Identity: Comparative Studies*, New Delhi, Oxford University Press.

Panofsky, Erwin, 1991, *Perspective as Symbolic Form*, New York, Zone Books.

Saussure, F de, 1974, *Course in General Linguistics*, Glasgow, Collins.

Sen, Samita, 1999, 'Recast(e)ing Class' in *Economic & Political Weekly*, 1 May.

Srivastava, Sanjay, 1998, *Constructing Post-Colonial India: National Character and the Doon School*. London and New York, Routledge.

Srivastava, Rahul, 1999, 'Power of the Image' in *Economic & Political Weekly*, 24 July.

Sulkunen, Pekka, 1982, 'Society Made Visible—On the Cultural Sociology of Pierre Bourdieu' in *Acta Sociologic a*, 25(2).

Thakkar, Usha, 2004, 'Culture and Politics' in *Economic & Political Weekly*, 25 September.

Thapan, Meenakshi, 1991, *Life at School: An Ethnographic Study*, Delhi, Oxford University Press.

Thompson, John, 1984, *Studies in the Theory of Ideology*, Cambridge, Polity Press.

Thompson, John, 1990, *Ideology and Modern Culture*, Cambridge, Polity Press.

Verdery, Katherine, 1994, 'Ethnicity, Nationalism, and Statemaking—Ethnic Groups and Boundaries: Past and Future' in Hans Vermuelen and Cora Govers (ed) *The Anthropology of Ethnicity: Beyond 'Ethnic Groups and Boundaries*' Amesterdam, Het Spinhuis.

Wacquant, Loic J, 2002, 'The Sociological Life of Pierre Bourdieu' in *International Sociology*, Vol. 17(4), December.

Wacquant, Loic J, 2002, 'On Bourdieu' in *The Chronicle of Higher Education*, Friday, 25 January.

Williams, Raymond and Nicholas Garnham, 1986, 'Pierre Bourdieu and the Sociology of Culture' in Richard Collins, James Curran et.al. (ed) *Media, Culture and Society: A Critical Reader*, London, Sage Publications.

Wolfreys, Jim, 2000, 'In Perspective— Pierre Bourdieu' in *International Socialism Journal*, No. 87, Summer.

Zeldin, Theodore, *France 1848 - 1945*, Vol. II: *Intellect, Taste and Anxiety*.

The Cause of the Unemployed, Petition, 1998.

The Collins English Dictionary.

The Fontana Dictionary of Modern Thinkers.

Who's Who in France 1983-1984.

Index